ROSABOWER:

A COLLECTION OF

ESSAYS AND MISCELLANIES.

BY

W. C. LARRABEE.

Cincinnati:
R. P. THOMPSON, PRINTER.
1855.

CONTENTS.

ROSABOWER:

A COLLECTION OF

Essays and Miscellanies.

THE BOWER.

WILL you come, gentle reader, to my bower, and take a seat by my side, and let us commune with nature and with ourselves? The place is beautiful—beautiful as ideal visions of fairy-land. Its influences are soothing as dreams of love. To reach the sequestered retreat I, many years ago, with the fair and gentle being,

> "Who unto my youth was given,
> More than all things else to love me,"

and the sweet little ones whom God had given us, and whose smiles threw sunshine along our pathway, wandered many a weary day, and compassed many a devious round. My cottage-home, on the Atlantic hill-side, disappeared beneath the eastern horizon. The cities of the Atlantic grew dim in the cloudy distance. The rough and rocky Kennebec, the clear and gentle Merrimac, the softly-flowing Connecticut, the magnificent Hudson, the dashing Delaware, and the long and winding Susquehanna were left behind in the "land of dreams." For many a day I glided along the waters of the "blue Juniata;" I ascended the Alleghanies; I descended to the valley of the fair and lovely Ohio—"la belle riviere." On its waters, amidst verdant hills and fairy landscapes,

I held my way for nearly a thousand miles. Up the meandering Wabash, amidst landscapes beautiful as were ever daguerreotyped on poet's soul; by vales lovely as Tempe or Cashmere; along fields fair as that

> "Of Enna, where Proserpina, gathering flowers,
> Herself a fairer flower, by gloomy Dis
> Was carried off;"

and through groves, sweet as that of Arcadia or of "Daphne by Orontes," was I urged by the resistless power of steam, till, on one lovely morning, there lay spread out before me, in the quiet beauty of summer sunlight, the *City of the Prairie.* Over all the landscape was diffused a soft and mellow radiancy, a gentle, wavy light, like the dim and dreamy hues of distant mountain scenery. With eye unvailed and undimmed, I stood looking on the fairy paradise, shadowy visions of whose surpassing beauty had often flitted before the magic mirror of the soul, amidst the dreams of childhood's reverie.

Midway between the City of the Prairie and the City of the Plain, on which stands Indiana's capitol, and midway between the gentle and fair Ohio and the broad and beautiful Michigan, by the side of a streamlet, whose waters run rippling by to mingle with the Wabash, smooth and softly flowing, nestles, in a cozy retreat, my summer bower. On the north may be caught faint glimpses of my vine-covered cottage, peering out among the trees, and beyond rise the steeples of the village. On the south there stretches away, in the dim distance, a shadowy valley dreaming of perpetual summer. On the east appear fields waving with the green grass and the golden harvest, and pastures cropped by lowing herds and bleating flocks. On the west rises a grand old forest of venerable and magnificent trees, whose memory reaches back to the silent and oblivious ages of the past.

One of the old trees, an original denizen of the soil,

throws its dense and impenetrable shade over my rural seat. Around me, clustering close, are thickets of evergreens. Here are growing, fresh and fair, as on their native plains, the pine, the fir, the spruce, and the tamarack, transplanted from my own native home on the Atlantic shore. Springing up amid the evergreens, and scattered all along the valley by the brook, are lilies of the purest white. The bright green leaves of the maple and the beech, which surround and overhang the bower, reflect from their polished surface the cheerful sunlight. Just in the vale, at the foot of the bowery dell, is a lakelet of pure, transparent water, whose quiet bosom reflects the shadows of the trees, forming a perfect daguerreotype of the sylvan scene.

There are voices here, gentle reader; the voices of Nature in her gladness and love. Lots of merry crickets are chirping in the tall grass. The incessant hum of the bee is heard in the air and on the trees overhead. On a little bush by my side sits the sparrow singing to its mate on her nest in the neighboring thicket. From the fence-corner comes the plaintive monotone of the robin. From the crevice in the old stump flits the wren twittering emulous. On the topmost branch of the maple sits the mocking-bird, most tuneful of nature's warblers, leaving, in her ecstasies of melody, nothing unimitated. From the adjacent grove comes the cooing of the turtle-dove, mournful and sad. Even the pines, in their waving tassels, furnish a harp for the winds, giving out music soft, soothing, and inimitable. And is it fancy, or do I sometimes hear, mingled with the melody of nature, soothing my soul with heavenly harmony, and cheering me onward and upward, the spirit-voice of my angel child, idol of my heart, and twin genius of my spirit, my own sweet Emma Rosabelle, whose grave, covered with violets and myrtle, is made beneath the same tree whose branches incline over me? Many a sweet summer hour did she sit here by my side, or blithely bound over the lawn, clapping her little hands for joy that summer was come. Then would she skip from flower to flower along the dell, and having woven, with tiny hands, a wreath, steal with light steps around my study-chair and crown me with a chaplet, to recall me from my dreamy reverie. Her fair hand failed never to smooth from my brow the wrinkles of sorrow or of care. Her voice to my soul was music—music sweeter than Eolian melody or the Orphean Lyre. Her soul was a mine of gems and of gold. Her heart was a fountain of affection, welling up spontaneous and pure from exhaustless depths.

One evening, in the merry month of May, she was rambling with me about this shady glen, and about the garden walks of home, till the fading twilight sent us to repose. To the night succeeded a morning of intense anxiety. There was hurrying to and fro about the house, and flitting forms of physicians and friends passed and repassed by me, as I was watching intent over my sick and dying child. Another night—a night of bitter agony, a night of intense anguish, a night of dying hope, a night of despair—passed slow and sad away. Another morning came—the morning of the holy Sabbath came bright and beautiful; but I can only remember the voice of wailing and of woe in my once happy home, the melancholy tones of the bell of death pealing on the air, the long funeral procession, the open grave, and by the side of it a coffin with its lid upraised, and in that coffin my own little Emma Rosabelle, with the sunlight of heaven beaming bright on her cold, pale, yet beautiful face. We buried her—buried her here in this rural spot. "When I am dead," said she, a few days before she fell sick, "they will not bury me in the cold graveyard, but they will bury me in the bower among the flowers, and my father and my mother will come and sit by me." So we buried her here, in this lovely bower, and for her sake we call it Rosabower.

Here she still sleeps. Unbroken are her slumbers, undisturbed her repose. She wakes not, though I call her long and loud. She sleeps on, though her poor mother, with a disconsolate heart, often kneels in prayer over her grave; though her only sister, at morning and at evening, strews flowers over the spot; and though her little brother, often as he passes by, sighs for the lost companion of his childhood. She slumbers on, though spring after spring has returned with its music and gladness, though summer after summer, with its flowers and its fruits, has come and gone, though autumn after autumn has strewed her grave with fallen leaves, and though winter after winter has howled, drear and bleak, with its wild winds, over the landscape.

To me there seems something bright and beautiful gone from earth. There is a blank in life. A cloud is on my brow, a shadow on my heart. Yet would I not call back my child to suffer and to die again. No, sleep on, my lovely one. Dark as may be to me my future pathway, there is one bright spot in the past. There is on my soul one beauteous picture that can never fade—a picture of loveliness, of gentleness, of purity. When my eye of flesh grows dim with age, my eye of mind shall still look, my child, on thy beautiful face. When my ear grows dull to passing sounds, the melody of thy voice shall linger still

> "Like an echo that hath lost itself
> Among the distant hills."

Come, then, gentle reader, come to my bower and let us commune together. I would, if I may, awaken in your mind some pleasing reminiscence of the past, and inspire some hope of the future. If I contribute, in ever so slight a degree, to afford you one pleasing emotion, I shall accomplish no small object. Happy is he who succeeds in smoothing one wrinkle from the brow of care, and in lighting up one smile of hope on the face of sorrow.

I may not aspire to furnish you any new ideas. My retreat is away from the busy city and the crowded thoroughfare. No one comes to see me unless he comes on purpose. I have only a few books, and them I read up long ago. In our free and easy interview let us not be cooped up by bars of iron logic, or entangled in split-hair nets of metaphysics. Forced all day to be solving equations, and developing functions, and deducing differentials, and summing up integrals, and measuring triangles, and moving in conic sections, I must, at evening, when I sit down to commune with you, have a respite from what men call science and reason, and must cultivate the sentiments and the affections, the noblest part of our nature.

Let us, therefore, with unembarrassed ease and familiar freedom, review the past, analyze the present, divine the future, develop the sentiments, and cultivate the affections of our nature, and occasionally make excursions into the domains of nature and of fancy, that we may pick up by the way something to amuse, or instruct, or interest us.

BARREN HILL.

I CONFESS that I had not the good fortune to be born in the west. I was going to say that few have; but that would be a sad mistake; for any one may perceive, from the legions of merry children about him, that the west is becoming quite a common birthright. I may, however, truly say, that few of my age have the pleasure of claiming the great and glorious west as their childhood's home.

I have to own for the place of my birth a spot known in the neighborhood as *Barren Hill.* Rather an unprepossessing name, surely. I here enter my protest against the practice of bestowing such villainous names on places and persons. There are places, and beautiful places too, where I would not live, solely on account of the horrid names attached to them. I would not, under any consideration, be obliged to speak or write such names. Often it happens that a beautiful place has an outlandish name billeted on it forever by some hypochondriac in a fit of spleen. While names are so plenty, and so cheap, and so easily manufactured, and so readily imported without custom-house duties, it is a pity there is not more taste displayed in choosing them. Barren Hill, however, is not so bad after all, at least not to me. It is true that corn obstinately refused to grow upon it, and that grass seemed uneasy and desirous of changing its latitude or longitude, it mattered not which. But it produced rocks in abundance. They were venerable-looking, primitive rocks. They seemed natives of the place, not strangers and intruders, like those we find occasionally in the west.

They were useful in many ways. A stranger, once passing by the hill, and seeing a flock of sheep upon it, cropping what little grass grew there, said that the shepherd should have a blacksmith-shop near by, so as to have the noses of the sheep occasionally new laid, as they might soon get worn blunt. But this stranger was evidently "green." The sheep had only to sharpen their noses on some granite whetstone, to keep them sufficiently pointed for cropping the tufts of grass in the crevices of the ledge.

These old gray rocks abounded in well-fashioned minerals. The tourmalin, and the beryl, and the amethyst, and the garnet, and the andalusite dwelt here in their native homes. It was curious to find these beautiful specimens of nature's handicraft, more finished in shape than any human artificer could form, in solid masses of granite. How came these delicate, beautiful, and fragile gems in these rough old rocks? One man, whom I once met in a geological expedition, thought the Indians must have happened along, and thrust the minerals in, while the rocks were soft. But when were the rocks soft, and how came they soft?

Not all the surface of Barren Hill was covered with rocks. There were little patches of thin soil, on which grew clusters of pines. The pine, the most beautiful of forest trees, loves the neat, clean, sandy surface of such soils as Barren Hill. Here the pine feels at home. The pine is a noble tree. It grew on Barren Hill in thick clusters, towering up, with its straight stem and conical top, high toward heaven. And what music it made! It answered the gentle zephyr in strains sweet as the Eolian harp. But when the storm wind blew, the pine answered in tones deep as the pealing organ. One cluster, on the very crest of the hill, formed a conspicuous object, last seen by the adventurous seaman, as he rounded the cape that bears the name of England's maiden queen, and sped away on the billowy deep. No daring ax has yet touched those noble trees. There they stand yet, projecting their well-proportioned forms against the sky, from whatever point you approach the hill. Long may they stand! Palsied be the hand that would cut them down! He that would destroy such noble trees, adding such beauty to the landscape, and connecting the present with the past, would hardly scruple to break his grandfather's neck.

On the hill-side was a lone old apple-tree. How it came there I know not. Its age, genealogy, and history were involved in oblivious obscurity, deep as that which has gathered over the temples and pyramids of Egypt. It held the right of possession to the place it occupied, by a tenure so ancient, that the "memory of man ran not to the contrary." It was the common benefactor of the neighborhood. Its shade and its fruit were free for all. The traveler oft stopped to rest him beneath its branches, the school-boy spent his noontide recess about it, and the youth went there at twilight to dream of love. I know not but the old tree is there yet. If so, it must be getting far advanced in life. I have a filial affection for it; and if it were not, as is usually the case with aged trees, as well as aged people, so strongly attached to its native place, I would invite it to come and spend its last days here, by the side of my old beech.

Bubbling up from the gravelly soil on the hill-side was a pure spring of clear, cold water. It was none of your intermittent springs, such as flow by fits and starts—very profuse in their supply of water in a wet time, when you do not need it, and totally drying up when you do need it, thus constantly reminding you of the friendship of the selfish—but a perennial fountain, flowing the more profusely as the season advanced, and water

2

became scarce. In summer its waters grew cold, and in winter they grew warm, thus exhibiting marked independence of character, scorning to be influenced by the ever-varying temperature of the air and the earth. How refreshing on a hot summer day—a day so hot as to cause the pitch actually to fry in the pine trees—to kneel at the spring, and drink the clear, cold, sparkling waters, as they gushed up from the pure bosom of earth, into a basin of clean, white sand! It really makes me want to drink now to think of it.

On the north side of the hill was the blueberry patch. Alas! my western friends know not what a blueberry is. Like the pine, it grows only in a thin, poor, sandy soil. It is the finest of all wild fruits. But the greatest thing about the blueberries is the pleasure of picking them. In blueberry time the hill was no longer barren, at least of visitors. Matrons and maids, and boys and girls, and little children of all sorts and sizes, were there with their buckets and baskets. Merry and joyous were the blueberry days. I remember them well. Could I take another blueberry excursion, I should feel young again. At the southern base of the hill was the cranberry meadow. This modest little fruit loves to hide its blushing beauties beneath the vines and grass. It comes, too, at a time when all the other fruits fail—peeping up through the ice of winter, and disappearing only when the last snows of spring melt away. It grew in copious abundance about Barren Hill. Beyond the cranberry meadow was the bog, as the natives called it, for want of taste, I suppose, to select a better name. The bog, however, despite its unattractive name, was a beautiful feature in the landscape. It was covered with a dense growth of the finest evergreens in the world. They were principally fir. Few of my western readers have seen the fir-tree in its native glory. You have seen small specimens in the gardens and yards of the city. But he who would judge of the appearance of a forest of firs in their native swamps by the single specimens he sees in our gardens, would be about as wise as the man who carried about a single brick, exhibiting it as a specimen of his house. The straight trunk, regular branches, and deep green of the fir render it decidedly the handsomest tree that ever grew this side of Eden. The bog was rendered more beautiful in summer by the intermixture of juniper with the fir. This tree has a variety of names, such as juniper, hackmatack, tamarack, and larch. It belongs to the pine family, but is not an evergreen. It forms, however, a beautiful forest. West of the hill, just over the river, was the city. A fine city it is, too A promontory makes out into the sea, terminating in a high headland. The promontory is some three or four miles long, and about one mile broad, and forms what is called a horseback ridge, inclining gently on each side to the sea. On this ridge the city is built. Every part of it is distinctly visible from Barren Hill. Its numerous spires, its noble Exchange, its lofty Observatory, and its forest of masts from the shipping in the harbor, afford a most enchanting spectacle to the dwellers on Barren Hill. Its bells, too, whether ringing merrily for nine at night, or chiming sweetly the call to church, or pealing sadly the knell of death, redouble their music by the echoes of the hill.

At the eastern base of the hill was the ocean—the old Atlantic, the deep, dark, dashing ocean. How wild its waves beat on the beach! How they dashed against the cliffs! How they bellowed in the dark caverns! When the weather was fair, the whole expanse seemed sometimes whitened with sails, and the waves seemed to sport and play on the beach. But when the storm came, the waters foamed, and dashed, and roared with incessant thunder. There is something peculiar in the sound of waters. Did you ever listen to it? The little brook that babbles by your father's door makes music such as is not soon forgot. The cascade, as some rapid stream tumbles over the projecting rock, makes a still deeper impression. Niagara produces a sound which you can never forget. But the ocean has a voice of its own. It speaks in deep, solemn tones. They move the very soul, and stir up the deep, hidden feelings of nature.

On the whole, Barren Hill is not so mean a place. I have seen a great many places, in whose favor I could not say half so much. And I have not told all yet. I have said nothing of the herrings in the weirs, nor the clams on the flats, nor the shad in the river, nor the mackerel and codfish a little distance out on the ocean. Verily, I should like to pay the old hill a visit. I think I should know it, though I doubt whether it would know me, so changed am I since last my foot trod its rocky soil.

EPHRAIM BROWN;

OR, THE UNIVERSAL GENIUS.

WHEN I entered the academy, in one of the beautiful villages of New England, to pursue the usual course of study, preparatory to college, the first acquaintance I formed was with Ephraim Brown. Ephraim was the son of a very respectable physician in a neighboring town, and was sent to the academy to acquire the education necessary for the study of medicine. He was a good-looking young man, and distinguished for his social virtues and gentlemanly habits. He was a fine scholar, of superior literary taste, and quite accomplished for a mere academician, in the classics, mathematics, and general literature. His moral character was irreproachable, and his sentiments religiously inclined. For several months he was my room-mate, and I learned to esteem him and to love him to such a degree, that a quarter of a century has not sufficed to annihilate, if at all to diminish, my high regard and warm affection for him.

Ephraim, however, in one respect, was a very singular case. He entertained an idea that he was a universal genius. At first he thought he would study medicine, and, if he did, he would bring about a thorough revolution in the study and practice of that art. He would reduce the science of anatomy to such perfection, as to leave nothing to be attempted. In physiology, he would make discoveries, which would keep all the world agog for a thousand years. In the healing of disease, he would become so skillful, that the people within range of his practice would have to move out of the country, in order, when tired of life, to die.

At the close of the academic term, we had an exhibition. Ephraim was head and body of the whole affair, having the salutatory, and valedictory, and chief part of a scenic performance. His success in the comico-tragic was encouraging, and he thought he would become an actor. He would restore the drama to its legitimate purpose. It was true, his religious sentiments would not admit of his becoming an actor in the theater, as now managed; but he would effect a radical change. In his hands the theater should really be a school of morals. He would himself write a series of plays, that would throw Shakspeare utterly into the background. In acting, he would excel all that ever had been done, or ever should be again. Such actors as Garrick, and Forrest, and Macready, would either be driven from the stage, or take subordinate parts under his patronage. Full of high expectations of success as an actor, Ephraim went home, and I heard no more of him for some months. On entering college, however, I found Ephraim in the neighboring village, studying law. He had entered his name in the office of a distinguished jurist, and had just finished Blackstone. He thought the practice of the law might be too small business for him. He aspired higher than that. He did not think he should ever open an office; but he intended to become an expounder of the law. He would yet be Chief Justice of the Supreme Court of the United States, if he did not think there might be too much drudgery in the business. He thought, on the whole, he would become a writer on constitutional law. He would write a treatise on government which should be translated into every civilized tongue on the globe, and should become the source from which the statesmen of the universe should draw their constitutional principles for a thousand years.

Having accomplished my college course, and taken charge of an academy, I unexpectedly received, one evening, a call from my old friend Ephraim. He had now concluded to become an astronomer. He had just read Mrs. B.'s Conversations on Natural Philosophy, a common school book of those times, and had mastered the chapter on astronomy, and was going out to lecture on the subject; and, as soon as he could, by the avails of his lectures, raise the funds, he would erect, on the top of a very high hill in his native town, an observatory, from which he would make discoveries of far more importance than Herschel had ever dreamed of. In this interview he could talk of nothing but planets, and comets, and fixed stars, and nebulosities.

Ten years or more passed away, during which I had heard nothing of Ephraim, when, on a cold, winter evening, as I was sitting, with my children, about a blazing fire, in our little cottage, on the Atlantic hill, a knock was heard at the door. Wondering who could be there on such a bitter and blustering night, I opened the door, and there stood my old friend, so changed in appearance, I had difficulty in recognizing him. Welcoming him to my fireside, right glad as I was to see him, I asked him where he had been, and what he had been doing, these many years. He cheerfully gave me a history of his life and adventures, with his various enterprises and successes.

Not succeeding as well as he had hoped, in his astronomical excursion, he concluded he would try preaching. Not being a member of any Church, though evidently a man of sincere piety, he determined to preach, as the Kentuckian fought—"on his own hook." He went among the frontier settlements, near the Umbagog Lakes, and began his labors with high hopes of success. He had no doubts but converts to the truth would be multiplied on his hands, like the rocks along the river valleys; and he would build up a new and prosperous Church, whose distinctive name he had not fully determined. His Church should be a nucleus, about which should gather fraternal societies, through whom the theology and moral philosophy of the world should be reformed. Ephraim's notions of theology were generally orthodox, but they were somewhat transcendental. He loaded so big a gun that he wasted all his powder on a few charges, and fired so high over the heads of the people, that he did no execution. After a few rounds there was nobody left to fire at. All had quietly left his congregation, and he wisely concluded preaching was not his *forte*.

He then strayed over the mountains, at the head waters of the Kennebec, and spent a year or two, working among the farmers, and making himself agreeable and welcome, by his intelligence, affability, and good-nature. At last, he concluded he would turn school-teacher. Being disposed to do good, as well as produce a sensation among the natives, he looked around for some place where his services might be needed. There was a country, known down east, in those times, as the Aroostook, about five hundred miles from any place, and thither Ephraim turned his steps. He found, in the Aroostook, some ten or fifteen families, happily blest, as families in out-of-the-way places usually are, with lots of children. Ephraim opened a school, and remained full three years in the same place, teaching the little children of the wilderness, "a, b, c," "baker," and "no man may put off the law of God," and other matters of science, discussed in Webster's Spelling-Book, with occasional lectures on the classics, anatomy, law, astronomy, and theology, much to the amazement of all down east, who had never heard of so much learning. The people had boarded him around among them, and contributed, in addition, sufficient to keep him in decent clothing, and to enable him to lay by enough to meet the expenses of a foot-journey to the Kennebec, to see his old friends. Ephraim was not determined, when he left my house the next morning, what he should do next; but he thought he should return to the Aroostook, and spend his days teaching the children in the little log school-house the people had erected for him.

I have never seen nor heard of Ephraim since, though some years have passed; but I presume he is yet as far as ever from realizing his high-wrought expectations.

I have never been acquainted with any genius just like Ephraim, but I have known many fail in success, from causes similar to those which affected him. His notion that he was a universal genius, led him continually on a phantom chase after that which ever eluded his grasp. Had he deliberately chosen any definite business of life, and soberly adhered to it, be it medicine, or law, or teaching, or, indeed, any other profession or pursuit, he might have become eminent. He had talents, taste, and good character—capital sufficient to set up any one in the world; but no man can expect to succeed in any business requiring time and talent, unless his attention be devoted to that only, with other congenial and auxiliary pursuits. The idea of universality of genius is utterly Utopian. We do not mean that genius is naturally limited to any one channel of enterprise, but that it can run only in one channel at the same time. Any one, of ordinary capacity, by diligent adherence to any one business or enterprise, may attain a respectable rank; but if he divides his attention and efforts between several enterprises, he will most surely fail in all.

Ephraim seemed greatly to lack independence of will and strength of personality. The least difficulty lying along his path was sufficient to deter him from the prosecution of a favorite enterprise. If one would succeed in the enterprises of life, he must ever love to meet difficulties for the pleasure of overcoming them. In all matters of responsibility, he must be unyielding and uncompromising. The more opposition and impediment he finds, the more energy, determination, and personal will he should exercise. I have seen many young men, of fine talents and amiable disposition, become utterly useless, and sometimes ruined, for the mere want of the "I take the responsibility" principle. Those of a temper yielding in matters of difficulty in enterprises, are usually yielding in moral principle, and hence are they easily seduced by the vicious. Ephraim, however, was as unyielding in morals as he was easily discouraged in enterprises. You could neither coax, nor drive, nor frighten him to do wrong. His conscience was impregnable. In this he differed from most of those who are deficient in personal energy.

On the whole, Ephraim was a right-down good, clever fellow. His faults were such as are common to all easy, clever fellows. If one be predisposed to be vicious and really bad, we can usually, if he have stamina enough about him to stay, when put into the right shape, make something of him; but, when one has not resistance enough to maintain his position, nor cohesion of character sufficient to retain any determinate form, but taking, like water, whatever form surrounding bodies and circumstances may give, there is little hope of accomplishing much by education and discipline. You may labor long and hard, and you can by no effort make water retain the permanent shape of a block of marble or of wood

THE EMIGRANT.

THE emigrant from New England, as he leaves his native home for a residence in the west, experiences some strange and hardly definable feelings. His home has become endeared to him by the associations of childhood, of youth, and of manhood. There is the sloping hillside on which he gathered the violets of spring and the lilies of summer. There is the little brook, among whose shady bowers he spent many a summer hour. There is the woodland plain, over which he rambled in autumn, when the leaves were falling around him, and every wild flower had disappeared before the chilling frost. There is the old orchard, whose ripe fruits he had so often gathered up—the meadow all waving with grass—the pasture with its glades and dells all grown over with brakes and ferns. There is the old elm, planted perhaps by the hand of his grandfather, with its long branches overhanging the house; and there is the pine, planted by his own hand, with its evergreen tassels sighing to the wind. In the distance are the blue hills, which have formed the background of the landscape on which he has looked from infancy; and nearer are the silver lakes, from whose mirrowy surface he has so often seen reflected the sunlight of morning.

The old cottage in which he was born and nurtured, and which has also been thus far the nursery of his own little children, has charms for him, which the princely palace might not equal. Its image, with the scenery around it, is indelibly stamped on his soul. Let him become a wanderer in distant lands—let new and startling scenes every-where meet him—let him make a new home wherever he may, the impress of his childhood's home will still lie too deep in his memory ever to be effaced. Wherever his waking thoughts may be, his dreams will still linger about this spot.

The emigrant, before he leaves this sacred spot, calls his children once more around him. Once more they kneel before the old family altar, and offer up their devotions to a protecting Providence. Then they walk together once more about the orchard and garden, instinctively bidding good-by to each floweret and shrub. Returning, they cast a "longing, lingering look" at their cottage halls, and close the doors to open them no more forever.

Slowly and sadly the emigrant proceeds on his weary way. From the topmost ridge of some long hill, he catches the last glance at his cottage home. The carriage stops. The family, little children and all, fix their eyes, full of tears, on that loved spot. There it is, in quiet, silent beauty, embowered in shrubbery, and rendered still more enchanting to the sight by the soft blue tinge which distance throws around it. A moment more—one other look, and the carriage moves on, and the cottage disappears forever.

Not yet, however, has every familiar scene gone from the emigrant's view. There is yet about him the scenery of his native state. These farms, these neat villages, these lakes, these crystal streams he has seen before. One by one, however, every familiar scene fades away, till the last hill of his native land sinks below the horizon. The whizzing steam car bears him on, and he stands on the summit of the Alleghanies. Here he stops again, to take one more look at the world he is leaving. He stands on the boundary line between the east and the west. On the one side is the world which he has long known and admired—on the other is, to him, an "undiscovered country." He looks back, and there rushes on his soul the thrilling memory of the past—the memory of incidents, and scenes, and friends which he had long since lost in oblivion. Philosophers tell us that there is reason to believe our thoughts and feelings imperishable; that relics of sensation may exist for an indefinite time in a latent state, and may all be brought up whenever any stimulus, sufficiently exciting, acts on the mind; and that, therefore, there are occasions when there is brought before the mind the collective experience of its whole past existence. Such an occasion occurs to the emigrant, as he stands on the Alleghanies and looks back, over hill and dale, toward his native home. Scenes long since faded away—incidents long ago forgotten—friends long since followed to the grave—all come up before him as vivid and as bright as though the events had just occurred. His eyes swimming with the recollections of the past, he can look no longer. He closes them; but yet he sees painted on the living canvas of his soul the land of his birth, with its mountains and valleys, its lakes and streams, the cottage where he lived, with all its rural attractions, and the friends he had long known and loved.

Gathering up his energies, the emigrant opens his eyes and looks before him. At his feet he sees a range of hills, lower than that on which he stands, succeeded by another, lower still, and still another, continually diminishing as they recede, till far away, near the distant horizon, he sees spread out, in quiet beauty, tinged with the sunlight of evening, the illimitable plains of the west.

The emigrant's heart is glad. He winds his way down the mountain side, and presses on his journey. On the banks of the Scioto he again looks back. The last hill has faded away in the east. He looks forward and there sees before him the fertile plains of western Ohio, of Indiana, and of Illinois. To him it appears one vast wilderness, without habitation or cultivated field—a dead level, varied by no elevation or depression, and enlivened by no rippling brook. Wending his way, however, westward, he perceives what he supposed a level plain to be an undulating surface, intersected by many a meandering stream, and covered with corn, wheat, grass, and forest trees in such abundance and magnitude as to defy all his former calculations of the productive powers of nature. Pursuing his way he reaches the Wabash, flowing through the most fertile valley ever wet with the dews of heaven, or warmed by the rays of the sun. Here there appears before him a variegated landscape of woodland and prairies, exhibiting a scene of beauty, to which, even in fair New England, his eye had never been accustomed. Still moving toward the setting sun, the emigrant soon finds himself on the interminable, tenantless, homeless, treeless prairie. Day after day he moves on, nor meets one human face, unless some traveler like himself may cross his path, and then all is loneliness again. The sense of loneliness is one that must oppress him, wherever he may make his journey through the interior of the great west. The dense and continuous forests, the prairies, and even the immense fields of corn, all tend to make him feel lost in the vastness of the scenes with which he is surrounded. He stands on the bluff and looks down on ten thousand acres of corn, all in one continuous field. He looks on the cultivated prairie, waving for miles with the golden wheat, all ready for the sickle. He goes into the forest, and the prodigious trees overwhelm him by their size, and make him dizzy by their hight. The calmness of the atmosphere, the stillness that every-where prevails, oppress him with emotions of sadness. He feels like the shepherd king of Palestine when he looked on the heavens in their grandeur, and then thought on the frailty of man.

In some retired spot, surrounded by primeval beauty, the emigrant makes him another home. The forest is cleared away, and the fields grow green with corn. Soon the little white cottage, resembling, as much as possible, his former home, erects its modest front. Up its walls climb the woodbine, the jessamine, the eglantine, and the honeysuckle; and around it cluster the sweet-brier, the almond, the lilac, and the rose, exhibiting the same beauty, and emitting the same fragrance as those around his home on the Atlantic hill. His cottage halls now again echo with the merry laugh of childhood. Tiny hands gather up the dandelions of spring, and little feet bound over the decorated landscape. The little ones—rambling from nook to nook, and dell to dell, gathering wild flowers of every hue, walking hand in hand along the garden avenues, admiring the shrubbery and flowers, and listening to the mocking-bird, the sweetest of all songsters, and unknown in the north—earnestly inquire of their mother if she supposes their old place can be so pleasant. Then is the emigrant's heart glad. The cloud of sadness is dispelled from his soul. He is lonely no more. He meets not, it is true, the familiar faces of his old friends; but he is content with the society of his own household. He misses the excitement and the stirring scenes with which he was once surrounded; but he heeds it not—he learns to find sufficient interest and amusement at his own fireside. He dreams of his old home; but his new home has, in his waking hours, sufficient charms to remove the sadness of his dreams. He looks in vain for the church of his native village, with its spire pointing to the blue sky; but he still may worship with renewed zeal at his own family altar. The pealing organ he hears no more; but sweet voices around his domestic hearth chant the morning and evening hymn of thanksgiving and praise. Wherever the loved ones are, there is *home*—wherever home is, there may be peace, and content, and happiness.

MT. AUBURN CEMETERY.

On a visit to the east, being detained a day or two at Boston, and being tired of the heat, and dust, and noise of the city, I made an excursion to Mount Auburn, the city of the dead. The distance from Boston is about five miles, through a succession of villages of the New England style, with their neat, shaded streets, fine gardens, white cottages, and steepled churches. The most important village on the way is Cambridge, the seat of the venerable Harvard University, rich in the associations of the past. About a mile west of Cambridge, I came to a large gateway, opening into a beautifully-wild and romantic inclosure, containing about one hundred acres. Over the gate is written, in conspicuous characters, these words: "Then shall the dust return to the earth as it was, and the spirit shall return unto God who gave it." Entering by the gate, I passed down an avenue between rows of pines and firs, to a small lake bordered by willows. Leaving the lake, I passed on a few rods, and saw before me a natural mound, surmounted by a neat monument of very beautiful Italian marble. Being the first monument we meet on entering the cemetery, it naturally arrests attention and excites curiosity. We readily suppose it may in many words record the history, describe the character, and extol the virtues of him who sleeps beneath. On approaching, however, this beautiful monument, I saw inscribed on it but a single word—the name of the philosopher and philanthropist, who came from a far country to visit our own fair land—who died here suddenly, far from his home and his friends, and for whom strangers had made a grave in this beautiful spot. It was SPURZHEIM. How expressive appears that simple inscription, that single word, *Spurzheim!* His name alone is sufficient to recall to the mind the history and the virtues of that great and good man, who held so distinguished a rank in philosophy. At the invitation of his friends and admirers in America, he had left his native land across the ocean, bringing with him a reputation as a lecturer on science and philosophy, such as few men had ever attained. He had been in this country but a few days when he fell ill of a fever, and died amidst the regrets of all who had ever heard his name. The following lines, written for the occasion by the Rev. Mr. Pierpont, were sung at his grave:

"Stranger, there is bending o'er thee
  Many an eye with sorrow wet;
All our stricken hearts deplore thee;
  Who that knew thee can forget?

Who forget what thou hast spoken?
  Who thine eye, thy noble frame?
But that golden bowl is broken,
  In the greatness of thy fame.

Autumn's leaves shall fall and wither
  On the place where thou shalt rest;
'Tis in love we bear thee thither,
  To thy mourning mother's breast.

For the lessons thou hast taught us,
  For the charm thy goodness gave,
For the stores of wisdom brought us,
  Can we give thee but a grave?"

Leaving this spot, I passed on over the grounds. Avenues and paths intersecting each other at various angles run in every direction over this city of the dead. Their names are derived from the vast variety of trees and shrubs with which nature has adorned this beautiful spot. There is Larch Avenue, Beech Avenue, Oak Avenue, Hazel Path, Catalpa Path, Jasmine Path, Hawthorn Path, Vine Path, Iris Path, Linden Path, and so on through all the vegetable vocabulary. Of all places I ever visited, this is the most remarkable for its diversified surface and for its variety of vegetation. There are hills, valleys, horseback ridges, lakes, glens, dells, and brooks, of every possible shape and variety. On the small space of one hundred acres may be found growing spontaneously nearly every variety of tree, shrub, and wild flower common in the north, with most of the exotics cultivated in the gardens of the vicinity. The mingling of wild and cultivated shrubbery, of indigenous and exotic flowers, in so rural and romantic a spot, produces a fine effect. I ascended a hill which commanded a view of the grounds and much of the surrounding country. Here you may see, through the openings of the trees, Cambridge, Brighton, Brookline, Charleston, Roxbury, Dorchester, and I know not how many more of the beautiful villages in the vicinity of Boston, and beyond them the towers and steeples of the great city itself, with the blue waters of the ocean stretching away in the distance. Looking west, you may see the green fields, and orchards, and gardens, and white farm cottages, which form so distinguishing a feature in a New England landscape. The scene was enlivened by the cheerful sounds of melody which nature was pouring forth from the forest, the earth, and the air. The robin was practicing his plaintive song from the top of a beech; the wren was twittering by her nest in a hollow stump; the cuckoo was uttering her monotone at a distance; the sparrow was adding her modest notes to the general symphony; the bobolink was fluttering round full of music; and the northern mocking-bird was imitating them all from a willow by the brook. To this was added the chirp of the cricket in the grass, the ceaseless hum of the bee in the air, and the sighing of the summer wind through the pines. It was a lovely summer day, as I stood on this hill, and cast my eye over this scene of beauty, and listened to these sounds of nature mingled with the faint hum of the distant city. The interest of the scene was hightened by the associations of the neighborhood. I was in the early home of the Pilgrims. I could almost step on the rock of Plymouth where they landed. Harvard University, founded by them, was in plain sight. So also was Bunker Hill, of glorious memory. Lexington and Concord were close at hand. In the midst of so much beauty, and so many associations of the past, I could hardly believe myself in the city of the dead. But a glance through the trees exhibited, in every direction, the monuments which the living had erected over the departed.

The ground is laid out in lots of sufficient size for containing the graves of a family. The proprietor, each for himself, incloses his lot with an iron fence, and ornaments it with shrubbery and flowers. In the center of the lot is a monument, on which are inscribed the names of those whose graves are made in the inclosure. There is great variety exhibited in the style of the monuments, each proprietor consulting his own taste. Some are of marble, some of sandstone, and some of granite. Their shapes and sizes vary, some being plain and neat, others gorgeous and extravagantly expensive. Some of the inscriptions are simple and beautiful, others labored and in bad taste.

Though nature has formed this place the most variedly beautiful that can well be imagined, and the resources of ancient and modern taste have been freely expended in adding to it the decorations of art, yet I would not desire to be buried here. There is too much pomp, and show, and circumstance about it. There is an apparent effort to carry the artificial distinctions of this world to the grave. Let me not be buried in so public a place, nor in the crowded city, where my body, hurried by the hired sexton through the busy streets, must be consigned to the grave, where the idle passer-by may disturb the loved one, that comes at night-fall to drop the tear of affection on the turf that covers me. When I am dead, let me be borne from my cottage home on the shoulders of sympathizing neighbors to the church where I was accustomed to worship. From thence let me be carried to the rural burying-place. Let there the beautiful burial-service be said over my poor body, and a hymn be sung by voices that have loved me. There let me rest, where the sparrow may build her nest unscared, save when the foot of an affectionate wife, or a beloved child, or a valued friend, may press down the wild flowers that grow on my grave.

There is something peculiarly interesting to me about the old graveyards of New England. You will sometimes, in traveling through the country, unexpectedly pass a graveyard, strangely populous for the place where it is located. It may be near a small village, or it may be away from the present population, surrounded on every side by a forest of pines. There lie successive buried generations. The old, dilapidated, moss-covered stones, in many a quaint inscription, tell the story of some old pilgrim of a generation long since past. You will often find in these ancient cemeteries many a name familiar to you—many a name highly honored in the history of the country—many a name that is handed down from generation to generation, associated with noble deeds. But it is not so at Mount Auburn. You find there the names of few known to the country. There is little there to associate the present with the past. The proprietors, with few exceptions, appear to be the merchants of Boston, known only in their own business circles. There are, however, a few monuments erected by societies and benevolent individuals over the remains of those whose memories will long be cherished. I noticed particularly a neat little monument erected by the scholars of one of the Boston schools in memory of their teacher, one erected by the ladies of a neighboring town over their pastor, one to Hannah Adams, by her female friends, and one by the Massachusetts Agricultural Society to Thomas G. Fessenden, who has done more, perhaps, for the promotion of scientific agriculture than any other man.

I looked in vain among these memorials of the dead for the name of one dear to myself—a name associated as it was in my mind with many recollections of the past, and with such genius and goodness as rarely fall to the lot of man—the name of B. B. THATCHER. I know not as he was buried here. I felt, however, disappointed; for I had reason to hope the world would not let such a man as *Thatcher* pass from among us without a stone to tell where he lies. I know not, however, but his friends interpreted literally, and sacredly obeyed his "last request," published a short time before his death.

"Bury me by the ocean's side—
O, give me a grave on the verge of the deep,
Where the noble tide,
When the sea-gales blow, my marble may sweep;
And the glistening surf
Shall burst o'er the turf,
And bathe my cold bosom in death as I sleep.

Bury me by the deep,
Where a living footstep may never tread;
And come not to weep—
O, wake not with sorrow the dream of the dead!
But leave me the dirge
Of the breaking surge,
And the silent tears of the sea on my head.

And grave no Parian praise;
Gather no bloom for the heartless tomb,
And burn no holy blaze
To flatter the awe of its solemn gloom;

For the holier light
Of the star-eyed night,
And the violet morning my rest will illume;

And honors more dear
Than of sorrow and love shall be strown on my clay,
By the young, green year,
With its fragrant dews and crimson array.
O, leave me to sleep
On the verge of the deep,
Till the skies and the seas shall have passed away."

but Thatcher can not soon be forgotten. His genius, his modesty, his goodness, his purity of character, have embalmed his memory in the hearts of all who ever knew him.

While I was thinking of Thatcher, I wandered along over many a ridge and many a dale, and unexpectedly came upon a scene that touched my heart more keenly than any thing my visit had yet presented. On a neat little mound rested a granite slab, surmounted by a marble table, standing on four small columns. On the granite, protected from the weather by the table over it, rested a sculptured marble couch, on which was reclining the perfect figure of a child, a little girl perhaps four or five years old, with her little hands folded on her breast, in all the sweet loveliness and melancholy beauty which often so strikingly appear in the early dead. The face was apparently beautiful by nature, but rendered still more interesting by the silent beauty of death. The smile of innocence was on the lips—the smile that death could not remove—the smile that appeared as if some angel had a hand in forming it—the smile that spoke of heaven. On the monument was simply inscribed the name, EMILY. I know not when I have met with any thing that so touched my heart. The scene brought up before me the image of many a lovely one whom I had seen in youthful beauty deposited in the grave. The emotions, the thoughts of that hour can not soon be forgotten. I lingered over the picture, nor minded the lapse of time, till the sun of a long summer day was gone down, and the shades of evening were falling around me. I looked up and found that the numerous visitors who had been wandering, as well as myself, among these haunts of melancholy interests, had all departed, and the gates were shut.

"I felt like one who treads alone
Some banquet hall deserted,
Whose lights are fled, whose garlands dead,
And all but me departed."

Slowly and sadly I retired. The keeper observed me approaching, and uncomplainingly, and even kindly, opened again the gate for me. Alone I returned to the city, where I arrived just as the last lights of evening were disappearing.

PROVIDENCE.

THERE is, in the constitution of the world, a wonderful relation of things, which can only be referred to Providence. The atmosphere surrounds the earth, and extends some distance from it. The water covers a large portion of its surface. Heat, drawn mostly from the sun, but modified by collateral influences, is constantly active. The combined action of these agencies induces and maintains the condition of things indispensably necessary to the existence of living beings. The absence of either of these agencies would be fatal to every man, and every animal, and every insect, and every plant on this globe. The undue preponderance of either over the others would be equally fatal. No human power could so combine these agencies, and mete out their several influences, as to produce the required result. The heat causes the winds to blow, while the winds temper and distribute the heat. The heat causes the water to rise in vapor. The air supports the vapor. The heat rarifying the air, the vapors descend in showers, tempering the heat as they descend. Thus is kept up an eternal round of action, in which each agent alternately acts on the others, and is itself acted on by each of them. It is in the managing and the controlling of these distinct and antagonistic agencies—in the effecting, from their combined action, a determinate result, and in the providing against disturbances that might arise from the undue influence of any one, that we see the wisdom of Providence.

The earth, however, forms but a small part of the material universe. There are known to be, in the solar system, other planets like the earth, and some of them inconceivably larger. There are also smaller bodies attendant on the planets. All these bodies are in motion. The earth moves in its orbit more than sixty thousand miles an hour—a velocity a thousand times greater than that of the steam car over its iron track. The secondary planets, or moons, have also a movement around their primaries, in addition to the movement of both around the sun. There are belonging to the system an unknown number of bodies, called comets, moving in very eccentric orbits, sometimes approaching very near the sun, then darting away into distant and unknown regions. All these bodies, moving with inconceivable velocity, and liable to a thousand disturbances by their mutual attractions, have yet moved on, each in its own path, and all in regular order and harmony, for six thousand years. It is the eye of Providence that watches them in their course—it is the hand of Providence that guides them—it is the intelligence of Providence that foresees and provides against the disturbances to which they might be subject.

But the system of planets moving about the sun is far from being the whole, or even a considerable part of the material universe. You may, on any clear night, see, without the aid of telescopes, at least one thousand stars, each as large as our sun, and each probably surrounded by a system of planets as numerous as those of our own system. When you bring the telescope to the aid of your eye, you may see, in the distant regions of space, thousands of thousands of stars, each surrounded by its own system of planets—each forming the center of that system, and distributing light and heat to every part. To all these systems of worlds the care of Providence extends. There is existing a relation not only between the several parts of each system, but all the parts are connected in one grand system—one whole—one universe.

There is a movement of the systems themselves around some common center. What that center is, and how long is the period of revolution, no human philosopher can tell. But the eye of Providence is over the whole. This movement within a movement, this complicated machinery of the universe, is all under his constant direction. The motions of each planet around its center—the motions of the systems around the common center—the times, directions, distances, and velocities, are all provided for. To human eye each planet might seem to pursue its journey unconscious of any connection with the other bodies of its system—each system might seem independent of all other systems; yet the unseen hand of Providence unites them all together in one harmonious whole.

Thus we see the wisdom and power of Providence in the material universe—in bodies having no intelligence, no will, no free agency. In the moral universe, in the history of man, there is another movement to provide for—the free agency of man—the power to will and to do according to his own pleasure. The acts of men are seldom intended by the performers to have any reference to the designs of Providence; yet all human agency becomes, in the end, subservient to the accomplishment of his great purposes. Men act independently of each other; and yet their acts are all linked together. In the history of the world, each generation of men, each nation, each community, each individual has pursued its own course, for the accomplishment of its own purposes, independent and regardless of those who went before and those who might come after; and yet each has contributed, perhaps equally, to perform the several parts composing the grand designs of Providence. The world is a stage. Each generation, as it comes on, performs its part, as it pleases, regardless alike of the acts of its predecessors or successors; and yet these independent parts, under the superintendence of Providence, form one grand and perfect drama. The free agency of man extends only to the performance of the act. It can not control the ultimate consequences of the act. When, therefore, the action is performed, the power of the actor ceases. But the consequences of human action may extend through all time. Over these human agency has no control. But Providence superintends, and overrules, and uses them all for the accomplishing of his own designs.

The history of the world abounds in illustrations of this view of the doctrine of Providence. That beautiful story, in the sacred writings, of the ten Hebrews and their brother, will readily occur to the reader. Envy toward Joseph induced his brethren to sell him to a company of strangers. The act was one of great enormity. Its ostensible design was to defeat the purposes of Providence. "Let us see," said they, as they were conspiring against the child, "what will become of his dreams." But the very act by which these men intended to defeat one of the great purposes of Providence, became, when once it had passed out of the power of the actors, the very means of accomplishing that purpose.

There are, in the history of the world, two great events, which, from their prominence, may be selected as illustrations of our subject.

The first is the conquest of Italy, and the western Roman empire, by the barbarous tribes of northern Europe. Italy, under the Roman emperors, was a civilized, an enlightened, a religious country. The refinement, the arts, the learning of the world, were all deposited there. The tribes of northern Europe knew nothing of refinement, nothing of the arts, nothing of literature, nothing of Christianity. From their primeval forests, from their rugged hills, they poured down in countless numbers on the cultivated vales of Italy. From their rude touch the arts shrunk. At their approach learning retired to convents and monastic cells. Humanity shuddered at the coming desolation of all that was good and fair. But the watchful eye of Providence was over the scene; and Christianity, daughter of heaven, stood her ground, when civilization, and art, and learning forsook it and fled. By her influence the conqueror was conquered, the vanquisher vanquished. The result was, that both parties, the Italian and the northern invader, were mutually benefited, and the interests of Christianity and of civil liberty promoted. A new order of things, a new form of civilization commenced, and the Christian religion was introduced into all the tribes and kingdoms of Europe.

The second great event of history to which we allude, is the fall of Constantinople, and the conquest of the eastern Roman empire by the Turks. During that long period usually called the dark ages, Constantinople formed one bright spot, around which yet lingered the twilight of literature. It stood on the soil of classic Greece. It formed the outpost of Christendom. For eight centuries the Christian world had been waging a doubtful war with Mohammedanism. The cross and the crescent had alternately prevailed in Asia, till Mohammedanism had acquired undisputed control over all those fair regions, and was now approaching the very gate of Europe. Constantinople was that gate. Let that be battered down, and the resistless tide of Moslemism might sweep over the lovely vales of Greece, dash over the Alps, and desolate every country of Christendom. During the storming of the city, which lasted for nearly two months, the world was looking on, awaiting the result with intense anxiety. At last the crisis came, the Moslems triumphed, and Constantinople fell. The tidings flew to every city and every hamlet of Europe. To the heart of the patriot the event brought dismay—to the friends of learning it appeared that the last glimmering of twilight had disappeared, and night—a night that might know no morning—had come upon the world—to the Christian it brought the extinction of his hopes for the universal triumph of the Gospel. An icy chill came over men. They sat down and looked at each other in sullen despair.

But the imperial city of Constantine fell not unobserved by the all-seeing eye of Providence. Her Christian Churches were not converted to Moslem mosques without his notice. The Saracen might do his utmost: his hour was come. Let him enjoy it. Here, however, was the "beginning of the end." He might take the city—he might disperse the inhabitants; but he could not control nor direct the ultimate consequences of his acts.

The city, falling into the hands of the Turks, was sacked and pillaged, and the inhabitants dispersed abroad. They fled for security and protection to the cities and villages of Europe. They were, in general, a refined and accomplished people, having a national and hereditary adaptedness to the pursuits of taste and literature. Of this their conqueror could not deprive them. He might destroy the books which he found deposited in the city, but he could not destroy the Greek language nor the Greek mind. The exiled citizens carried with them their learning and their taste. They became teachers in the villages of Europe. Every stray particle of that twilight which had so long hung around Constantinople, now became a sun, dispensing light to those who sat in darkness. The result was glorious. The morning soon appeared. The darkness of the thousand years was dispelled. The human mind arose from its long sleep. There followed the discovery of the art of printing, of the mariner's compass, of the telescope, and of the new world.

The conquest of Constantinople, which seemed, to human view, to secure permanent and universal success to the Ottoman power, laid the foundation for its ultimate ruin. Mohammedanism belonged to a dark age. It could not flourish in the light. Intercourse with other nations must, in the very nature of things, modify, and in the end essentially change those peculiarities of circumstance and of character to which it owed its success. This the Moslems of the fifteenth century, when they were storming the walls of Constantinople, did not foresee. It is true, the Turk still has a name and a place among the nations; but that name no longer strikes terror to the heart of the Christian, and that place is far down in the scale of nations. The crescent has long been waning, and is now but a single line of light. The Turk still dwells in Istamboul; but he has been driven from Athens, and from Sparta, and from Thebes, and from Corinth. In the onward march of the nations, and in his own obstinate, pertinacious, and sullen refusal to adopt their improvements, he reads his doom.

The two great events to which we have alluded, are by no means the only ones in which is clearly seen the overruling hand of Providence. The history of the world would seem to form one great chain. The several links were made, each by different men, at different shops, and in regions far distant from each other. None knew, as he was hammering out, and shaping his own part, that it was to have any connection with any other link. But Providence, by an unseen hand, has joined the parts all together, and formed a chain encircling the globe, reaching back to the time when the morning stars sang together at creation's birth, and terminating only when the same stars, at the evening twilight of time, shall sing its requiem.

As Providence effects his designs by human agents, it

may be that the errors and the faults of men, in enterprises of reform, may retard, though they can not defeat the accomplishment of his purposes. Yet even apparent delay in the accomplishment of a good enterprise, may be the very means of ultimate success. There is a winter in the moral as well as in the physical world. In winter ephemeral vegetation dies, but not the perennial plant. To this, winter is the season of rest and of preparation for a more vigorous growth. So is it in moral enterprises. Seasons of rest there may be; but it is only to gather strength. Moral enterprises may seem to suffer retrogression; but it is only like the river which reaches some barrier thrown across its way, and which flows back till it may gather such an accumulation of weight as to break down the obstacle. The history of the world, indeed, forms a great river. Its sources, like those of our own Mississippi, are far distant from each other—one in the mountains of the setting sun, and another where first falls his rising beam—one in the icy fountains of the frozen north, and another in the broad plains of the sunny south. Its tributary streams may seem to flow in any and in every direction, and may continually be changing their course, winding around hills, and meandering through vales, but their destiny is onward, onward still. An invisible power controls them, and at last they all unite in one broad, deep channel, and flow on, through time, toward the illimitable and fathomless bosom of eternity.

Providence regards not only the elements of nature, the universe of matter, and the prominent events of history, but also the personal interests of individuals. That same eye that watches the motion of the stars, regards the humblest of his creatures. Without his notice time plucks not a hair from the temple of age. Nor need we fear lest we be overlooked amidst the profusion of his works. We can not go where he rules not. Could we mount the wings of the morning sunbeam, and be borne away to the most distant isle of the ocean, his power would be there still.

> "Should fate command me
> To the farthest verge of the green earth—
> Rivers unknown to song, where first the sun
> Gilds Indian mountains, or his setting beam
> Flames on the Atlantic isle, 'tis naught to me,
> Since God is ever present, ever felt,
> In the void waste as in the city full;
> And where he vital breathes, there must be joy."

THE WHITE MOUNTAINS.

THE White Mountains of New Hampshire form a conspicuous and interesting point in the scenery of New England. From earliest childhood I had gazed on their aerial summits with admiration and wonder. From the hill near which I first opened my eyes on this beautiful world, I might see, far above and beyond the towers and steeples of the distant city that arose in that direction, the snow-colored peaks of those magnificent hills. When I left the place of my birth, and went many miles east, to spend the maturer days of childhood, there still towered up before me those noble piles. From the hills that skirted the evergreen plains, on which was located the venerable institution where I spent the maturer days of youth, these mountains might still be seen. And when I had become a man, and settled in my own humble cottage, on a hill far from the ocean-dashed cliff where I had listened to the incessant roaring of the waves, there still rose up in solitary grandeur, far above all intervening peaks, the granite summit of Mount Washington. Nor could I travel in any direction without encountering, often as I ascended an eminence, the distant view of these everlasting mountains. They had become associated with the dreams of childhood, the reveries of youth, and the sober thoughts of manhood. I had often looked, at evening, on those lofty peaks, looming up into the clear sky, illuminated by the rays of the setting sun, and wondered what might be concealed among their dark ravines and gloomy dells—what scenes of picturesque beauty might be enjoyed from their bright summits—what "better land," what fairy region might lie beyond.

In the summer of 1836, having a few weeks of leisure, I resolved to visit these mountains. In company with several friends I started on the excursion. We proceeded through a delightful country of varied scenery—lofty hills, deep valleys, broad rivers, and mountain torrents—till on the second day we arrived at Fryeburg, on the Saco river, thirty miles from the White Mountains, although it appears at their very base. Fryeburg is one of the most lovely spots on earth. It is a village of about one hundred houses, in a beautiful valley, through which the Saco winds with a course so meandering as to make a distance of more than thirty miles within sight of the village. This valley is encircled by lofty hills, rising one above another, with the White Mountains towering above the whole. Lovely, quiet, and peaceful as this place now appears, it was once the theater of one of the most desperate and bloody battles that history or tradition has ever recorded. A century ago this was the home of the Saco Indians, the most warlike and powerful of all the tribes of the north. It was also the grand rendezvous of all the hostile tribes in this region, and was the principal link in the chain of communication between the tribes of New England and those of Canada. From this point they issued out in hostile incursions, carrying death to the settlements for a hundred miles in every direction. Many a mother fell bleeding under the tomahawk—many an infant was dashed against the stones. A company was formed at Boston, under one of the most intrepid leaders of those brave times, for the purpose of breaking up this haunt of merciless savages. They went prepared to effect their purpose, or perish in the attempt. They made their way through an unbroken wilderness, more than fifty miles beyond the frontiers; found their enemies in their native recess; posted themselves by a small lake that admitted of no retreat; and there fought, some of them in single combat by deliberate challenge, till scarcely one on either side was left to tell the story. The trunks of the trees, yet standing on the borders of the lake, attest, after the lapse of a century, the desperate conflict, of which they are the only surviving witnesses. Countless marks are yet seen where the ball lodged in their trunks, and has been since extracted by the curious or the idle.

After viewing this memorable battle-ground, and resting for a night in the hospitable mansion of a venerable friend, we proceeded on our way, up the valley of the Saco, winding among precipitous hills, exhibiting at every turn the most varied scenery. When near the celebrated notch, where the hills approach so near the river's brink as to leave scarcely room for a carriage, we suddenly met a thunder-storm. The river dashing along from rock to rock—the hills towering precipitously high up beyond the dark clouds—the rain pouring down in torrents—the thunder redoubled manifold by its reverberation among the hills, and the lightning leaping from peak to peak, formed altogether a scene sublime beyond description. The whole company, overwhelmed by their emotions, involuntarily stopped in the open road. One of them, unable to restrain his feelings, leaped from his carriage, fell on his knees, then prostrated his face to the earth, and uttered ejaculations of admiration to the name of Jehovah. It was near this spot, where, a few years before, a whole family had been overwhelmed by an avalanche from the mountain. A slide had started from the summit and come down with resistless force, bearing the huge rocks and trees with it. It was night. The family, as it is supposed, were aroused from sleep by the thundering approach of the avalanche. They leaped from their beds, they fled from their home, they ran for their lives, but rushed into the grasp of death. The avalanche, just before it reached the house, divided, going off in different directions, leaving the house uninjured, but overtaking the family, and burying every one of them deep beneath the ruins of the mountain. The house was standing when we passed. No living creature was seen about it but a solitary mouse, which we scared from one of the deserted rooms.

A few miles beyond this spot we came to the narrow defile called the notch. Here the river, now dwindled to a brook which a child might leap over, makes its way through a pass so narrow as to afford but barely sufficient space for a carriage, while on each side the granite cliffs rise to a great hight, sometimes perpendicular, and sometimes jutting over as if about to fall and crush the unwary traveler. After passing the notch, we came to an open but elevated plain, where we found a comfortable house of entertainment. Here we rested for the night, intending to ascend the mountain in the morning. Arising in the morning, bright and early, we procured a guide and prepared for the ascent. We plunged into a dense forest of evergreen, and with many a weary step clambered up the steep ascent. As we proceeded the trees became "few and far between," and dwindled to mere dwarfs. After climbing up, up, up, for a distance of about two miles, we reached the summit of the first mountain. This was a plain of great extent, commanding a fine view in every direction. Here we saw the summit of Mount Washington, the highest of the group, distant four miles. For more than three miles the path lay along this elevated table-land, with slight depressions and elevations, though gradually rising, exhibiting new views of distant scenery with every change of position, till we reached the foot of the last peak, that of Mount

Washington itself. Here we rested for awhile, and took a refreshing drink of water from a clear and cold spring. Thus prepared we commenced the tedious ascent over naked rocks, broken into countless fragments, piled one above another, and bleached by the storms of ages. At last we gained the highest peak of this enormous pyramid. The atmosphere was clear, only a light cloud occasionally passed over the sun. This, however, added to the interest of the scene. The flitting shadow of a cloud, moving rapidly over the mountain, and traced in its progress for many miles, as it was borne south by the north wind, was a spectacle which I had often admired in a hilly country, but which I had never before seen on so grand a scale.

The view from Mount Washington combines the beautiful, the grand, and the sublime. You have before you, on the south, the Saco, winding its devious passage among precipitous hills, till it escapes in the broad plains of Fryeburg. Far away in the south is spread out before you the illimitable Atlantic. On the east you see the Androscoggin, winding, for many miles, through an unbroken wilderness, then issuing out among cultivated fields and beautiful villages. On the west you see, far over the hills, the valley of the Connecticut, and the distant range of the Green Mountains beyond. On the north you look on an ocean of mountains of various forms and sizes, covered with forests of every variety of evergreen. So elevated is Mount Washington above all other hills in the neighborhood, that you may look down on every object as far as the laws of vision will permit. I recognized many a town, lake, and stream, which I had known in the regions below. I looked for my own humble cottage, three days' journey distant, but it was lost in the dimness of distance.

I can never forget my visit to those magnificent piles

of nature's own forming. Years have since passed away. In the mean time I have exchanged the magnificent hills, on which my eye rested from childhood, for the equally-magnificent plains of the west. But still the beauty and grandeur of the view from Mount Washington, form a vivid picture on which I love to look. This picture seems to form a part of my very soul. It is to me one of the connecting links that bind the present to the memory of the past.

THE VOICE OF THE PAST.

FROM the deep, dark recesses of the past, there comes to the ear of philosophy and of religion a voice of warning and of wisdom. It comes from the plains of Chaldea; it rises from the vales of Palestine; it murmurs out from the tombs of the Nile; its echoes are heard from Parnassus, and from Helicon, and from Olympus; it is heard booming over the waters from the shores of the old world, and from the isles of the ocean. Let us listen what it says.

1. The past speaks to us of the vanity of human greatness. Its language seems to be addressed to me, and to all, who have affinity of soul to appreciate its teachings. It seems to say, Who art thou, O man, son of earth, being of a day, who exaltest thyself with the vain notion of greatness? Listen to the story of those who have, in my time, traveled the same road in which thou art now journeying. There was once a great king, who ruled over the land of the Nile. All whom he met paid him reverence. Millions rose up at his bidding, and came and went again at his command. In the pride of his heart, he built him a city, from whose hundred gates there issued out a hundred thousand warriors, all clad in armor, ready to carry dominion, destruction, and death wherever he listed. He erected a statue, which, by some curious mechanism, saluted, with strange music, the rising sun. He called for his obeisant slaves, and they went to the quarry of living rock, and dug from the mountain side the gigantic block, and by means unknown to modern times transported the huge masses to

the plains, and there erected a pyramid, to serve as a place of burial for his body, and to perpetuate his name. But of his hundred-gated city nothing but ruins remains. His statue has fallen, and no longer emits its tones of music. His pyramid yet stands; but of the body it was intended to preserve, not a vestige, not a particle of dust remains; while his name, his very name is lost, lost forever, nor will its echo ever again fall on human ear.

There came another, and he ruled over the plains of Chaldea. His dominion extended over the Euphrates and Tigris, famed in song. By unhallowed, yet successful war, he extended his sway over the Jordan, whose waters were sacred to the chosen people of the Most High, and over the sweet-gliding Kedron. At noonday, he walked out on his palace roof, and looked over the magnificent city he had built, and boasted that he was greater than all kings, and even aspired to equal the Most High, saying, Is not this great Babylon, which I have built for the city of my glory, and for the eternal habitation of my people? But while he was yet speaking, there came a voice from the deep, saying, "How art thou fallen from heaven, O thou son of the morning! How art thou, which didst weaken the nations, cut down to the ground! Thy pomp is brought down to the grave with the voice of thy music. Hell from beneath is moved to meet thee at thy coming. It stirreth up the dead for thee, even the chief ones of the earth. It hath raised up from their thrones all the kings of the nations. They all speak to thee, and say, 'Art thou also become as one of us? Art thou also weak as we? Thou that didst strike the people in wrath with a continual stroke; thou that didst rule the nations in anger; thou that didst say in thine heart, I will ascend into heaven, I will exalt myself above the stars of God, I will ascend above the hights of the clouds, I will be like the Most High, even thou art brought down to the pit, thy staff is broken, thy arm palsied, and from thy iron grasp the oppressed hath escaped.' " And where now is the great city of the Chaldean monarch? Where is Babylon, the metropolis of cities and the glory of kingdoms? Alas! it is swept by the besom of destruction. The Arabian pitches not his tent there; the shepherd makes not his fold there; but the wild beast of the desert makes his lair there, and the moping owl hoots out from the broken fragments of fallen fanes, and the bittern screams over the stagnant pools that cover the plain where the great city once stood. As for the boastful hero himself, his name only remains on the records of time. Not one remnant of his greatness, not one vestige of his power, not one monument of his pride survives; not one drop of his blood flows in the veins of any human creature.

Next came he of Persia's wide-extended realms. In his arrogance he scourged the sea for having interfered with his plans. Along Thermopylæ's defiles he marched his countless hosts. A hundred years passed, and his warriors were gone, his obeisant followers gone, all gone; his kingdom was subverted, and himself forgotten.

There came another, he of Macedon, pre-eminently called the Great, the self-styled son of Ammon. On the utmost boundaries of the habitable globe the tramp of his fiery steed was heard. From the jungles of the Indus the tiger was startled by the clattering of his hosts. When he had conquered the world, he sat down on the shores of the Indian ocean, and wept that there was not another world to conquer. But where is he now? What remains of him but his name? Who knows the place of his grave? Where is his kingdom—his kingdom of universal dominion?

Next came he of the sunny Tiber. Before him the swift Parthian fled, and from his warlike strokes the fierce Gaul recoiled. The rude Briton, dwelling in the *ultima thule* of the ocean, trembled at his name. Tc him the liberty-loving people of republican Rome offered a crown, which he wisely refused in name, yet received in fact. His empire he bounded by the ocean, his fame by the stars. The city where he dwelt men called the eternal. And what now remains of him or of the eternal city of his home? Of the one it was long ago said, there were none so poor as to do him reverence, and of the other, nothing but the wreck is left.

There came another. From the shores of the frozen north he rushed down on the plains of Italy. He boastfully said, that not a blade of grass ever grew beneath where his horse had trod. His legions of wild and savage barbarians did his bidding in spoiling the earth, and sacking its cities, and deluging its plains with blood. But his horse's tramp has long since ceased to sound, and the grass has grown green again. Himself lies unknown and unhonored beneath the Busentian waters. His hosts have vanished like a shadow, and the earth is at rest again.

Ages passed away, and there came another. The thrones of Castile and Arragon, and of the empire of the Rhine and the Danube, he molded into one, and sat upon it. Across the ocean waste he sent his ships to the Indian isles, and to the continents of the north and the south. His standard was erected, his name and authority proclaimed on the Cordilleras of Mexico and the Andes of Peru. The empire of the Montezumas and of the Incas fell an easy prey. Gold was poured into his coffers, and glory surrounded his temples. An age passed, and the glory and the greatness of Europe's Charles was voluntarily laid aside. Tired of his crown, as a child of its toys, he threw it away. He let go his hold on power, came down from his throne, and hid himself away in a retired monastery. Another age passed, and the empire he had yielded up had fallen to pieces. Its Germanic possessions were passed to other hands; its Indian islands, all, save one, were fallen to other owners. Of the transatlantic continent, Mexico, with its mines of silver, and Peru, with its rivers of gold, nothing remained.

There came another still. From the Mediterranean isle he suddenly blazed with dazzling brilliancy on the eyes of men. The darkness of despotic power retired before him. At his approach the thrones of kings tottered, and fell, and crumbled. Kings and queens came down on the plain, and bowed the knee, and kissed his hand. He stamped on the earth, and there sprang up men armed to the teeth, ready to do battle for him, either on the burning sands of Egypt, or along the sunny plains of Italy, or amid the interminable forests of Russia. He brought down the eagle of Austria, grappled with the bear of Russia, and kept at bay the lion of England. His power knew no resistance, his ambition no bounds. The people flung their caps in the air, and cried, Long live Napoleon, Emperor of the French! But over the spirit of his dream there came a change. His star, which had shone resplendent on all the landscape, was shorn of its beams in the murky atmosphere of Waterloo. It finally set, quenched forever of its fires, in the Atlantic Ocean. Far away in the waste of waters, where gallant ship seldom sails, rises high toward heaven a bleak and barren rock. Here were spent the latter days, and here was made the grave of him who made the earth tremble.

"Hark, comes there from the pyramids,
Or from Siberia's wastes of snow,
Or Europe's fields, a voice that bids
The world he awed to mourn him? No.

The only, the perpetual dirge
  That's heard there is the seabird's cry,
The mournful murmur of the surge,
  The cloud's deep voice, the wind's low sigh."

Thus speaks the past of human greatness. Alas! how vain is greatness! It passes like the shadow of a summer cloud over the landscape. The eye is upon it, and it is not.

"The rush of numerous years bears down,
  The most gigantic strength of man,
And where is all his wisdom gone,
  When dust he turns to dust again?"

2. The past speaks of the perfectibility of human nature. Greatness is only comparative. It implies that one is above another. Were there no object of comparison we could have no ideas of greatness. In estimating greatness we usually limit our comparisons to the present; but in estimating the improvement of man, and his progress toward perfection, we compare one age with another. As man in his individual character passes through four stages of existence—childhood, youth, manhood, and age—so in his collective or national character there are four similar periods. Every nation, every government, has its infancy, its youth, its maturity, and as surely its decline. As surely as the human body has in its inmost nature the elements of decay, so every human institution has in its constitution the elements of dissolution.

Man, as a race, has had his infancy and his youth, and he may have, somewhere in the future, his maturity, and away in distant ages, his period, not of decay, but of change of sphere. But the past speaks to us only of infancy and of youth. She knows nothing of maturity, nothing of decay, in the history of human nature. While individual man dies, while nations cease to be, the race dies not, human nature ceases not to exist.

Man improves in knowledge. From the very dawn of human existence the race has gone on constantly increasing in science. From the time when Tubal-cain first began to handle brass and iron, man has been advancing toward perfection in the arts. The ancient mariner ventured not beyond the isles of the Ægean, or the Mediterranean, while the modern sailor explores

"Seas not his own, and worlds unknown before."

The ancient message-bearer trusted only to the speed of his foot, or of his horse, while the modern express is whizzed along by steam or flashed by lightning.

Man improves in virtue. There are several species of virtue. The principal are political virtue and moral virtue. Political virtue is connected with forms of government. Political, social, and personal freedom are ever in proportion to the virtue of the people. In this species of virtue the progress of human society is evident. The earlier forms of human government were despotic. The one governed the millions. Under the republics of Greece and Rome the tens were free, and the thousands slaves. In the feudal ages the hundreds were free, and the thousands still slaves. In modern days, the tens, the hundreds, the thousands, the millions, the universal race, are rising emancipated, disinthralled, regenerated, to the full measure of perfect and unrestrained liberty. Nor is less evident the progress of man in moral virtue. Every age develops some new application of moral principle, and adds something to the sum of human virtue. Nothing has been lost, but much gained. There has never been any human virtue, which does not yet exist. There have been vices which have ceased to exist, and there are new virtues constantly generating. So that, on the whole, the race of man is progressing in virtue. In the progress of humanity there is no retrograde; the tendency is ever upward; each age forms a stage in the advancement. The primitive ages cleared away the rubbish, and leveled off the site. The classic ages prepared the materials, and left them to season. The feudal ages laid the foundation. Modern ages are carrying up the structure, stage after stage. Up still goes the edifice, the great temple of humanity, each age taking up the work where the preceding age left it.

Such are the teachings of the past on the questions of human improvement. Her doctrines are sustained by the facts of human history, and are delightful to the heart of the Christian philosopher, who sees therein sure indications of a glorious future.

3. The past speaks of the omnipotence of truth. Truth is a rock in the midst of quicksands. It lies on a deep and firm foundation, immovable, though all around be fluctuating and changing. Truth is the pure gem, which rusts not, and changes not its luster, but shines on from age to age with increasing light. Truth is the lever which moves the world. By means of it the great work of human improvement is effected. Whoever wields this lever may be sure of success.

On the omnipotent prevalence of truth the past speaks in language distinct, explicit, and certain. The past tells us of One, who, some two thousand years ago, in an obscure village of Palestine, appeared in human form, and with human feelings, as the representative of truth itself. His message, however, was disregarded, himself despised and rejected, and his life sacrificed to appease an angry mob. Before his departure, however, he called to his side twelve men of like passions with ourselves, and committed to them the truth which he had come to reveal. To these men he assigned the task of changing the faith and the religion of the world. They were obscure and unknown among men, unlearned in the wisdom of the world, and unaccomplished in the arts and refinements of society. But truth rendered them invincible. They went before the Jewish Sanhedrim; they stood up before governors, and kings, and even the emperor himself, and spoke the words of truth and soberness. Truth made them omnipotent. By its power they changed the habits, the faith, and even the civil institutions of society.

Blessed be the man who happily presents to the eye of humanity a new truth! He does a work which never can be undone. He plants a seed which can never be uprooted—a seed having in itself life and immortality. It may, through unpropitious circumstances, lie for awhile dormant. It may be trampled by the rude foot of recklessness. But

> "Truth crushed to earth will rise again—
> The immortal years of God are hers."

What matters it, then, O thou that lovest truth, whether men hear thee, or smite thee? What imports it though the world believe or scoff? Truth is immortal, and thou shalt share her own immortality.

4. The past speaks to us of the wisdom and power of Providence. Though individual human greatness is nothing, yet man is great. Though the individual dies, yet the race lives on, ever advancing. Though truth may lie long scoffed and neglected, yet she will in the end make her voice heard. All this is owing to the superintendence of Providence, a power incomprehensibly higher than human, watching incessantly over human affairs. One age has no power to connect itself with the past or the future; but He that sitteth on the circle of the heavens; that hath stretched out the north over the empty space, and hung the earth on nothing; that leadeth forth Arcturus, Orion, and the constellations of the south, and that dispenseth the sweet influences

of the Pleiades, joins the past, the present, and the future together by indissoluble links.

Thus speaks the past for the comfort and hope of man. Her voice is one of gladness to the human race. But she has another voice, which she sometimes utters in the ears of mortals. To me she often speaks with the gentle voice of the venerable one, who breathed her prayer over my sleeping infancy, but who for thirty years has been sleeping on the hill-side that looks out on the Atlantic waters. Again she comes, and speaks with the musical voice of the fair one, companion of my childhood, who rambled with me over the meadows, and by the brook, gathering flowers, in the spring-time of life, but whom we laid to rest long ago beneath a bower of evergreens on my native plains. She comes again, the past—alas! she comes too often—amidst my garden walks, and at the bower, calling me with the voice of the beauteous being,

> "Whom I laid to rest in the lonely bed—
> The lost and the lovely, the early dead."

I can not but listen to the voice with which the past speaks to me, nor can I dispel from my heart the sadness which her echoes produce. Though the picture which her flitting forms cast on the mirror of my soul be one of deep shades, yet I must look on it.

> "O, unrelenting past,
> Strong are the barriers of thy dark domain,
> And fetters sure and fast,
> Hold all that enter thy unbreathing reign.
>
> Thou hast my better years;
> Thou hast my earlier friends, the good, the kind;
> Yielded to thee with tears,
> The venerable form, the exalted mind.
>
> My spirit yearns to bring
> The lost ones back—yearns with desire intense,,
> And struggles hard to wring
> Thy bolts apart, and pluck the captives thence.

6

In vain. Thy gates deny
All passage, save to those who hence depart,
Nor to the streaming eye
Thou givest them back, nor to the broken heart.

Thine for a space are they,
Yet thou shalt give thy treasures up at last;
Thy gates shall yet give way;
Thy bolts shall fall, inexorable past!

All that of good and fair
Hath gone into thy tomb from earliest time,
Shall then come back to wear
The beauty and the glory of its prime.

They have not perished, no,
Kind words, remembered voices, once so sweet,
Smiles radiant long ago,
And features, the great soul's apparent seat,

All shall come back, each tie
Of pure affection knit again;
Alone shall evil die,
And sorrow dwell a prisoner in thy reign.

And then shall I behold
Her by whose kind, maternal side I sprung,
And her, who, still and cold,
Fills the lone grave, the beautiful and young."

"THERE THE WEARY ARE AT REST."

THERE seems a sweet repose about the place where rest the dead. The very air seems hushed, or breathes, if it breathe at all, a low, plaintive sound, that appears like soft music. Whether I visit the graveyard on a bright summer day, or in the depth of winter—in spring or in autumn—at early morn, at noon, or at twilight—the same quiet, peaceful spirit seems presiding there. I love to ramble alone among the graves. To me there is something inspiring—something holy about the place. Especially are peculiar emotions excited, while standing by the graves of those who, while living, occupied a high rank in usefulness or fame. I recollect the vivid emotions I felt, when, many years ago, wandering about an old graveyard, on the banks of the Connecticut, I unexpectedly found myself by the grave of M'Donough. I had read of the terrible battle of Champlain, and heard much of M'Donough, but I knew not that the warrior was buried there, till I stood before the stone that marked his resting-place. Similar emotions were excited, on looking at the spot where lie the remains of Whitefield. But my feelings were never, on such an occasion, more highly excited, than when of late I visited the graveyard of a neighboring city—a small, but beautiful and retired city, stretching over a lovely plain, on the banks of one of our picturesque rivers. It was an evening of springtime, when all was green, and quiet, and beautiful. Proceeding some distance from the city, on a street unfrequented, save by the hearse and the funeral train, I came to the place of rest—the city of the dead—already rivaling in population the living city near by. Here was spread out an area of considerable extent, laid out in beautiful order, in family lots, and tastefully ornamented with shrubbery and flowers. Here is the home of the dead. On this sequestered spot nature bestows her gifts of beauty and her cheering influence, as well as on the homes of the living, in the city of cottages and of gardens, whose inhabitants are now inhaling the sweet odors of spring, and enjoying the mild sunshine of a beautiful May day. The same zephyr that whispers through the trees of the garden, breathes mildly here, but revives not the dead. The same flowers that bloom before the cottage door, disclose their beauties and shed their perfume here, but not for the dead. The same sun that pours his morning beam into the cottage window, awaking beauty from her slumbers, shines here, but brings no morning to those who sleep in these graves. And there is music here, too—the sweet, plaintive music of nature—the music of bird, and of insect, and of gentle breeze, mingled with the lowing of cattle from the green pastures, and the merry peal of the bell in the city; but those who lie here heed it not.

I passed on among the avenues, by the neat mounds raised over the dead, and read the names inscribed on the stones. But to me few of the names were familiar. I was a stranger here in this city of the dead. Far away from this spot are the graves of those whom I have known and loved, and who have loved me, as I may never hope to be loved again. They lie, some beneath the ocean wave, and some on foreign coasts. The grave of one is made on the plain of evergreens, beneath the spreading branches of the pine, and of another by the side of the mountain stream; and I stand here, a stranger among the living, and may lie here, a stranger among the dead.

The grave of a stranger never fails to affect me. I can not stand over it, without suffering the deep fountains of feeling to be broken up, and wave after wave of sadness to flow over my soul. Many years ago, when a mere child, I was rambling in the populous graveyard of the city near my native home; I read the names of hundreds familiar to me, with no peculiar emotions; but I happened on one grave which made my young heart bleed. It was that of a foreigner, a young and gallant officer, who fell in a naval engagement in the harbor of the city. True, he fell fighting against my country, in a desperate battle in the last war, and by his side there lies his antagonist, the brave captain of the American ship, who fell at the same time; and they lie side by side, as quietly as if they had been in life brothers, instead of enemies. But while standing on such a spot, I could not think of him as a foe and a warrior, but as a man and a stranger—one who had a mother yearning for his return, and whose sisters had been long looking, with aching eyes and bursting hearts, for him to come home. There he lies among strangers, far away from his home; and no mother—no sister will ever look on his grave. No friend may ever plant a shrub or train a flower on the sod that covers him. The skeptic may deride me, the philosopher may smile at me, and the Christian may pity my weakness; but yet I would not that my last resting-place should be among strangers. I would sleep, during the long, moonless, starless night of the grave, by the side of those whom I have known and loved while living. I would that when the night is gone, and the shadows and darkness of the tomb are dispersed, and the resurrection morning breaks, my opening eyes may meet the eyes of friendship and love. I would that the faces on which I may then look, may be those familiar to my childhood and youth. I would not, then, that my grave should be the watery deep, though Ocean might wind her funeral shell in a requiem over the spot; nor on a foreign shore, though my countrymen might erect the monument of marble or of granite to commemorate my name; nor even here, where I now stand, though the spot be beautified, and many a friend of former years might, as he wends his way toward the west, turn aside to look at the place where I might rest. But let my grave be made in some rural, quiet spot, where may lie also my companions and friends, my wife and my children. No matter, though, in the long lapse of ages, our names be obliterated from the decaying stone on which they may be recorded, and the very place where we lie be neglected and forgotten. Let us lie there together in peace, and in the morning of the resurrection, let us together awake, together arise, and together meet our blessed Savior, the Lord Jesus Christ.

Near this neat and orderly cemetery, over which I was rambling, and which gave rise to these desultory reflections, is another of more ancient date, if any thing can be called ancient in this youthful country. This latter was even more populous than the former. Multitudes of graves, unknown and undistinguished, were all around me. Little order seemed observed in the location of the graves, and little attempt to ornament the grounds. Most of those who sleep here were early settlers of the country. Their surviving friends, if any survive, have moved away, and the old burying-ground is left to be overgrown by the wild luxuriance of nature. Near the center of this old graveyard is an area of a few square rods, inclosed by a plain rural fence. Within the inclosure are native shrubs and wild flowers, growing in all the freshness and vigor of this climate—a climate better adapted to variety and strength of vegetation than any other on the globe. In this green spot is a grave, at whose head is an upright slab of sandstone, on which is the following plain and simple inscription:

"In memory of
REV. JOHN STRANGE,
who died
Dec. 2d, 1832,
In the 44th year of his age, and the 22d of his
itinerant ministry.
'They that be wise shall shine as the brightness of
the firmament, and they that turn many
to righteousness as the stars forever and ever.'"

Here, then, lies that remarkable man, whose face I never saw—whose voice I never heard, but whose name is one of the first and the last which the stranger hears in Indiana. In every part of the state, from the valley of the White Water to the Wabash—from the Ohio to the shores of Michigan—in the populous city and in the obscure hamlet—the name of Strange is but another word for eloquence. The old men will sit down in their rude cabins, and talk of him by the hour, and relate anecdotes of his eccentric genius and irresistible eloquence.

As I stood over the grave of Strange, and thought of the glowing and animated descriptions I had heard of his eloquence, I could but regret that it had never been my happiness to listen to those thrilling tones which had so often fell on many a delighted heart. His eloquence must have been unique, peculiar, inimitable, and irresistible. Indeed, some have told me that it could not be described. But death heeds not the "voice of the charmer, charm he never so wisely;" and Strange has gone—gone in the prime and vigor of life, and in the full career of his power and usefulness, to the grave, "even to the land of darkness and the shadow of death." Nor may any Orphean lyre call him back. Rest thee here, then, eloquent and beloved brother! Not yet has thy memory perished from among the living. Some fair hand has even just now planted over thy grave a rose, which is just opening its petals to the breath of spring. Thy impress is left on many a heart. Nor can it be obliterated with the present generation. The mark which thou hast left on the moral and religious character of this youthful, this rising state, must remain indelible. The stone that stands over thy resting-place may crumble and perish, and thy name be forgotten, but the impression for good which thou hast made on this community will remain through all time.

THE SPIRITUAL.

"WHAT is man?" asked the shepherd of Palestine, as he was watching his flocks by night, and looking up to the heavens. The same question has been asked, again and again, age after age; but who has answered it? Who *can* answer it? Who can clear away the mystery that hangs over man's being and nature? Of the first consciousness of our own existence we have no memory. By which of the senses we first obtained a knowledge of the material world we can not now tell. Reason and philosophy teach us that by touch we first derived our notions of materiality. We wave our hand in the air and feel a slight sensation, which we call resistance. We wave it in the water, and feel a stronger sensation of the same kind. We place our foot on the ground, and feel a still stronger impression of resistance to our will. We thus learn that there is something external to us—something that resists us—something beyond the control of our will.

This first fact which we learn is repugnant to our nature. We abhor resistance. It is painful to the soul. The soul exhibits its antipathy to resistance in those dawnings of the love of power, which the child exhibits among its earliest acts. The struggling of the soul to overcome the resistance of external nature, shows that the connection between soul and body is unnatural. Confinement suits not mind. It aspires to be free—to roam at will through space—from star to star—from sun to sun—from world to world. In its pure, essential state, it knows nothing of limits—nothing of a resisting medium.

The sense of touch furnishes us only the knowledge of resistance, with form, hardness, magnitude, and extent, as modifications of resistance. Taste and smell acquaint us with qualities of matter of very little consequence to us as means of knowledge, except the practical knowledge, which enables us to choose proper articles of food.

Another organ of sense is found in the ear. Material bodies, when acted on by any force, have the power of vibrating. The vibrations are imparted to surrounding bodies—solid, liquid, or aerial—and by them communicated to the ear, which is so organized as to take up and repeat the vibrations, and thus furnish the mind the sensations we call sound.

Another instrument of the soul is sight. The various bodies in nature have the power of reflecting, each for itself, different shades of light—some blue, some green, some red, and others various colors formed by a combination of primary colors. The eye is so constituted as to receive these colors, and thus afford the mind the sensation we call vision. The only notions, however, we primarily obtain by sight are color, light, and shade.

We see, therefore, how small is the sum of human knowledge directly derived through the senses—resistance, taste, odors, sounds, color, light, and shade; that is all. From whence, then, derive we the innumerable ideas forming our stock of knowledge?

The senses are merely instruments of mind. The eye does not see. It sees no more than the telescope does. It enables the mind to see. The ear hears not. It hears no more than the drum hears its own beating, or the organ its own music. The drum beats, the drum of the ear answers to the beat, and the mind hears. The organ sounds, the organ of hearing sounds in unison, and the mind hears. Whatever sound is made by sonorous bodies is repeated by the material organ of sense, and the mind is affected by the sensation.

The same power which enables mind to use the eye as the instrument of seeing, the ear as the instrument of hearing, and the hand as the instrument of feeling, also enables the same mind to combine and modify the notions of color, sound, and touch, so as to acquire the wonderful variety and amount of knowledge we possess. Wonderful, indeed, is the variety of ideas derived from sight, combined with touch, and modified by intellect. From my rural seat I see the surface of earth covered with vegetation. The green grass is springing in a thousand spires at my feet. At my elbow a youthful and vigorous pine is throwing its tassels to the summer breeze. At my side is blooming a rose on its native stock. Just before me is a cluster of lilies, white and pure as virgin innocence. Behind me, leaning gently over my head, and by its dense foliage protecting me effectually from the burning heat of the sun, is an old beech, and close by it a tall maple. A thousand varying lights and shades are beaming before me. I recognize within the sphere of vision innumerable objects of God's creation—the cedar, the fir, the spruce, the birch, and the tamarack, from my own native north; the orange, the lemon, and the cactus, from the sunny south; and the pink, the violet, the locust, the oak, the elm, the pear, the peach, the plum, the apple, and the grape of this fair land. Along the valley is leaping the brook. On the ridge beyond appears the tender blade of green corn. On the north appears the village with its spires, and on the south a rural landscape, with flocks and herds feeding on the hillsides. Can it be that all these variant ideas are derived merely from color, light, and shade? Even so; nothing but color, light, and shade. All else is the work of mind—of mind which can thus, from a few simple elements, create so vast an amount of knowledge. Did we, from the fact that the elements of all our knowledge in the present state of existence are derived through the senses, restrict our belief within the range of sensuous existence, we should reason contrary to experience and philosophy. And few are found to reason thus. Few there are who believe in the existence of no beings beyond the cognizance of the human senses. Is there, indeed, one solitary human creature, of common intelligence, on the surface of this earth, who believes in no personal existences except those of flesh and blood? The bird in its cage, though he may never have had a mate, nor tried the free air with his pinions, seems yet conscious that there is a world about him, and other beings related to him; so the imprisoned spirit of man, looking out from its dark abode only through the grated windows of the senses, has, deep in its inmost recesses, a consciousness of some mysterious connection with congenial existences—spirits of the air, of the earth, or of the deep.

The notion of some connection between us and a spiritual world and spiritual beings, is not with us so much a matter of belief as a sentiment—an instinct. It seems born in us. It grows with our growth, and strengthens with our strength. He that believes nothing—the utter skeptic—if such a one there be, feels this sentiment in its full force and influence. With our ideas of spiritual beings is usually associated superiority. This led, in ancient times, to acts of devotion and propitiation. The polished Greeks and warlike Romans peopled their forests and their fields, their hills and their valleys, their rivers and their seas, with spiritual beings, whom they invoked and worshiped. They worshiped Jupiter; but, with them, Jupiter personified the air, and was a substitute for that great spiritual Being who presides over the seasons, the atmosphere, and the weather. They worshiped Venus; but Venus, with them, was the ideal of beauty, whose forms they saw every-where in nature—on the earth, in the sky, in human action, and in human face. They were led to believe in some ideal being of spiritual nature, whose care and skill arranged the beautiful, and whom they worshiped under the human female form. The Egyptians worshiped the Nile; yet no intelligent Egyptian ever believed the Nile conscious; but he *felt* that there was some unseen agent—some spiritual Being presiding over the river, and whose providence superintended its overflow and its ebb. They worshiped the ram, not that they believed it superior to any other beast, but because it was a representative of that great constellation in the heavens whose annual return brings the spring, and over whose revolution presides the great Being who governs the universe.

In all ages men have *felt* that they have yet some connection with the spirits of those departed from earth. The sibyl of Endor believed she could call back the spirit of the prophet. Orpheus attempted to call back from the realms of Proserpine, by the tones of his lyre, the spirit of Eurydice. Æneas believed he saw the spirit of Creusa, who perished in the sacking of the city, and that of Palinurus, who was drowned in the waves.

So deep-rooted in the human constitution is the belief in the personal and conscious existence of those who were once of us, but are now gone from earth, and of their continued connection with us children of earth, that it seems to have entered into the religious creed of a great portion of the Christian world. What but this induces the devotee to kneel to the Virgin and pray to the saints? He only feels, as we all do, that there are spiritual influences and spiritual beings around him. He is taught to believe that the spirits of the good may have with the Divine presence access, which is denied him, and that they may serve as mediators between him and the great Spirit that rules all things.

And who of us may not have felt the influence of the same all-pervading sentiment? Who has not kneeled over the grave of his mother, or his companion, or his child, and felt so strong attractions of communion of spirit with the loved one sleeping below, as to force audible words from his lips? At such a time, and in such a place, there are holy thoughts springing up in the soul. Visions of glorious scenery appear spread over the broad ethereal landscape of mind. Forms of beauty—beauty such as earth knows not—pass and repass before us. We seem to hear sweet voices from the spirit-land, and the gentle whisper of peace and of holy delight from lips whose earthly prototypes have long since been pallid and cold. Tell me not, ye groveling, miserly, sensuous mortals, tell me not there is no communion of soul with soul—no commingling of affection—no intercourse of feeling—no reciprocal breathings of spirit between the sojourner in materiality and the sainted spirit who has put off this mortal vail, and assumed the white robe of spiritual fabric. There is but a thin partition between this earthly house of our tabernacle and the apartments of the spiritual mansion in which dwell the happy ones. With ears attuned to spiritual harmony, and from which the grosser sounds of earth are shut out, we may, even now, hear, as did the apostle when caught up to heaven, words of spiritual import, which mortal tongue may not utter. There is but a light mist—a shadowy cloud—a thin vapor of sensuousness, which conceals from our eyes the glorious landscape of the spiritual world. Occasionally the cloud may be broken, the mist dispersed, and there may appear glimpses of a fairer world, and more lovely forms than earth ever disclosed, or humanity exhibited. Elevating is the effect and holy the influence of these spiritual communings. The enraptured mortal, who has had one glimpse of the immortal, would fix his eye forever on the scene. The famishing child of earth, who has had one earnest of spiritual communion, would hold forever to his parched lips the delicious cup. Insipid after this become the intoxicating draughts of sensuous pleasure. The soul becomes elevated above the damps, and vapors, and fogs of sense, and lives in a higher, a purer, and more transparent atmosphere.

The consciousness of the spiritual forms the foundation of our belief in God. The ancients, in their reliance on second causes, fell short of the great First Cause. Their error lay not in believing in no God, but in too many gods. Spiritual influences they could not deny. To these agencies they imputed all the operations of the physical world. On them, as well on us, the inherent sentiment of the spiritual forced the idea of Deity; and revelation teaches us, what nature did not teach them, that God is *one*. The older revelation does not so much reveal the fact that there is a God, as that there is but one God. The former man's own reason and nature teach him. The latter revelation only teaches. Our belief in a future existence rests on the same foundation. We feel that we are connected with the spiritual world, and with the spirits of the departed. We feel, too, that we shall live in spirit, though dead in body. We feel that death forms no part of the destiny of mind. Death seems to us only sound, undisturbed, wakeless sleep. To the Christian philosopher, the only difference between the sleep of a night and the sleep of death is one of time. The sleep of the grave is long. Nor can we wake at will, nor be aroused, though wife and children call us long and loud. But to both—to the night and to the grave—there comes a morning. To the sleep of night there comes the sunshine and the day—to the sleep of death there comes a brighter sunshine and a day to which there comes no night. Our faith in divine revelation rests, also, on this spiritual sentiment of our nature. This sentiment forms a foundation which, in the well-balanced mind, may defy the spiteful dashings of Deism, and the deep-rolling surges of Atheism. We but see, in the book of revelation, the reflected image, from a bright and polished mirror, of the spiritual creations of our own consciousness. Our faith is not so much founded on logic and reason, as on sentiment and consciousness. The words of Jesus become to us spirit and life. We drink them into the soul. The truths of religion become a part of our constitution and of our mental furniture. Our faith in Christianity thus becomes living and active. Its effect is diffused through the whole character. It forms the warp which, interwoven with the practical filling, constitutes the web of a religious life.

Our belief in spiritual existence leads us to form ideals of whatever we love or admire. We personify truth, and love, and goodness, and whatever is beautiful or admirable. The same law of human nature led to the ideal creations of gods, and goddesses, and nymphs, and naiads of classic mythology. The genii of the Arabian tales, and the fairies of the English nursery, may be traced to the same source. And may not the passion for fiction have its origin in the same cause? There is generally some poetry in fiction, and always fiction in poetry. In its ideal creations we find food for our mental appetite more congenial than the every-day furnishings of human life. The only antidote for fiction is the habitual contemplation of the lofty and noble subjects of the Divine attributes and a future life. He who, in his hours of philosophic meditation and religious devotion, converses with angels and spirits, will have little appetite for communion with the characters that teem in the brain of the novel-writer. He who is accustomed to the lofty thoughts of the moral sublimity and the ineffable glories of spirituality, will find little pleasure in the puerile plots and flash language of players and novelists. His soul becomes elevated above all reliance on these futile means of excitement and pleasure. He needs not fiction for an antidote to ennui; for he is never alone. Angels and spirits are his companions, and holy thoughts form to him a delightful substitute for the sensuous imaginings of the groveling heart.

It is evident that while the senses are aids to the mind in acquiring knowledge in this corporeal state, they, in their present imperfect condition, would be obstructions in the way of pure, unembodied spirits. The body itself will, however, become, in a future life, spiritual, and all its senses spiritual. The grossness of materiality will be all worked out of the system. Dullness of hearing and imperfection of seeing will trouble us no more. The senses we now have we shall possess, in our spiritual and immortal state, in greater perfection than ever fell to the lot of humanity. We shall taste of the fruit of the tree of life, and of the water that floweth forth from the throne. We shall certainly hear—for there is music in heaven—music sweeter than the tones combined in harmony of the lyre of Apollo, the lute of Orpheus, and the harp of the winds. There is the music of sweet voices—voices, alas! no more heard amidst the rough sounds of earth—voices of a great multitude, which no man can number, all tuned in harmony, with an accompaniment of the harps of heaven, singing a new song—the song of redemption and salvation. Do our mortal ears ever catch the distant echoes of that heavenly music? The shepherds of Palestine heard the song of the angels when the Savior was born. And if our hearts be pure, and our thoughts turned toward heaven, we may seem to hear the voices of the loved ones of the soul, gone from earth, mingled with those heavenly strains. Then, let the corporeal senses perish; let the rose bloom and shed its odors in vain over the senseless nostril; let the hand be palsied in death, and folded for the last time over the sleeping bosom; let the ear be untuned to sounds, nor vibrate at the voice of the birds, nor of music, nor of love; let the eye be closed—let the sleep of death come over it—let the sod cover it, nor the sunlight of earth ever reach it: the soul has other ears and other eyes, far more perfect than these material ones, and with them it will hear heavenly harmonies, and see heavenly prospects.

Tell me not that there is no future life for the soul. Tell me not that this earth is the boundary of mind. Tell me not that beauty fades—that memory fails—that ideas are erased—that thought is evanescent—that knowledge is lost. I *feel*—I *know* it is not so. Should you present your mathematical diagrams, and prove, with a rigidity that Euclid, nor Newton, nor La Place ever attained, that man has no connection with a spiritual world—no future life—no immortal existence, I should not believe you. I should know there must be some fallacy in your reasoning; for I should *feel* that your conclusion was inconsistent with my own consciousness. Let, therefore, the sensuous wallow on in the mire. Let the earthy grovel in the dust. Let the miserly ransack the rubbish. Let the groveling plod along in the by-roads and muddy lanes of sense, asking no question but, "What shall we eat, and what shall we drink, and wherewithal shall we be clothed?" But, thou child of immortality, ethereal creature of spirituality, heir of heavenly inheritance, leave the beggarly elements of earth, and elevate your thoughts, your affections to that spiritual world, with which you are now connected by those surpassingly-constituted organs of interior life—those perfect instruments of the intellect and of the soul—for which mortals have yet found no name. And when your corporeal senses have done their work and perished with the body, your spiritual senses will acquire an acuteness, and exhibit a perfection, which will leave nothing to be desired as a means of knowledge and of happiness through eternity.

MUTATIONS OF HUMANITY.

THE elements of change enter deeply into the constitution of all human things. Nature herself, though, to our view, her laws remain invariable, exhibits one continuous series of changes. Nothing earthly continueth in one stay. The plant that springs from the earth, passes through rapid gradations, till it comes to maturity, and then it declines and perishes. Another rises in its place, flourishes for awhile, and, in its turn, gives way for its successor. Every animal, from the microscopic insect to the lord of creation, exists in a state of perpetual transition. The earth herself escapes not the fate of all her children. The beautiful scenery of nature, whose brilliant colors are stamped on all the impressions of childhood, and woven with all the dreams of maturer years, might, in the lapse of centuries, become strange to us.

Nothing, however, is more subject to change than the works and the institutions of man. Should the wise king of Israel be permitted to revisit the earth, he would look in vain for the temple of Jehovah, or the city in which it stood. Memnon would not recognize, in the broken columns on the banks of the Nile, his hundred-gated Thebes; nor would Zenobia find among the palm-trees her Palmyra. The Roman of the Augustan age would find little or nothing in the modern city to remind him of the Rome of the Cæsars.

Nor are the social and political institutions of man less instable than his works of art. The laws of Lycurgus and of Solon exist only as history. The institutions by which Lacedemon, and Athens, and Rome rose to greatness, and maintained, for ages, the chief place among nations, have long since passed away. The institutions of the middle ages exist no longer. Forms of government, modes of living, and social habits have all changed, and all keep incessantly changing still.

Changes in the institutions of man are connected with the progress of humanity, and, indeed, are essential to it. Conservatism is ever hostile to improvement. The mutable constitution, therefore, of human creations is made, in the wisdom of Providence, subservient to human progress. There are, also, involved in the mutations of humanity, other principles, which will appear as we trace the progress of society.

In the interior of Africa, among the mountains of the moon, at the sources of the Nile, dwelt, in early times, the people called by the Greeks the Ethiopians. Little is known of the extent of their country, of the number of the people, of the form of government, or of their social institutions. The shadows of forty centuries have gathered around them. But that there was the cradle of civilization and of art, and that the immediate descendants of the Ethiopians arrived, in some of the arts, at a degree of perfection which modern nations have not equaled, are facts attested by monuments as enduring as the granite hills. The story of their greatness was yet fresh in the time of Homer, who says that Jupiter, out of respect to their attainments, annually made them a visit, with all his train, for twelve days.

From Ethiopia colonies emigrated to the plains of Chaldea, and to the valley of the Nile. The most important member of the family was Egypt. It was the glory of kingdoms. To her the polished nations of modern Europe owe the origin of art and literature. While the nations of the Caucasian race, now so distinguished in the world, were scarcely yet in the rudiments of being, the people on the banks of the Nile were erecting edifices, which modern art can hardly equal, and writing on them a language which modern science can hardly interpret.

The Labyrinth is declared by Herodotus, the earliest of the Greek historians, to be the greatest triumph of human art, far exceeding all the works of Greece. The pyramids, those stupendous masses of gigantic blocks of granite, have withstood the ravages of unknown centuries. Scattered all along the Nile, over the plains of Memphis, and of Dendera, and of Thebes, are remains of works of art which no modern nation may attempt to rival. The catacombs are populous with the dead of thirty centuries, preserved in substance and in form by means unknown to modern science. The literature of this wonderful people is engraven and sculptured in characters inimitable by the moderns, on the pyramids, and obelisks, and ruined temples.

Brilliant was the career of this remarkable race. For a thousand years or more its star was high in the ascendant. It had, in the order of Providence, its mission to fulfill, and then its place was supplied by another. It accomplished its work, and then it went to its reward. It acted its part in the drama of humanity, and then disappeared forever from the stage. Its part was a showy one. Its work was one of physical cunning and artistic excellence. Its mission was one of concentrated human effort under the direction of absolute monarchy. The cities, pyramids, and temples of the Nile, were the result of physical effort directed by one mind, absolute in authority over the millions.

"Those ages have no memory, but they left
  A record in the desert; columns strown
On the waste sands; and statues, fallen and cleft,
  Heaped like a host in battle overthrown;
  Vast ruins, where the mountain's ribs of stone

Were hewn into a city; streets that spread
In the dark earth, where never breath has blown
Of heaven's sweet air, nor foot of man dares tread
The long and perilous ways, the cities of the dead!
And tombs of monarchs to the clouds up-piled—
They perished, but the eternal tombs remain;
And the black precipice, abrupt and wild,
Pierced by long toil, and hollowed to a fane;
Huge piers and frowning arches forms of gods sustain,
The everlasting arches dark and wide,
Like the night heaven, when the clouds are black with rain;
But idly skill was tasked, and the strength was plied—
All was the work of slaves to swell a despot's pride."

From Egypt we pass to Greece. The Grecian republics once formed a brilliant constellation in the world of science and of art. Like the lost pleiad their place is vacant; but the light which they emitted has not yet faded away from our sight.

The mission of the Greeks was one of literature and of taste. They excelled in poetry and the fine arts. Homer yet holds the first rank among epic poets. Neither Shakspeare nor any other modern author has produced a tragedy more powerful to excite intense interest in the mind, or to break up the deep fountains of human feeling, than the Edipus of Sophocles, or the Medea of Euripides, or the Prometheus of Eschylus. Herodotus and Thucydides are yet models for the historian. No age has ever produced finer specimens of biography and memoirs than the sketches of Socrates by Plato and Xenophon. Demosthenes yet holds his place as prince of orators. The geometry of Euclid yet forms the text-book in the highest seminaries of Europe.

In the fine arts, those which distinguished a polished people, the Greeks excelled the moderns. The various styles of architecture are yet known by Grecian names. In statuary and painting they reached a point of eminence, unattainable by the most highly gifted of later times.

The Greeks were not inattentive to the diffusion of knowledge. In the earlier days of their career, histories and poetry were rehearsed by the author in the theaters and other public places. In this way Herodotus published his incomparable histories, and Homer his immortal poems.

The mission of Greece was a mission of taste and of poetry. Glorious was their career, but it soon closed. Brilliant shone their sun, but it has long since gone down, and darkness has gathered over the whole land. The same blue waters, the same fairy isles, the same grand hills, the same fertile vales, and the same meandering streams are there, as when these scenes kindled up the light of genius in the poet, and people are there, too; but, alas, how changed!

> "He who hath bent him o'er the dead,
> Ere the first day of death is fled,
> Before decay's effacing fingers
> Have swept the lines where beauty lingers,
> And marked the sweet angelic air,
> The rapture of repose that's there,
> And but for that sad shrouded eye,
> That looks not, wins not, weeps now,
> And but for that chill, changeless brow,
> Some moments, ah! one treacherous hour,
> He still might doubt the tyrant's power,
> So fair, so calm, so softly sealed,
> The first, last look by death revealed.
> Such is the aspect of this shore:
> 'Tis Greece, but living Greece no more."

To the Grecian succeeded the Roman. The science and the knowledge, but not the taste and the poetry of the Greeks, passed to the Romans. The mission of the Romans was to conquer the world and themselves.

The conquest of the world was effected by the indomitable energies of her generals and her soldiers. The hand of Providence was in it, for thereby was the world prepared for the advent of the Savior. The fierce barbarian was subdued, the restless Parthian quieted, and the fickle African subjected to law. The world was at peace. The gates of the war temple, turning on their unused and rusty hinges, were closed.

But the conquest of themselves was a higher achievement of Roman virtue, than the conquest of the world. And self-conquest was the great and leading idea of the Roman age. The Roman times were times of sternness of moral character—of determined purpose—of unrelaxing energy—of unyielding virtue—of devotion and self-sacrifice to the public interests. The glory of the age was the subjugation of the propensities, the passions, and even the affections of nature.

But this form of humanity, though its chief ingredient might be iron, decomposed and crumbled away, like its more perishable predecessors. It answered the purpose for which Providence designed it, and then ceased to be. From the everlasting forests and the frozen hills of the north there poured down on the sunny fields of Italy countless multitudes of strange men, before whose frosty fingers the arts withered, and at whose rude approach literature and taste retired.

Strange were the mutations of humanity that followed during the period of at least one thousand years. It is difficult to determine the peculiar mission of the middle ages. It was the winter of humanity—the season necessary, in human as well as vegetable life, for gathering up the energies and preparing and maturing the materials for a more vigorous growth. And long as was that winter, it at last wore away, and spring returned. And how glorious was that spring! New life was infused into every department of human interest, and man, prostrate for ages, appeared again walking erect in the image of his Maker.

Time would fail us to notice the characteristic, the

leading idea, or, to use the word we have adopted in this article, the *mission* of the various communities of modern times. There is, however, one characteristic strongly marking the present age. The principle is more fully developed in our own, than in any other country. It is *independence of thought and freedom of action.* The Pilgrims who first settled North America were men who sacrificed every thing for

"Freedom to worship God."

Toleration they might have had in their own country; but with this they were not satisfied. They demanded freedom and independence. To secure it they left their home, their dear native land, and sought a new home on the bleak and barren coast of the north Atlantic. The principle of independence, though beginning in religious interests, ended not here. It soon naturally extended to politics. The declaration of American Independence was the legitimate result of the principles the Pilgrims had adopted.

Perpetuity of national existence is not to be expected in the present condition of humanity. Each nation, as well as each individual, has its work to do, and when it has done that work, it gives place to its successor. We, too, must depart in our turn, when our work is done. Nor may any nation hope for a resurrection. Nations live but once. When they die, they die forever.

THE TOLLING BELL.

There are sweet sounds here, dear reader. Over my head, on the topmost branch of the beech, sits a mocking-bird, sweetest of singers, emulously tuning his mellow throat to every variety of song. Just over the brook is a robin singing to his mate that is sitting on her nest. From amidst the maple boughs chirps the black-bird. The plaintive cooing of some lone turtle-dove is heard from the dry branch of a leafless poplar. The grass seems alive with the shrill notes of the merry cricket. I like that same cricket. Its sound is such as I used to hear at my native hearthstone. I cheerfully welcome whatever sight or sound revives in my heart the memory of other days. Welcome the sunshine that used to fall on my childhood's playground! Welcome the moon, whose silvery light is the very same that gleamed from the quiet lake near my native home! Welcome the stars—Orion with his band, Arcturus with his sons, and the Pleiades with their sweet influences, and the shining galaxy of a thousand gems, that shed their mellow light on the flowery path of my youth! Welcome the spring, with its buds of promise, and its genial influences! Welcome the summer, with its flowers, its inimitable green, and its merry voices! Welcome all to my heart; for they sometimes, for a brief season, make me feel as I once did, before care had wrinkled my brow, or years blanched my temples, or sorrow wrung my heart. But not the sunshine, nor the moonlight, nor the starry evening, nor budding spring, nor flowery summer, nor the merry music of nature's thousand voices, brings back the glad heart, nor the buoyant hope of childhood. I look on the world of nature—it is as beautiful as ever; but there are those who once enjoyed its beauties with me, now gone forever from earth. I look upon the world of men; but it appears not to me as it once did, when every successive view presented the beautiful and ever-changing colors of the kaleidoscope.

But I am wandering away I know not where. I was speaking of pleasant sounds. My nerves are suddenly startled by a sound whose meaning I know full too well. The deep tones of the college bell come booming over the fields, and awaken thrilling emotions in my soul. The sound is not that which calls me to my daily duties, nor that which betokens the hour of prayer, nor that which calls the wanderer home to the house of God; nor is it that which marks the grave and measured march of the funeral procession. But it is the knell of death. It tells us of the departure of the amiable and manly youth, by whose bedside we have watched for the last few days and nights, wavering between hope and despair. Not an hour ago I left his bedside. His father was standing over him with intense anxiety. His mother was bathing his fevered brow, and shedding bitter tears. His youthful associates in the pursuit of knowledge were around him. I left him for a time, and I came here to soothe my agitated feelings; and now that tolling bell tells that all is over.

To-morrow that bell will toll again, as with sad hearts we bury the lovely youth by the side of his companions, who have gone before him to the place of the dead, whence they return no more. Alas, alas, for human life! what is it? and what is it worth? Surely it is as the grass of the field, or as the morning flower—cut down in its beauty and its prime.

THE MORAL SUBLIME.

THERE is a passion, excited in the mind of man by natural scenery, called by philosophers the emotion of the sublime. The occasions on which the emotion is raised are many and various. There is sublimity in our magnificent forests and illimitable prairies. There is sublimity in the starry heavens, as we look, on a clear night, at the innumerable shining lights that stream forth from their exhaustless fountains. There is sublimity in the clouded sky, when the red lightning darts along its resistless way, and the thunder echoes over the hills. There is sublimity in the water, as it pours over Niagara's precipice, and plunges in the abyss below. There is sublimity in the ocean, as it rolls up its waters, wave after wave, and dashes with thundering roar on the beach. Yes, there is sublimity in the ocean. It was the ocean that first raised in my infant soul the emotion of the sublime. I listened to its grand music when the morning sun arose dripping from its watery bed, when the twilight of evening was waning, and when the deep-toned bell of the distant city was striking the hour of midnight. The ocean, the boundless, the fathomless, the illimitable, when shall I again stand on its rock-ribbed shores, and see its wild waves play! The ocean alone, of all whose images are stamped on childhood's tablet, remains unchanged. The friends whose faces were then familiar, are all gone. The old house has fallen to ruins. The elms that grew about it are blasted by lightning, or prostrated by the tempest, or cut down by the ax. The snorting steam-horse, dashing along with his iron hoofs, has scared away all the sylvan associations of the evergreen forest. The ocean alone is there in its sublimity, as I first beheld it, unchanged amid surrounding changes, an image of the throne of the Eternal, that stands immutable amidst the wreck of matter and the crush of worlds.

There is sublimity in the mountain, as you look up to its lofty summit, peering above the clouds; or, as you stand on its airy hights, and look down its dizzy sides into its dark ravines, walled up by precipices a thousand feet deep. There is sublimity in the volcano, as you stand on the verge of the crater and look down deep into the bosom of earth at the boiling sea of melted rock, while the deafening roar of nature's artillery might drown the battle sounds of Austerlitz, and of Marengo, and of Waterloo—while the red flames flash toward the sky, and the waves of lava sweep over the plain.

But not natural scenes alone excite in man the emotions of the sublime. There is a sublime in morals as well as in nature. Acts of daring enterprise, of unconquerable virtue, of magnanimity, of patriotism, of benevolence, and of heroic fortitude, may excite emotions of sublimity not less overpowering than those caused by the grandest scenes of nature.

There is not wanting sublimity in the pursuit of knowledge. The youth, struggling with poverty, with neglect, with difficulties and embarrassments, yet urging his way upward to the temple of science, presents an object of thrilling interest. The triumph of philosophy and science over nature; the lightning quiet and the thunder silent before the master-spirit of Franklin; the same power which heaves ruin and desolation from the volcano's crater, rendered, by the genius of Fulton, subservient to the interests of man, propelling the steamship across the ocean, and urging the chariot wheel over its iron track, may afford occasions of the moral sublime.

Instances of patriotic enterprise, illustrating the moral sublime, may be found in the history of every nation. But there is in the sacred records, one that, from its peculiar circumstances, deserves to be classed first among acts of moral sublimity. I refer to the patriotic sacrifice which Moses made for his people. Moses, the Hebrew, was the adopted son of the daughter of Egypt's king. He might be heir to unlimited power and exhaustless riches. Egypt was then the glory of kingdoms. Her kings had conquered the greater part of the known world. Her philosophers were skilled in all the arts and all the sciences of the day; so that the historians, and the poets, and the philosophers of classic Greece went to Egypt to enrich themselves with the learning of that renowned country. Her temples, her palaces—the world has never seen such. Her Thebes poured forth from its hundred gates its hundred thousand warriors. Her Memnon's statue with strange music saluted the rising sun. Her pyramids, which yet remain, though beat upon by the winds and rains of forty centuries, were then fresh and fair. The Hebrews were slaves in the land—abject, degraded, miserable slaves. The blight of four hundred years of oppression had fallen on their spirit. Their father-land was in the possession of strangers. Their heritage was poverty—their life unceasing toil—their home a dreary, comfortless mud cabin. To Moses was given the choice, either to remain the son of the king's daughter, and enjoy the power, the riches, and the glory of the kingdom, or to suffer affliction with his people—to associate with princes, or with slaves—to live in a splendid palace, or in a mud hut—to be buried, when life should be over, in a pyramid, or on a desolate mountain, where no man might know his sepulcher. He chose the latter. He cast away the pleasures, the riches, the honors of Egypt's court, and became the leader of those who had nothing to give him in return. History records no instance of patriotism like this.

The records of benevolent enterprise may furnish many illustrations of the moral sublime. Acts of pure benevolence—acts prompted merely by the love of human kind—acts performed at the sacrifice of one's ease, pleasure, and personal interest, are eminently calculated to move the deep fountains of human feeling. Among pure philanthropists, those whose lives and fortunes have been devoted to ameliorate the lot of the unhappy, stands first the name of Howard. He chose for the field of his operations that department of human suffering which all others had overlooked. He went to the prison—he entered the deep, dark, damp dungeon cell—he listened to the prisoner's tale of woe. He administered medicine to the sick, and consolation to the broken-hearted. He went from city to city, exploring all the prisons of his native land, and bringing to light the secret horrors of the prison-house. He then visited the continent, and went from state to state, and from kingdom to kingdom, not, like the warrior, to subdue cities and subvert thrones, nor, like the philosopher, to seek for knowledge, but to remember the forgotten, to attend to the neglected, to visit the forsaken, and to sound the depths of human suffering. He has thus invested his very name with a halo of glory.

The class of philanthropists known as reformers furnish many instances of the moral sublime. The reformer has often to stand solitary and alone against the world. The stormy waves of popular opinion are beating about him. He must not only stand firm against those waves, but he must direct their current to another channel. It is his to change long-established opinions and customs, fortified by prejudice and interest. Men ardently love their opinions; they love their interest better. It hence becomes a herculean task to change public opinion, when the change necessarily interferes with the business pursuits of community. The last century furnishes an example of a single individual, humble and unpretending, one of the people, having nothing to entitle him to special attention, attempting a measure of reform, and succeeding in it, with the entire British empire and all the world beside against him. When Wilberforce first mentioned to his friends his design to subvert the policy of the British government in relation to the African slave-trade—a trade which had existed for centuries—a trade in which were employed British ships, and British sailors, and British capital—a trade whose profits found their way, by a thousand channels, to every man, and every woman, and every child in the kingdom—he was met by one universal burst of opposition. On making a motion in Parliament for the appointment of a committee to investigate the policy of the trade, he was treated with positive rudeness, and utterly refused a hearing. But the British Parliament, though its laws govern half the world, could not restrain the rising spirit of Wilberforce. The British treasury, though it had at its command the wealth of the Indies, could not buy off his conscience from its righteous decisions. The British government, though on its dominions the sun never sets—though it might crush half the kingdoms of Europe at a blow—though it might wrest the scepter from the powerful grasp of Napoleon, and imprison him in the rocky fortress of a sea-girt isle, far away in the Atlantic, could not subdue the soul of Wilberforce. Onward he went, in spite of the world, till he saw the British Parliament, the British nation the British empire, submissive at his feet. Noble and happy old man! The greatest empire of earth arose to do him homage. He reached the goal of human life with his silvered brows covered with laurels of victory and of triumph. Yet were those laurels not dripping with blood, nor wet with the tears of the captive. No curse, no blight shall rest on them. They shall remain ever green, ever fresh, so long as the human heart shall respond to deeds of noble philanthropy.

Our own times are not wanting for illustrations of the moral sublime, in the department of Christian benevolence. The missionary enterprise has for its object one of the grandest conceptions that ever entered the human mind—the enlightening, educating, elevating to the dignity of its nature, the whole human race. Its field is the world—the world with all its continents and islands, its hills and valleys, its mountains and plains. Its line of operation extends from India's coral strand to Oregon's boundless forests—from Hudson's frozen bay to Magellan's misty straits. Its subjects are the men of every clime, and every color, and every tongue—the fair Circassian, the swarthy Indian, and the dark African. Its efficient force is a band of heroes, such as the classic soil of Greece never produced, and the sunny vales of Italy never nourished. Leaving his home, his country, his friends, all that the world holds dear, the missionary, bearing aloft the standard of the cross, boldly marches forward in the face of difficulties, such as neither Hannibal, nor Cæsar, nor Napoleon ever encountered. No clarion of war, no alarum drum, but the silver-toned trumpet of the Gospel, announces his approach. No blood-stained battle plains, no ravaged fields, no smoking ruins mark his passage. The earth grows green where his foot has been, and the horn of plenty pours out her exhaustless gifts. No groan of grief, no sigh of sorrow, no wailing words of woe, no weeping widow, no helpless orphan's cry is heard along his path. The blessing of him that was ready to perish rests on his name. Humanity rises to do him honor, and the voices of earth and heaven unite in saying, "Blessed is he that cometh in the name of the Lord."

History affords several examples of heroic fortitude, which none can contemplate without emotions of sublimity. But there is a scene often occurring within our own observation, unspeakably sublime. I refer to the triumphant death of the Christian. There is something in the idea of death appalling to every human being. The very grass beneath your feet instinctively shrinks from it. The worm that crawls along your path shudders at it. Man, thinking, reasoning, foreseeing man, looks at it with horror indescribable. All that he hath will he give for his life. This dread of death, so deep, so appalling, can only be subdued by some extraordinary influence. The warrior may meet death with what the world calls courage. The culprit may meet it with sullen obstinacy. The philosopher may meet it with resignation. But only the Christian can meet it with triumph. He approaches that dark valley of the shadow of death, from whose gloomy precincts none ever return. He sees before him that black stream, on whose banks there grows no living thing, and on whose leaden waters there floats not even a wreck of all that has been. Of all his friends, not one can go with him through that dark valley—not one can cross with him that oblivious tide. That he should meet death with resignation would be grand—that he meets it with triumph is inconceivably sublime.

Such a scene we witnessed not long since. There was among us a man in his maturity—a man whose eye was not dimmed by age, nor his natural strength abated by infirmity. Time's frosty fingers had scarcely touched his brow. He had selected him a spot where he hoped to spend a long life. He had built him a cottage, and surrounded it with beauty. The wife of his youth was with him. The children of his heart clustered about his hearth. Beloved at home, honored abroad, he was just prepared for a long and happy life. In the midst of all, death—death that respects none—death that accepts no substitute for his victim—death that gives back those whom he calls hence not to the weeping eye, nor to the broken heart—death knocked at his door, and summoned him away to that undiscovered country from whose bourne no traveler returns. Short was the time allowed for preparation. Yet the good man could not leave this beautiful world, with all its loved scenes and fond associations, without casting one longing, lingering look behind. Rising up in his bed, looking out of the open window on the earth, smiling in summer beauty, he exclaimed, "My native land, farewell!" Casting his eyes on his wife and children, and waving his hand, again he exclaimed, with indescribable emotion, *"My native land, farewell!"* Then there seemed to appear before him the ladder which old Jacob saw, extending from earth to heaven. His intercourse seemed to be with another world. Pæans of triumph were sung with his dying voice; shouts of "victory! victory!" seemed to die away on his expiring breath. Long will it be before those who beheld that scene of triumph can forget it—long will it be before those songs of victory will cease to echo on our hearts. The Christian may enjoy in his dying hour such a scene of triumph as none of earth's chieftains ever enjoyed. They were sometimes drawn, through the open gates of the city, in a chariot, with the captives taken in war following behind. But the Christian, in the triumph of the last hour, seems to mount that chariot of fire which appeared to Elijah, the prophet, and to be borne through the gates of pearl, and along the golden streets of the New Jerusalem, with death a captive, and bound to the chariot wheels.

GOING HOME.

"Mother, let us go home. Why did we come here?"

On an evening of early autumn, in a rural cottage, on one of the most retired streets of our pleasant village, a fair young girl lay on her dying bed. She had left, some two years before, her home on the Wabash, and had come to this place to spend a few years at school. In her were associated unusual sweetness of disposition, and extraordinary power and refinement of mind, with great beauty of person. She seemed one of the highly-gifted children of earth, who partake more of the spirituality and intellect of angels, than of the materiality and imperfections of mortals. She had pursued her studies with extraordinary success, and saw before her the highest honors of the seminary of which she was a member. She fell sick of fever, and for many days her friends were suffering the agitating anxieties of fluctuating hope and ever-recurring despair. We had gathered around her as she lay quietly sinking under the influence of disease and slightly affected with delirium. For a moment she aroused, opened her eyes, and saw her mother leaning over her bed. "Mother," said she gently, "let us go home. Why did we come here?" She closed her eyes again, and quietly fell asleep to wake no more. Her last thought seemed of home—the home of her childhood. A few weeks before she fell sick, while apparently under the influence of some presentiment of her early death, she wrote, as a school exercise, the following delightful passage:

"The heart has memories that can not die. They are

memories of home, of early-loved home. Home! there is magic in the very word. The sound sends a thrill to the heart, vibrating on every nerve. Home! how dear and cherished are its remembrances! How hallowed is the spot! There passed sweetly our childhood's rosy hours. O, I sympathize with the lone wanderer, who has not in all the world a spot he may call home. Sad must be his heart when, weary, forsaken, and forlorn, he finds no asylum, where the weary rest, where the forsaken find comfort, and the forlorn hope. Though separated from my own cottage home, my thoughts often wander back to its rural charms. Sometimes I fancy I am wandering by the crystal brook that winds by the cottage door, and gazing on its lucid stream as it goes singing and dancing along in the bright sunshine, or sparkles in the silver moonbeams. Along the verdant and flowery brink of that little brook I have passed some of the happiest moments of my life.

"Often, at the sweet hour of evening, when memory's sacred spell was on my soul, have I strolled out, while the dew-drops were sparkling in the moonlight, and sat down on the soft carpet of green, sprinkled with little tufts of beautiful wild flowers, and listened to the waters as they murmured through the vale. Oft was my heart enraptured with the scene, and I thought this was the 'happy land where care was unknown.'

"Near by the cottage stands the old school-house, in which I first was taught to read. And there, too, about that dear cottage home, was my favorite garden walk, my pleasant arbor, my beautiful flowers, the rose-bush that twined about my chamber window, 'and every loved spot that my infancy knew.' I wonder if my flowers still bloom as fair and as sweet, and if the rose-bushes twine as lovingly about the window, as when I used to trim them. Ah! lovely flowers! you may bloom on, but not for me. Other footsteps will tread my garden walk; others will sit in my shady bower.

"But my cottage home throws a still stronger spell over my heart. There, on the brow of a hill, beneath the floating branches of a tree, sleeps sweet Ellen, my only sister. I weep when I think of Ellen's grave. Who will train the rose-bush over the spot? Who will plant the myrtle and the snow-drop, and bedew them with tears of affection? Who will kneel at twilight beside her grave, and say to her, good-night?"

This lovely human angel, more seemingly a native of some bright, heavenly sphere than of earth, for some months before her death, and when in full health and blooming in beauty, appeared conscious that her days were few, and that she was standing on the very verge of the spirit-land. The following beautiful essay was written on her nineteenth birthday:

"The morning smiles with cheerful beams of rosy hue. The pearly dew-drop, in its chariot of cloud, glides away to its 'bower in air.' The lark sings sweetly, as he upward flies to greet the glorious king of day, now approaching in sublime grandeur, cheering all nature with his refulgent rays. Calmness and serenity sit smiling on the beauteous face of Nature. The gentle whispering of a lonely, wandering zephyr, as it plays among the lovely flowers, or sports in the leafy groves, falls upon my listening ear. A romantic charm seems floating on the soft gale, leaving a fairy impress on every object.

'O, there is joy and happiness
In every thing I see,
Which bids my soul rise up and bless
The God that blesses me.'

"Again I hail the return of my birthday; and though amidst joyful salutations and happy wishes that are wont to greet me—though surrounded by Nature arrayed in her loveliest garb, yet there is a pensive sadness pervades my would-be gay and happy heart. In vain do I wear a cheerful smile and an air of careless mirth and gayety; for naught can exile the melancholy vision that hovers about my spirit, or obliterate the deep impression made upon my heart by the return of my birthday. Methinks I hear a visitor from the land of silence softly whisper, 'Every birthday finds thee nearer a visionless sleep and a couch of clay.' Yes, a few more fleeting birthdays, and who will think of Minerva? Who will ever dream that such a being appeared on the stage of existence? Who will cherish her name and love her memory? O, none! Another will take her place, the vacuum occupied all will be well, and not one will hold her in sweet remembrance.

"Ah! I have planned full many a scheme of earthly happiness; but how soon may the hand of the fell destroyer throw a chill blight on all my budding hopes and blooming prospects, crush all my bright anticipations, and hasten me to the shades of oblivion, there to slumber alone and forgotten! That word 'forgotten,' how sadly it falls on my pensive heart! It is a mournful theme to dream of the land of oblivion. All shrink from its dark and gloomy shades, with a kind of instinctive reluctance to enter its dismal abodes. How transient is our mortal existence! Flowers are truly our emblems. In the morning we gaze on the sweet rose-bud, with its petals folded in tender infancy—the emblem of pure and innocent childhood; at noon it bursts forth, in exquisite beauty and loveliness, 'the queen of flowers,' displaying its irresistible charms as it proudly and gracefully bows to the gentle breeze and basks in the sunbeams, captivating its unnumbered admirers—the emblem of the most interesting period of life—our blooming, gay, and happy youth. But mark the change of the scene. For an hour we see it the pride and admiration of all, a perfect flower; but soon the destroyer comes; it begins to droop; the rude blast is too much for its delicate and fragile form; its richly-tinted petals wither, and when evening throws her sable mantle around us, the work of destruction is complete, and naught remains to tell its mournful fate. It dies, the emblem of our transient being. And think ye the flowers that bloomed by its side, the companions of its youth, wept long for the untimely fall of their lovely sister? No! they breathed, 'Our sister is no more;' the bud that grew by her side, half entombed in her robe, sprung up in her place, and she was from memory forever erased. Such is her fate; her knell unrung; her requiem unsung; her epitaph unwritten; and such shall be mine. Yes! I shall sink like that flower. Perhaps a few more scenes of youthful pleasure, interspersed with those of pain, a few more sips at the cup of happiness, mingled with drops of sorrow, and the curtain will fall. Perhaps a few cherished and devoted friends may mark my decline, and breathe a sigh of sympathy. A tear of sorrow and regret may tremble on the cheek of some fond and loved associate, as she gazes on me for the last time; a soft whisper of, 'Peace to the lone and silent couch of her who sleeps forever!' may pass round my humble tomb; they turn away, the occurrence assumes the mystic form of a dream, and vanishes. Yet why am I sad? Why thus dejected? Is it not sweet to pass from earth so quietly; and with such calmness and serenity to leave the afflictions, cares, disappointments, and thorny paths of this mundane sphere? 'Yes, unhonored and unknown let me live, unwept and unlamented let me die.' It is a beautiful thought, that, when I sleep that last, long, dreamless sleep, they will place my lowly couch in some sequestered grove, 'far from the world's gay stroll,' by the side of some gentle, murmuring brook, beneath the green-decked bows of a towering forest-tree, that may wave in silent grandeur over my peaceful home. No deep-toned knell shall wake the forest birds. No massive block of marble shall tell who slumbers there. The soft, plaintive notes of sweet Philomel shall be my dirge, while the waters of the crystal brook shall chant for me a requiem. I would that the gentle hand of one, whom once I loved, should plant the myrtle, snow-drop, and teach the woodbine and rose-bush to twine above my grave. I would that none but kindred spirits should ever wander there, and, as a token of their remembrance, 'bring flowers to the place where my dust is laid.' O, how sweet is the contemplation of that tranquil, beautiful sleep, when the soul is inspired by the hope of a blissful immortality in the bright mansions of Elysium!"

Whence come these presentiments of approaching dissolution? Does some sister spirit,

"From the land which no mortal may know,"

whisper to the inner ear of the soul "of things which must shortly come to pass?" Or is it true, as the ancient philosopher taught, that the soul on earth is an exile, banished for a time from its native home, yet conscious of its inheritance of immortality, and pining for its rest in heaven? Is there associated with the recollection of our early home, our home of childhood and innocence, inspired suggestions, and spiritual connections of a better home in the paradise of God?

Life is indeed to the good but a pilgrimage—the journey of a day. Our earthly homes are but temporary bowers, in which we may rest from the fatigues of our journey, and gather strength to go on our way. The exile of earth will soon end, and we shall go home. The mansions of permanent rest are fitting up, and the loved ones who have already arrived are waiting our coming. We are on our rapid way to join the inmates of that heavenly home. And yet with strange inconsistency we are lamenting their early removal. We are yet, though years have passed since she went *home*, weeping over the departure of the talented, amiable, and beautiful Minerva:

"Yes, there still are bending o'er her
Eyes that weep;
Forms that to the cold grave bore her
Vigils keep.
When the summer moon is shining
Soft and fair,
Friends she loved in tears are twining
Chaplets there.
Rest in peace, thou gentle spirit,
Throned above;
Souls like thine with God inherit
Life and love."

THE FOREST SANCTUARY

In a charming grove, on a beautiful hill, overlooking a lovely landscape of valley, plain, lake, and river, the people of the Most High were met for prayer and praise. It was an evening of early autumn. The people, quietly seated on the rude benches, with eye intent, and listening ear, were hanging enraptured on the lips of the man of God, whose eloquent tones fell like music on the heart. He was one of the pioneers of the Church—a tall, old man, of form erect, of noble bearing, and of strictly-expressive countenance. His head was gray with years and with toil. Long years ago, he, a mere stripling from the Green Mountain land, had been sent on a mission of salvation to the people scattered over these hills and valleys. He had returned to his mountain home, and labored for many years in his Master's work. Now he had come back to the scene of his early labors; and with a voice even more musical than in youth, and with an eloquence that had lost none of its power, he was speaking the words of truth to a vast multitude of deeply-devout worshipers. There were, in that forest congregation, old men, who, in their youth, had, under the persuasive power of that same eloquent voice, yielded themselves up to holy influences and a life of piety. To hear that voice again seemed to them like the return of youth, bringing back to their hearts the joyous emotions of other days. By their side were their children, and their children's children. The man of God spoke of Jesus, and of the cross, and of redemption. He depicted the scenes of the resurrection, of the judgment, and of eternity. He closed with an appeal to the sinner, of such power and eloquence, that the hardest heart seemed melted—the most stubborn will subdued. He closed his sermon, came down from the rustic desk, proceeded to a large, open space, within the inclosure of tents, and, with a voice sweet as the harp of Ariel, sang the following words:

"Come, ye disconsolate, where'er you languish,
Come, at the shrine of God fervently kneel;
Here bring your wounded hearts—here tell your anguish;
Earth hath no sorrow that heaven can not heal.

Joy of the comfortless, light of the straying,
Hope, when all others die, fadeless and pure,
Here speaks the comforter, in mercy saying,
Earth hath no sorrow that heaven can not cure."

When he had concluded, there were gathered about him in a large circle hundreds of worshipers. Among them was a multitude of penitents. With gentle words and soothing tones he invited the mourner for sin to come and kneel at the rude altar near him for confession and prayer. A multitude rushed to the devoted spot. They came—the mature man, the comely matron, the sprightly youth, the fair maiden, and the child. They dropped on their knees before the good old man, and he continued telling them of the love of Christ. Then the multitude all kneeled on the ground, and the good man offered up the earnest prayer of faith. He then arose and sang, a hundred voices joining—

"Arise, my soul, arise,
Shake off thy guilty fears;
The bleeding sacrifice
In my behalf appears;
Before the throne my surety stands;
My name is written on his hands."

Struck with the sublimity of the scene, I stood at a short distance, on a little knoll, looking on the place and the people. The grove was composed of tall maples, and grand old oaks, and gigantic hemlocks, with here and there a tall, straight pine. Lamps were suspended from the branches of the trees, lighting up the whole scene. The trunks of the trees seemed like variegated and massive pillars upholding a canopy whose gorgeous colorings, touched by the brush of autumnal frost, no painter's pencil might imitate. The mingled voices of the immense multitude, all tuned in native melody, rose up amid the forest leaves, like the deep tones of the pealing organ, chanting in some old cathedral the *Te Deum* in strains of harmony. I looked on the people, and I seemed to see a vision of angels. Among the happy converts was a fair young girl, who stood with her eyes half closed, yet raised toward heaven, and gently clapping her hands in ecstasy. She spoke not a word, but no angel face to human eye ever seemed more heavenly.

An angel hand might paint that scene, an angel tongue might tell it, an angel pen describe it; but no human effort can avail to express either the depth of the emotion, the beauty of the sight, or the harmony of the sounds, that went up to heaven from that forest sanctuary.

That spot seemed holy ground. No Gothic temple could seem half so grand as that primeval house not made with human hands. No costly chandelier, with diamond reflectors, would give so pure a light as those rustic lamps suspended from the green branches, and their rays reflected from the autumn-colored leaves.

It is a glorious place, that forest sanctuary, the place where the Most High delights to meet his people. Not the temple of Jerusalem in its highest glory was more dear to the dweller in Palestine than is the memory to me of the forest temple, on whose rustic altar I have seen the dearest friends of earth bring their gift—the gift of a broken heart, and a contrite spirit—and offer it up to Him, to whom such a sacrifice is more acceptable than earth's richest treasures.

THE FALLING LEAVES.

It is the time of the falling leaf. The frost has come with its biting nip, and the forest leaves have felt its power. They are falling thick and fast from the beech and the maple, that have, during the long summer, furnished me so grateful a shade, beneath which I have spent many an hour. Here they drop, one by one, in the quiet and stillness of this bright and beautiful morning. O falling leaves, sad seems your fate! One summer only have you enjoyed, and now you fall to rise no more. But such is the doom of all like you, children of earth. Even now as you drop, one by one, you rest on the grave of youth and beauty. Already, and while I have been standing here, you have formed a covering over the bed where sleeps the long and dreamless sleep of the grave my own bright and beautiful one, who, like you, passed away. But yours is still a timely fate. You have filled your destiny. But she, alas, fell before the frost of winter or of age had come! She perished in the springtime of the year and of life. On a bright May morning, while the soft breath of spring and the genial sunshine were bringing out the flowers in all their budding beauties, she suddenly passed away. And we laid her beneath the overhanging beech. Here let her rest. O falling leaves, gather yourselves about her bed, and protect it from the beating rain, and the rude blast of the wintery wind, and the drifting snows!

Leaves of autumn, you forewarn me of my own fate. My own spring-time has past—my summer is gone—gone from my brow, gone from my heart. Gone is the buoyancy of youth, gone the cheerfulness of the happy days of childhood, gone the sunshine of the heart. The merry voice that once cheered my soul is hushed forever. The sunshiny brow that once reflected joy on my heart lies low beneath that bed of leaves. The gentle hand that once played with my whitening locks, and smoothed the wrinkles from my brow, now lies motionless on the breast where once beat the gentlest of human hearts.

And I, too, am on my rapid way, and soon must reach the resting-place of all that is born of earth. I must come and lie here by the side of

"The pretty child I lov'd so well."

Another will then stand where I now do, and watch your graceful descent as you drop on the grave of the child and the father.

THE BURIAL OF BALCH.

AGAIN we meet at the sad sound of the tolling bell. Again there lies shrouded for the grave, before the sacred altar of our quiet village church, one whom we have all known, and all loved. On the declivity of the hill, whose summit is crowned by the temple of God, a grave by friendly hands is made, and there we soon must lay the manly form of Balch. Fitting place is it for the long rest of the youthful and the good. The quiet lake sleeping in rural beauty at the base of the hill, seems an emblem of the rest of those whose souls no more are disturbed by the rippling undulations of emotion, nor the deep surges of human passion. It is a spot so retired, so still, so quiet, that the genius of repose might choose it for her permanent home. To that spot have we, during the last few years, borne many a lovely one—age with gray hairs, manhood in its vigor and strength, woman in her loveliness, childhood in its beauty, and now we bear youth with all its hopes of success and of usefulness.

Spring, in all its loveliness, had opened on the fields and about the lakes that surround this beautiful hill. The sky was clear, and the earth was beautiful. But death was here. Before this altar lay the inanimate form of as beautiful a child as human eye ever saw. Her home was far away. She had come here with her parents on a visit. A few Sabbaths she had occupied one of those seats in the Sabbath school, the personification of sprightliness and of beauty. But suddenly she fell sick. A few days only passed, a few nights of feverish agony, and, lo, she lay there arrayed for the grave! It was sad to see the mother weep over her beautiful one, her unreturning first-born. Who, that looked beneath that coffin-lid, can forget the loveliness and beauty that slept on those cold features! We bore the little stranger to the grave that was made for her amid the shrubbery and flowers. Who may tell the sad feelings of anguish with which her parents returned to their home!

* * * * * * * *

The yellow harvests of autumn were gathered in; the grass had become sear; the forest leaves were tinged with their variant hues, and some of them were fallen. Before the altar lay, shrouded and coffined for the grave, the wife and the mother—the mother whose children had daily received instruction from our lips. Who that ever knew her did not love her? Who ever looked on her benignant countenance without being reminded of the gentleness, the benevolence, the affection of the female character? But there she lay cut down in her full strength. The rose was in its maturity; it was not faded, nor blanched by age—but the reaper's scythe had ruthlessly struck it, and its life-blood gushed out. Her we deposited in that quiet spot, and strewed the earth over her. The mother that bore her, the sister of her heart, the husband that loved her as man seldom loves, and the children of her bosom, returned to their desolate home. Who can guage the deep fountain of anguish in those bereaved hearts? Who will venture to approach them with the mockery of words?

* * * * * * * *

The winter had passed, the warm breezes from the south had melted away the snow, the first flowers of May were peeping from under the dry leaf. Placed before that altar was a man of mature years, and great physical and intellectual strength. He died while yet his eye had not become dim, nor his natural force abated. Before that coffin, which contained all that remained of the companion of her youth, sat a woman, broken-hearted, the image of sorrow. By her side were her children, on whose cheeks were written, in characters of paleness, the grief of orphanage. With measured steps we bore the lifeless form to the spot consecrated to the dead. The procession stopped—the bier was lowered, the body was deposited in the grave. The procession was about to return, when one of those orphan children, a beautiful little boy, leaped from the carriage in which he was sitting with his mother, and from which the family had not alighted, and rushed, regardless of all around him, to the grave, and, standing on its brink, cast a longing, lingering look at the coffin of his father. The indescribable look of that child, as he bent over that grave, went to my heart. It brought out, in bold relief, on my soul the image of many a loved one over whom the grave has closed forever.

* * * * * * * *

It was winter. The tones of the bell called us again to this house. There was seen in the congregation many a hoary head, on which had fallen the snows of fourscore winters. Before the altar lay one of their number, a mother in Israel—one whose years had numbered a century—one who had seen the forests cleared away, and her children's children grow up and become old by her side. Full of years, full of honor, full of grace, and ripe for heaven, God had called her home. She seemed like a plant, whose seed becoming mature and perfect, mounts the air on its wings, and soars away, leaving the stock, which has fulfilled the purpose of its existence, to be resolved into its constituent elements.

* * * * * * * *

The summer came. Its first roses were plucked, and

its first fruits were becoming ripe. Before that altar lay an infant—an infant that had seen the snows of but one winter, but had never seen an autumn. Its mother gave it birth, and fell sick. A few months she nursed it in feebleness. The spring painfully wore away. When summer came, she left her home to go on a visit to her friends in pursuit of health. On her journey she expired in her husband's arms, before he could take her from her carriage. The bereaved husband went on his way with his dead wife to the home of her childhood, where he buried her in the church-yard of her native village. With his motherless infant he retraced his steps toward his desolate home. Arriving thus far on his way, the child fell sick and died, and we buried her yonder. Happy child! she knows not the sorrows of orphanage.

* * * * * * * *

Another summer was gone. The mellow autumn, with its fallen leaf, had come. The storm of wind and of rain, that had been raging for several days, was cleared away, and the calm and bright September sun was shining cheerful on the bosom of earth. The sky had resumed its delicate blue. The winds were all hushed, and a stillness befitting the occasion had come over all things. Before that altar lay the charming little Roscoe. Scarce had he lived two summers ere he sickened and died. Alas, that so much beauty must fade! His bright eyes were dimmed; his cheeks were pale, his lips were motionless; but the smile was there—the smile that death could not remove—the smile that spoke of heaven. On his breast and in his little hands were flowers, such as autumn produces. He, a fairer flower than earth is wont to produce, had been suddenly nipped, and had untimely fallen. Beneath the waving branches of a pine we made his grave. As we gathered around his place of rest we sung the mournful requiem, composed by the heart-stricken father in the hour of bereavement:

"I walked the fields in early morn,
And saw a rosebud on a thorn,
It sparkled in the dew so bright,
Methought I ne'er saw lovelier sight.
An hour had sped, and o'er the dewy lawn
I turned my steps again—the rose was gone.

At noon I went to view the flood
That dashed in torrents from the wood;
Down, down it rushed in foamy pride;
Two bows there spanned it side by side;
Another hour—the sky was darkened o'er;
I saw the sunbeams in the spray no more.

'Twas eve—I turned my wandering eye,
To trace the meteor through the sky;
A radiance beamed from off the pole,
That shed a sunshine on the soul:
A moment gone—I raised again my head
To view those flashing beams—and all were fled.

So like the rosebud from the thorn
That looked so gay in early morn;
Or like the rainbows o'er the flood,
That dashed so furious from the wood;
Or nearer like, to mortal eye,
The changeful meteor of the sky;
My cherub child is snatched from me away—
But O, sweet thought! to live in endless day,
Where neither rose, nor bow, nor sparkling beam,
To angel eyes does half so lovely seem!"

When we had sung this dirge, and commended ourselves to God, we with mournful steps and many a longing look behind, came from the spot where we left the child; and there he sleeps unmindful of the sports of childhood—of the anticipated hopes of the future—and of the love and grief of his parents. There he hears not the song of the robin that chirps on the bough that hangs over him. He sees not the pleasant light of the morning sun that calls his cousins to their sports. He smells not the wild flower that grows on his grave. He heeds not the voice of love that utters its mournful tones over him. Beautiful child, sleep on! Such as thou my Savior blessed. "Of such," he said, "is the kingdom of heaven." Lonely as appears thy rest, thou art not alone. The genius of Christianity sits over thy grave. Invisible to mortal eye, she there guards thy dust, waiting for the signal of thy Savior's appearance from heaven, when, starting from her seat, her renovating voice shalt thou hear, "*Roscoe, come forth!*" At that voice shalt thou awaken, never, blessed child, never to die again.

* * * * * * * *

And now it is summer again, and again we are here. Alas! alas! why are we here? From a neighboring city there returns to meet us here on our classic hill, one who lately went out from among us, in all the vigor of youth and perfection of manhood. He comes to his loved spot, his chosen retreat, his adopted home. He comes to his friends, to his classic associates, to his old companions, to the house of God, where he used to worship, and now he is before the very altar where he used to kneel and pray. Why speaks he not? Pupil, friend, brother, why liest thou there silent, motionless? Alas! the hand of death is on him, nor can he shake it off. The manly form lies low. The strong arm lies powerless on the cold bosom. The eye that flashed with intelligence, and beamed with benignity, is sealed up in darkness. The voice of eloquence, under whose tones our hearts used to melt, and our eyes overflow, is hushed forever. The heart once beating with life, and with sympathy for human suffering, and full of all kindness, and generosity, and sincerity of affection, is still, nor can its pulses ever stir again.

Melancholy end this of all his high hopes of a long and active life of usefulness. With a mind of unusual gifts, a body of unimpaired health, and a character combining all the elements of success, he had devoted himself to the Church of Christ. He had assumed the badge of a missionary of the cross. For this he had educated himself, laboring with his own hands to defray his expenses. The field of his future labors had been early selected, and his studies directed to the acquisition of the language of the people among whom he was to labor. He had finished his literary preparation, and was making arrangements for his departure. He was expecting before this present day should arrive, to have bid his friends farewell, and to have been on his way to the land of the south, where the La Plata and the Amazon flow over the luxuriant plains, and the Andes rise in grand sublimity. The farewell words have been spoken, but spoken with a faltering voice, and on a dying bed. He has gone his journey, but not the way he had fondly hoped. He has gone—not to the land on whose sky rises the cross of the south, and on whose horizon float the misty clouds of Magellan, but

> "To that undiscovered country, from whose bourne
> No traveler returns."

As in the providence of God he was not permitted to lay himself to rest as he had hoped, in a foreign missionary land, he asked to be brought to this place, that he might rest within sound of the bell that had so often called him to recitation and to prayer, and in sight of the classic dome beneath which so many pleasant hours he had enjoyed. And now the grave is waiting to receive him. Take him up, friends, and bear him on his bier to his resting-place.

* * * * * * * *

And now you have buried him. The earth has closed over him, and the grass will soon grow green over the spot. Here sleeps he alone. No one of his blood lies here. No mother, no sister may ever come here to weep over him, and no kindred may ever be laid to rest by his side. There was one dearer to him than sister, dearer than mother—one whom he had chosen for his bride. She sleeps, too, but not here. A thousand miles and more toward yon setting sun, by stranger hands her grave was made, and there she sleeps, without a stone to mark the spot, nor can any one tell which, among the nameless graves of that prairie cemetery, holds the moldering remains of the amiable and accomplished Maria. Would that, since it was the will of Heaven she should die, she had died with us, that we might have laid her and her betrothed side by side in this rural cemetery. But the will of God is otherwise, and so it must be.

And now farewell, brother, a long, a sad farewell! We leave thee here to rest. Here naught shall disturb thy repose. The peaceful lake that laves the borders of this resting-place of the quiet dead will never be disturbed by the discordant clatter of traffic. The bell that hangs on yonder classic hall will be alone heard, as it rings merrily for the hour of prayer, or tolls sadly for the dead. Here long wilt thou sleep. Thousands of times may yonder lofty mountains throw their deep shadows over thy grave. A thousand winters shall cover the earth with a white winding sheet; a thousand springs shall revive the flowers; a thousand summers ripen the fruits of the field; and a thousand autumns prostrate the leaf, and yet still shalt thou sleep on. We too shall come, one by one, and sleep by thy side. Our children in their turn, too, and our children's children, shall come and lie down with thee. Ages after ages shall glide away, and we shall be be forgotten by the children of earth. The storms of winter shall level the mound raised over us to the ground. Time's "effacing fingers" shall wear our names from the marble and from the hearts of the living; and Oblivion shall spread her dark shroud over our memory. Long,

long will be the night, whose shadows gather over us—night, moonless, starless, lightless. Yet when the morning comes—for come the morning will—the glorious resurrection morning—thou and we, who may share with thee this resting-place, together shall rise to meet the Lord our Savior, Jesus Christ, coming in the clouds of heaven to gather home his people.

PASSING AWAY.

Accidentally opening a book lying on my table, my eye fell on these words, "*This, too, shall pass away.*" The motto is said to have been chosen by an eastern sage, as a talisman, alike effectual in the days of prosperity and the sorrows of adversity. Much of life with us, gentle reader, is already passed away, nor can it return again. Our earliest recollections, now dim and fading, are of the mother who clasped us to her breast, and hung sleepless over our helpless infancy—the mother who watched our fitful slumbers through many a long night of sickness, breathing over us the prayer of faith, and of hope, and of love—the mother who taught us to speak, to walk, and to pray—the mother whose gentle tones soothed our ruffled temper—the mother whose bright eye beamed delight when we were good, and filled with tearful sorrow when we were bad. That mother has passed away. Her voice no longer animates us to youthful exertion. Her lip smiles no more. Her eye is closed—closed forever; nor will it look again on the light of morn, or evening twilight, or the green earth, or on us. The long grass of many a year's growth has become matted with many-twined roots in the turf that forms her covering in that silent bed where she sleeps the long sleep of the grave.

Our next recollections are of our little brothers and fair sisters, with whom we whiled away before the door the long summer day. Brother and sister, with hand twined in hand, we ran up and down the garden walks, or rambled over the fields, picking flowers on the hill-side. With tiny hands we dabbled in the brook—with light foot we chased the shadows over the lea—with stealthy tread we crept to the butterfly on the rose—with ringing laugh we skipped among the lambs. At early morn we rose to look out on the summer sky, and to listen to the caroling of the lark, the monotone of the robin, and the mellifluous music of the thrush. At noon we lay reclined in the shade by the brook, admiring the springing grass, the wild-wood violet, and peeping leaf bud. At night we returned tired of play, and, amidst sweet dreams, reposed till morning. The world was all bright and sunshiny. The hill, the vale, the wood, the brook, all furnished sources of amusement and pleasure. Those days are passed away. With them have passed the little brother and the fair sister. The little foot that tripped lightly with us over the lawn, lies motionless in the grave. The soft hand that was clasped in ours, is folded helpless on the breast. The voice that sounded so merrily, is hushed and silent forever. Tuneless is the harp that emitted so joyous tones, and moldered the form that stood in beauty by our side. In the churchyard, by the side of the mother, sleep the little sister and the little brother.

Though passed are the days, and gone on a returnless journey are the associates of childhood, yet faded are not the pictures of memory. Every beautiful scene has left daguerreotyped on our soul its image, and there will it remain forever, fresh and fair, in primeval beauty. To it in the darkened chambers of the heart we may often turn, and look on it, as on the image of a lost friend; nor will the review be profitless. Go on, then, happy child. Gather up while you may the glittering gems scattered like dew-drops along your pathway. Though to others but common pebbles, to you they are pearls. Build your castle in the air. Beautiful is it while it stands, and when it tumbles, its fragments may be beautiful still.

The colors of the soap-bubble are no less beauteous because evanescent. The hues of sunset are not less gorgeous because followed by gloomy darkness. The meteor while it shines is often more brilliant than the fixed star. Admire the butterfly while it is spreading its gay wings, and before winter comes, when you will see it no more. Chase your shadows while there is sunlight to see them; for soon darkness will gather over all the horizon. If fairies invite you to the enchanted bowers of imaginary beauty, go along with them. The substances of childhood are, it is true, evanescent. But the pictures thereof are permanent. They form a gallery in the inner chambers of the mind. When the eye grows weary with the bleak and barren prospect of age, you may turn to the gallery of childhood's pictures, and in the conceptions which they restore find relief from hideous forms.

Seek not, then, too soon to break the spell which fancy throws over childhood. The enchantment will of itself give way full soon enough. The dreams of childhood are as essential to the moral as sleep to the physical development. Let the child, therefore, by Fancy's pencil, delineate pictures to lay up in store for future requisition. Let the seed of moral truth be early implanted in his young mind. It may long lie imbedded beneath unpropitious circumstances. No sprout may shoot out, no germ appear, and no signs of life be exhibited. The day will yet come when, under favorable influences, it will push out its bud, open its flower, and mature its fruit.

If paradise can ever be realized on earth, it is to be found in the retired, quiet, beautiful, rural spot, surrounded by domestic influences. The ties that bind us to the home of maturity take hold of the heart. The domestic relations open in the heart of man fountains of feeling of whose existence he was unconscious. Deep seated in the inmost recesses of the soul, unobserved by the passer-by, hidden even from ourselves, they remain sealed up till the domestic key unlocks them. Then they gush forth in one unremitting and perennial stream, making green the sear spots of earth.

Beautiful to the eye of mature life is the scenery of home—a cottage embowered in roses and honeysuckle, and looking out on green fields and waving forests—a garden with winding walks and shady bowers—a stream flowing by and losing itself in a valley perpetually green—birds singing in the branches of blooming trees, and children playing on the grass-plot, and running to meet you returning home, peeping with their bright eyes through the fence, and clapping their little hands for joy that you are come.

"This, too, shall pass away." Over all this bright scene there may fall a shadow deep and dark. Let but one of these little voices be hushed in death, and never to your ear will sound the music of nature so soft and sweet as before. Let but one of those light hearts cease to beat, and never again will your own be merry as before. Let but those bright eyes be closed, and the coffin's lid, and the heaped-up earth, shut out from them the light of heaven, and never again to your eye will the sunshine of earth be bright as before. There will seem to have passed from earth something beautiful which can never be restored.

When once, in the maturity of life, we have known sorrow—when once the heart has been frozen by the cold sympathy of the selfish world—when once our hopes have been blighted by disappointment—when once the spirit has been crushed by misfortune—when once the soul has been overwhelmed by bereavement, we never shall be again what once we were. For the sake of others we may smile as before, but when the smile is most cheerful the heart may be most sad. The world, however, may know nothing of it; for we shall learn in time that "every heart knoweth its own bitterness, and a stranger meddleth not with its joy."

In the busy whirl of human life, we are hardly aware of the changes which are constantly passing over us. If, after an absence of years, we return to the home of childhood, we may become sensible of the transformation which we have undergone. I saw a man of mature age wending his way along the winding path he had often trodden from school, in boyhood's halcyon days, to the home of early life. A very happy child had he been—buoyant in hope, elastic in mind, cheerful and irrepressible in spirit. His eye was not yet dimmed by age, nor his physical strength abated by time. He came to the play-ground of his childhood. He climbed the hill, from which he saw the lovely landscape whose beauties had never faded from his memory. He went to the spring gushing out beneath the rock, and drank one long, deep draught of the waters, sweeter to him than those of Parnassus, or Helicon, or Arethusa. He followed the brook meandering through the vale, and drew, as in youth, the wary trout from the deep waters. He sought the evergreen bower on the plain, and laid himself down and slept beneath the very same cluster of pines whose rustling leaves had often, by inimitable music, lulled him to repose in happier days. Yet all would not do. The wanderer's heart was sad. The changes of earth had passed over him. The bright and the beautiful had faded from his sight. The lovely of earth were sleeping wakeless, some in his seagirt native land, and others far away toward the setting sun. The gray-haired man arose, looked once more on the landscape of childhood, then turned away toward his forest home, despairing of ever again restoring the sweet fancies of other days.

We, too, ourselves, shall pass away. The places that know us will know us no more forever.

> "Yet a few days, and thee
> The all-beholding sun shall see no more
> In all his course; nor yet in the cold ground,
> Where thy pale form was laid with many tears,
> Nor yet in the embrace of ocean shall exist
> Thy image."

The morning shall come to earth, and the sun send forth his brightest beams, yet shall not the darkness that has gathered around thee be dispelled. Spring shall return, and the earth put on her new robe of green, and in place of the decaying stock shall come up the fresh flower.

> "But when shall spring visit the moldering urn,
> Or when shall day dawn on the night of the grave?"

It is often said that time is passing away. It is not, however, time, but the mutable and material relations of time that are evanescent. Time is a stream ever flowing, never resting, but it leads to the great, shoreless, bottomless ocean of eternity. This never passes away—never—never—never.

The material universe itself shall also pass away. The heavens shall be rolled together as a scroll and disappear. The earth and all the works therein shall vanish. But there shall be in place thereof a new heaven and a new earth, of spiritual and eternal fabric, and in which shall be gathered all of the good and true to dwell forever.

SPRING.

SPRING, with its ethereal mildness, its budding beauty, and its gentle music of bee and of bird, is come again. The soft south wind fans the fevered cheek, and gently rustles among the branches of the old beech-tree. The leaves are putting out, like beauteous childhood bursting into youth. The grass is green again. The wild flowers bedeck the hill-side and sprinkle the sod of the valley. The bees are busily humming about the flowers and among the green leaves. The birds are chirping and hopping from sprig to sprig of the forest-trees. On the fence sits the robin, singing her plaintive monotone. On the bush the little sparrow chirps with a sweet though sad note. Perched on the topmost branch of the maple sits the mocking-bird, sweetest of nature's songsters, not inferior even to Philomel, pouring from her mellow throat sounds of entrancing melody. From the grove comes the moan of the turtle-dove, soft and sad.

Delightful is the return of spring. Happy the eyes that look on her in her beauteous drapery! Happy the ears that hear her joyous sounds! Beautiful is earth, reviving is the air, pleasant is the light.

Amid the gladness of nature my heart reverts to those to whom spring returns no more—to those who have been among us, once of us, but who now are sleeping in the grave, unawakened by the exciting sounds of a spring morning; unaroused by the morning bell that calls to prayer; unconscious of the soothing influence of the balmy breeze returning from the warm south-west; unmindful of the return of bird, and of flower, and of morn. In deep, unbroken, undisturbed repose they lie, nor answer they, though we bow our face to their lowly bed, and call them long and loud. They wake not, though the sun rise and set in brilliancy over them. They slumber on, though the rains fall, the lightnings flash, and the thunders roll. The springing plant and blooming flower arouse no emotions in them. The leaves of autumn fall, and wither on their bosom, but bring to them no emotions of sadness. They heed not the coming of summer, with her gorgeous drapery; nor of autumn, with her yellow harvests, her falling leaf, and her thoughtful melancholy; nor of winter, though its blasts blow bleak and furious over them; nor of spring, though it bring joy and gladness to childhood, and to youth, and to manhood. To them all seasons and all earth's changes are the same. Spring after spring will return, summer after summer will come and be gone, autumn after autumn will clothe the fields in mourning, winter after winter will spread her white winding sheet over all the beauty and the bloom of earth, year after year will be numbered, generation after generation will sweep along, age after age will pass away, cycle after cycle will revolve, and yet they, the loved, the lost from earth, will sleep on. Their forms change. Their images fade from every thing but the heart of love. But enshrined, sacred in the heart of affection, is the memory of the beauteous and loved ones. Nor will we forget them; but we will love them still, till we ourselves follow them

"To the land which no mortal may know."

THE ABSENT ONE.

I HAD stood on the summit of the Alleghanies, and looked back, with a "longing, lingering look," on the fair land I was leaving forever—the land of green hills and sequestered vales, of running brooks and placid lakes, and cultivated fields. From the summit I had looked down on the interminable plains of the west, spread out before me in misty beauty, presenting a scene new and mysterious. For many a long day had I been borne down the Ohio's smooth surface. With slow and tedious movement had I been urged up the meandering Wabash, till, one fine morning, the lovely prairie, decked in the beauty of spring-time, suddenly opened to my view. But my course was onward still, and many a muddy mile lay between me and my future home. Wearily was the way passed, and my place of rest seemed receding as I advanced. The country seemed one interminable forest of trees, such as put to defiance all my ideas of vegetable magnitude. At last, however, I espied, as I was gazing through an opening between the trees, the magnificent structure of the University, as it stood out against the blue sky, with the spires of its cupola gleaming in the midday sun. At that moment the bell struck a merry peal, and its deep tones fell in musical cadences on my very soul.

The village was at last in safety reached, and with some difficulty a place was found, where I and my loved ones might rest. But the village was not like my native one on the Atlantic hill. The house was not my neat little cottage, embowered with shrubbery. There was no garden, nor flowery ground, where my children might play, as they were wont to do in the home we had left.

Sadly passed the day of my arrival. Weary and sick at heart, I retired, but not to rest, for my sleep was fitful and dreamy. All night long I was wandering among the evergreen bowers of my native home, and calling my children to play with me on the green grass plot and flowery parterre. At early morn I arose, and rambled forth for a survey of the whole village, to see if I could find one beautiful spot, one familiar shrub, one favorite flower, one place that had any thing to remind me of home. In the course of my rambles I came suddenly and unexpectedly on a beautiful garden. It was in a retired spot, away from the haunts of business and the crowded thoroughfare. It was laid out in good taste, and abounded with flowering shrubs and plants. I stood astonished and delighted, gazing at the beauties of the spot, till I fell into one of those absent-minded reveries, which frequently come on me, and which cause those who do not know me well, to deem me an odd, unsocial, icy-hearted fellow. From this dreamy reverie I was aroused by the light step of a lady, who was approaching the place where I stood, along one of the garden walks. On meeting me she kindly addressed me, stranger as I was, with a gracious smile, and gave me a cheerful welcome to her garden and her father's house. To me she seemed some fairy angel, the guardian genius of a little paradise which she had formed for herself in this sequestered place. That garden seemed an oasis in the desert; a sunny spot in the midst of surrounding gloom; and that lady seemed some bright and beautiful being of another clime.

Years have passed away, and the garden is there yet. But the fairy one, whose delicate taste arranged the grounds, and whose hand trained the flowers, is there no longer. The garden walks know her light step no more. The flowers, forsaken and neglected, mourn for the lovely one, whose fair hand planted them. Alas, alas! she heeds them not. Their odors are breathed not for her. Their colors shine; but she sees them not. She sleeps. She sleeps not here among her friends, nor in the grave-yard near, where some congenial hand might plant a rose over her grave, but away among strangers, toward the mountains of the setting sun.

Farewell, gentle spirit, farewell. Thou art gone from earth, gone forever. Thy home is not among ephemeral flowers, but in the paradise of God. Hast thou, sainted spirit, yet met, in the evergreen bowers of that fair land, my little, beauteous one, who used to run, clapping her hands in joy, about the garden-walks of my cottage home?

"O, tell her, companion of the sainted ones,
  How my footsteps are haunting that lowly bed,
Where we laid her to rest on the flowery ground,
  Our lost and our lovely, the early dead.

And say, at the flush of the season's prime,
  Or when hearths are light with the evening blaze,
How we pine for the heart of our summer time,
  And the smile that could gladden our wintery days.

O, tell her we weep through the lonely years,
  For the dearest and sweetest that love ever won,
And though hope, like a rainbow, gleams over our tears,
  Yet we weep, O we weep, for still we love on."

THE CHANGES OF EARTH.

MANY and mournful are the changes which time works among familiar things. Returning, after years of absence, to the home of your childhood, the very face of nature seems changed. The field, which seemed a domain worthy a king, has contracted to a few paltry acres. The brook, which to childhood's eye seemed a great stream, has almost dried up. The house, which seemed to you a palace, has dwindled to a small cottage. And that house, too, is occupied by strangers, and no familiar face meets you at the door; or, what is worse, it is not occupied at all, but is left deserted, desolate, and decaying. You wander through the vacant rooms, and hear no sound, except that of the cricket beneath the hearthstone, and see no living thing, except the little mouse scudding off at your coming. A deserted house, especially if that house has ever been your happy home, is the most desolate of all desolate places, and the most gloomy of all gloomy objects. I once had a pleasant little cottage, which had for years been my home, and the home of my little children. I had rendered the spot beautiful by ornamental and useful culture, and I really loved it for its own sake and for its associations. Often, in my busy life, after a long and dreary ride, I had reached, after dark, the top of the hill, and looked down on the lights streaming forth from the window. The lights of home—the lights of home falling on the eye of the benighted, wayworn, and weary traveler—nothing but the lights of heaven, that stream forth from the throne of God, to cheer up the pathway of the Christian, as he passes through the valley of the shadow of death, can equal the lights of home. Since my removal from that cottage, I have visited it once again. I arrived, as usual, at evening on the brow of the hill, and looked down, but no lights met my longing eye. I drove up to the house; but all was yet dark and silent. I knew that my wife, who used to meet me with her gentle smile, and my children, with their merry laugh, at that cottage door, were quietly reposing in sleep in their new home in the west, more than a thousand miles away; yet I seemed to expect to meet them there, as formerly. I knocked at the door, but received no answer. I walked around the house. All was silent, gloomy, desolate.

There are seasons—seasons of sorrow and sadness—when the heart instinctively turns to the scene of its former associations, however far removed by time or distance, and however desolate and forsaken the place may be. There are moments when the sensations of the past are revived with such distinctness and freshness as to appear real. Familiar sounds, long since forgotten, are echoed back, and familiar sights, long since faded from the eye, reappear to the imagination. It is said by a late traveler in the east, that after journeying many a day in the Arabian desert, as he was riding along beneath the burning sky, under the scorching sun, and over the hot sands, weary, hungry, thirsty, and sick, thinking of his home and his mother far away, he suddenly heard the merry peal of the church-bells of his native village. He stopped and listened. Those merry peals still rang on, as they used to do in his childhood, of a Sabbath morning, ending in the sweet and solemn toll that calls the wanderer to the house of God.

After all, it may be well that the heart, though it searches incessantly for it, should find nothing on earth on which it may surely, and with unfailing confidence, rest. God designs not earth for our permanent resting-place. He has stamped mutability on all tangible things, that we might raise our souls to things above. While change comes over all our relations, God kindly permits us to look, even with mortal eye, on some objects which seem to change not. The sun, the glorious sun, shines on the eye of age as on that of youth. The moon, the silvery moon, looks forth in the heavens, fair as she did to the eye of man in Paradise. The stars, the brilliant constellations in the heavens, unchanged and unchanging, maintain, from age to age, the same place in the sky. The heavens exhibit the same appearance to us as they did to Newton, and to Galileo, and to old Abraham, when, on the Chaldean plain, God told him to number them, if he could. There are, also, immaterial ideas, or conceptions of the soul, which are immutable—ideas of the good, the beautiful, and the true, which know no change nor decay.

By these God teaches us that there is, beyond the stars, a world which knows no change—that there are things which are eternal. Happy, then, is he who sets his affections on things above—on things heavenly and divine—on goodness, and on truth, and on God.

THOUGHTS ON YOUTH AND AGE.

On all things outward is written, by the pen of Time, in characters *deep*, *legible*, and *effaceless*, change, mutation, perishability. Not even the aggregate forms of nature escape the common doom. The compact rock, itself a noted example of solidity and permanence—the conceded emblem of the eternal One—yields up its form, disintegrates, and crumbles under the influence of heat, moisture, and frost. The mineral, beautiful in appearance, perfect in shape, and curious in structure, becomes impalpable dust under the action of atmospheric or chemical influences. The iron, dug from the deep recesses of earth, gathers rust on its surface, and yields up its distinctive form to the law of change. The earth herself, the solid earth on which we tread, through the long cycles of ages past, has been passing through changes and revolutions; nor is the time of permanence yet arrived. Her mountains are elevated by volcanoes, and worn down by winds and storms; her rivers are, by changes of current and of course, constantly modifying her hills, her plains, and her valleys; her oceans are making land in one and destroying it in another quarter of the globe. Nor are the solar or the stellar systems of the universe less subject to the inevitable law of mutation. The bosom of the moon is heaved, and her face torn by volcanoes. The sun is marked by spots betokening, from their varying appearance, incessant action and change. The stars, though removed too far for accurate observation, exhibit unquestionable indications of revolutions and changes.

If the works of nature thus obey the great law of change, still more readily do the material works of man yield to the same law—works, too, which were designed for permanence, and built for eternity. Thebes, the hundred-gated; Babylon, the city of palaces; Tadmor, that flourished amidst palm-trees; Baalbec, of mysterious origin and unknown founder, have all disappeared from the face of earth, leaving only broken ruins to mark the place where once they stood. Even Jerusalem, the city of the chosen ones; and Rome, called by her builders the Eternal, no longer rear, the one its magnificent temple, and the other its Capitol, as in days of yore.

The law of change extends to the immaterial organizations of human ingenuity. Political organizations have been ever yielding, and are yet yielding to the inevitable decree of change. The old Assyrian empire, the earliest on the records of authentic history, and for many centuries limitless in extent, and omnipotent in authority, long since wholly disappeared, leaving not a vestige of itself among men. The empire of the great Cyrus, though long the most remarkable in the annals of time, exists now only in the dim pencilings and the shadowy recollections of semi-fabulous history. The Grecian republics, the Grecian kingdoms, and the Grecian empire, all equally and effectually have disappeared forever from earth. The Roman organizations, beginning with a monarchy, passing through the mutations of a republic, and terminating in an empire of boundless extent, irresistible power, and exhaustless resources, long ago crumbled like a disintegrating rock exposed to the furnace, and its fragments were blown away like comminuted dust.

Among the kingdoms, empires, and republics of modern ages, changes in precedence, relations, constitutional organization, and distinctive characteristics have ever been and are yet varying, with all the facility of the ever-changing colors of the kaleidoscope. Organizations founded in philosophy exhibit no lasting form. We read of the schools of the Peripatetics and of the Stoics, of the philosophical systems of Plato and of Aristotle, of Pythagoras and of Epicurus; but where shall we find even a vestige of the magnificent temple of philosophy which they built and adorned, and which they hoped would stand forever?

Nor have religious organizations formed favored exceptions to the general law of change. The mythology of antiquity was beautiful, extremely beautiful. The religion of Greece was conceived by poets, and adorned with all the beautiful drapery within the power of exuberant fancy and exquisite taste. For ages it sat enthroned in the respect and affections of the people. Yet was its foundation unsubstantial as the dreams of fairy-land. Nor has the form of religion yet ceased, through the successive ages of modern history, to change its phases. It would seem that the religious sentiment is, in man, inherent in nature, incessant in action, and perpetual in duration. But the form in which it embodies itself is ever-changing. The dwellers along the valley of the Nile embodied and adored the great powers of nature. The accomplished and educated Greeks personified and worshiped the intellectual and moral attributes of humanity. The Jew satisfied the religious sentiment by ceremonies, sacrifices, oblations, and observances. The early Christians were taught a more spiritual worship. To preserve, during successive ages, in any particular sect the same uniform usages is matter of exceeding difficulty. The spirit may remain the same, but the form will change. As well might you hope to preserve the same substance of body under all the changes of growth and decay.

Living forms are not less liable than are aggregate or

immaterial to mutation. Change is not the exception, but the law of animal and of vegetable nature. The process of growth and of decay is natural and certain. Each act of the living being is supposed to use up and destroy some definite portion of its substance. But living beings, unlike aggregate forms, unlike immaterial organizations, have in their own nature the power and the means of renewal. The consumption and the renewal of living matter seem thus continually going on to such an extent as to effect, as is supposed, in the human body, an entire change in seven years. In youth the waste is less than the supply of matter, and hence the body increases in size and weight. In maturity the waste and renewal are equal, and the body maintains its uniform proportion. In age the waste exceeds the renewal, and the body languishes, decays, and dies.

All outward human appendances seem to have a specific purpose, and when they have accomplished it they proceed rapidly to decay and dissolution. All the political organizations, all the theories and dogmas of philosophy, and all the varying forms of religion of antiquity had their end, which they accomplished, and then they perished. The spirit which animated these incorporeal forms passed, when the set time was come, into other, higher, and nobler forms. The spirit of religion, which had animated the typical and ceremonial forms of the Jewish worship, did, on the bringing in of the better covenant, forsake its old and dilapidated habitation, as would the winged butterfly its effete and defunct chrysalis, and assume the living and inexpressibly-improved form of Christianity.

Each individual particle of the human body has, probably, in like manner, its end. That purpose accomplished, the effete particle is thrown from the system, and its place supplied by another vital particle. Each age of man has its purpose. Infancy has its purpose, childhood its purpose, manhood its purpose. To some specific end all the powers of nature are for the appointed time directed, and then the system changes, and can never again become what before it had been. There is, therefore, no return of infancy, no return of childhood, no return of manhood. Decrepitude, decay, and dissolution are inevitable. We must in body grow old. The muscles will grow hard and stiff. The bones will become brittle. The hair will grow gray. The wrinkles will come on the forehead. Furrows will mark the cheek. The outward man will perish. There is no preventive—no elixir—no charm—not even a respite or suspension.

Yet, it would seem, we have two natures—one outward, the other inward. Man has a physical and a spiritual life. His physical life is limited in duration. As a physical being he grows old and dies. This is the outward man, which perishes. His spiritual life is endless in duration. This is the inward man, which never grows old, never dies.

The inward man has two modes of development, or two departments of action—intellect and affection. To the development of intellect and affection there is no limit. In their nature they are imperishable, and to the efficiency of their action there is no end. But, in order that we may secure all the advantages which our spiritual nature is capable of using; in order that we may be renewed and may increase, day by day, in intelligence and in moral perfection; in order that we may never grow old in mind or in heart, we should observe the laws and conditions of development and of perpetuity, which observation and experience have determined. It seems to be a well-ascertained law, that those only grow not old in mind who diligently avail themselves of both the great sources or means of intellectual development—observation and reflection.

The external senses, particularly seeing and hearing, are given us to help us observe. Observation is an exhaustless source, and an effective means of mental development. Observing, however, implies something more than mere seeing. The ox sees, but he never observes. He sees the flower he crops, but he observes not its beauties. The hog sees the pebble he roots from the ground, but he observes not its structure nor its form. The horse sees perhaps better than his rider the road along which he journeys, but he observes not the beauty of the landscape. Some men observe scarcely better than the ox, the hog, or the horse. To them the fairest flower is but a weed incumbering the cornfield. The noble tree of the grand old forest is only material for firewood or for lumber. The beautiful river, meandering through the vale, suggests only thoughts of profit in driving a rattling saw-mill. The mountain, rearing its head sublime among the clouds, suggests no thoughts of interest, because it can not be plowed. Before such men Nature spreads her beauty with as little profit as might accrue from casting pearls before swine.

Habits of observation the beast might never acquire. It is not in the nature of the hog to distinguish the pearl from the pebble; nor can the ox learn the difference between the rose and the thistle; nor can the horse ever appreciate a romantic landscape. But man may acquire habits of observation, and derive thereby instruction from the most common occurrences of nature. Newton, by observing an apple fall from a tree, discovered the law of gravitation. A boy, by observing the motion of the cover of his mother's tea-kettle, discovered the power of steam. The Grecian philosopher, by observing the quantity of water displaced by his body in the bath, discovered the law of specific gravity. Galvani, by observing the action of metallic substances on the muscles of a frog, first noticed by his wife, discovered the wonderful science of galvanism; and Morse, by observing the action of galvanic wires, discovered the science of telegraphing. By observing in childhood and in youth, we lay up nutriment for intellectual support in age. Youth collects and age uses the material of thought. Beautiful scenes, lovely prospects, fairy landscapes, and delightful images are constantly flitting before the eye of youth. If we only look at these scenes of interest and loveliness, no distinct image is formed, and no lasting impression made. But if we *observe*, the image becomes distinct, the picture formed, the impression fixed, by a process more mysterious and wonderful than the daguerreian, on the tablet of the soul. In manhood those pictures may be obscured by the flitting mists of care and the floating dust of business. But in age they are restored in pristine beauty and freshness. Their colors seem even more vivid, and their outline better defined, than when their impression first fell on the soul.

The renewal in age of pictures of observation in youth is clearly illustrated in a few interesting cases, in which men of careful observation and exquisite taste have been in age deprived of sight, the most efficient of the senses. Homer is said to have become blind in age. "The old blind bard of Scio" is a well-known description of his person. Yet, in youth, he had been a careful observer of nature and of men. In age, when he could no longer look on nature, or observe the ways of men, the pictures of youth returned with brightness more than real, and he lived amid beautiful scenes and lovely landscapes, such as seldom ever blessed the material eye of man.

Milton in age became blind. Lover of beauty, as he

was, he could but lament the deprivation. "Thus," said he,

> "With the year
> Seasons return, but not to me returns
> Day, or the sweet approach of even or of morn,
> Or sight of vernal bloom, or summer's rose,
> Or flocks, or herds, or human face divine;
> But clouds instead, and ever-during dark
> Surrounds me; from the cheerful ways of men
> Cut off, and for the book of knowledge fair
> Presented with a universal blank
> Of nature's works, to me expunged and razed,
> And wisdom at one entrance quite shut out."

Yet with what vivid distinctness returned to him the lovely visions of early days! His heart was with its early dreams, and sweetly he sang of Paradise and of heaven, touching his pictures of heavenly scenery with a living pencil and with divine colors.

Reflection is an agent of intellectual development even more efficient than observation. We see, we observe, and then we reflect. Observation transfers to the mind, and fixes indelibly there, the individual images of persons, and of events, and of scenes. By reflection we combine these individual and elementary scenes and images, forming a great gallery of pictures. Few are the elementary ideas obtained by observation. Innumerable are the pictures which reflection forms by combining elementary images. So that, in reality, reflection, though not the primary, is yet the principal agency of human knowledge. By the external senses ideas are admitted through the door into the workshop of the soul. By observation those ideas are assorted, classified, and arranged in appropriate places. By reflection they are combined, modified, and wrought into new forms. Often so many elementary ideas are used, and so curiously are they combined by reflection, that the product bears as little resemblance to the raw material, as does the magnificent steamship to the rough wood and native iron ore of which it is composed.

The habit of reflection acquired in youth becomes, in age, a sure preservative against mental imbecility and decaying dotage. Those who use only the external senses, who merely see, resemble one who only looks out of the window on beautiful objects flitting before him. Those who observe resemble one who should seize those objects, transfer them to his room, and deposit them in appropriate places for future use. Those who reflect resemble one who should manufacture for himself, out of the objects or materials presented, an exhaustless supply of every thing needful for age.

The *heart* of man need never grow old. It may increase in depth, and grasp, and power of affection till it ceases to beat. But in order to this, in order not to grow old in heart, the affections must be exercised. And they must be directed toward objects of worth and of permanence. If you love the world, your heart will grow old. If you love the riches of earth, you will become a miser. If you love the honors of the world, you will become a disappointed misanthrope. If you love the pleasures of the world, you will become nauseated and sick, and will loathe the very objects that excited your passions. But if you love virtue and goodness—virtue and goodness as ideal abstractions, or as embodied in the virtuous and the good of your companions and friends—your heart will be as young at sixty as at sixteen. We sometimes are cautioned against loving our friends too well. But if our affections be directed to the good, the virtuous, the amiable, and the true, we can not love too well. It is true the form, in which the qualities that secure our affection are embodied, may disappear from our sight. The material organization of the bright and beauteous ones, the loved ones of the heart, may perish. But the soul, in which the qualities that gained our heart are embodied, yet lives, as much a legitimate object of love as when it animated the mortal body. They are not dead, those loved ones; no. They have only changed their state. They have only left a mortal tabernacle, dilapidated, inconvenient, and decaying, and gone to live, to live forever in a heavenly habitation, in the midst of society perfect and congenial. We love them still; and they love us still; and they may yet welcome us to the house of our Father in the heavens, where there are mansions for us as well as for them.

Though, therefore, we must grow old in body, yet if we grow old in mind it is our own fault. He who merely sees and hears, who observes not, reflects not, and loves only transient things, may grow old. He is like the thoughtless insect, that flutters and sports the summer away, and makes no provision for winter. When the summer is gone, and winter, with her chilling blasts and driving snows, is on him, he must either die outright, or retire to his cell, and remain torpid till spring returns again. But he who observes, who reflects, and who loves the substantial, the permanent, the good, and the true, may feast in age, like the industrious and prudent bee in winter, on sweet and substantial substance gathered during youth and manhood.

Disease and decay of the material organs do, indeed, sometimes obscure the manifestations, and obstruct the action of mind, but never affect the nature of the mind or the heart. Decay is not an incident of intellect or of affection. We may ascribe limits to the duration of human existence so far as the body, but not so far as the mind is concerned. Annihilation of itself, termination of the existence of its being, is an idea of which mind can form no conception. Often in the dying hour, when friends tell the sufferer, and facts convince him, that he is dying, there seems an utter absence in the mind of all consciousness of change in itself. The soul feels that it is not dying, but only leaving its tenement for another and a nobler habitation. And while friends, gathering about the bed, are uttering cries and shedding tears, the dying one himself is calm and tearless, the spirit resisting the laws which destroy the body, and the soul triumphing over death, and defying the grave. Talk not, then, of growing old in mind or in heart. Talk not of failing faculties of intellect—of decay of mind. Talk not of withered affections, and of exhausted sympathies. But observe and reflect, love the true and the good, and you need never be conscious of change or alteration, except for the better, in mind or in heart.

SUMMER.

SUMMER—sweet, joyous summer, how many delightful associations are linked to the word—associations of childhood, and of home! I have read a story, in some old school book, of little Frank, who, on the return of each of the seasons, would wish that particular season to last always, and the little fellow received a scolding from his father, for indulging in what the old gentleman pleased to call inconsiderate and presumptuous wishes. But I never could find it in my heart to blame the child. In autumn he was delighted with beautiful skies and mellow fruits: in winter, with his hand-sled and skates, he amused himself on the ice and snow: in spring, the green grass, fair flowers, and beautiful birds made him leap for gladness; and in summer, the waving fields of grass and grain presented new scenes of pleasure before him. Nor was it unnatural, that he, child as he was, should think each season more pleasant than the former, just as every mother thinks her youngest child the most interesting of the family.

Summer has beauties not inferior to those of spring; though following so closely upon spring, it does not present so strong a contrast to the preceding season, and, therefore, it makes less impression on us. The fields of summer exhibit exquisite beauty. To stand at this season on some gentle eminence of our prairies, and look over many thousands of acres of green corn and golden wheat waving in the breeze, ready for the harvest, is worth a voyage across the Atlantic.

Come with me, gentle reader, and look upon our beautiful Wabash plains. The fair-haired Ceres, while wandering over earth in search of her lost daughter, must have visited these lovely plains, and been charmed with the beauty of the region, for see how she has scattered over the ground her priceless gifts! And well might she, goddess though she was, be delighted with the place, for who ever saw such a country? Look over these plains. What exhaustless fertility! See what beautiful clusters of trees, seeming like green islands in the ocean! Neither Calypso's sea-girt isle, nor the fairy land of song, nor Eden, as depicted by Milton, could equal, in exquisite loveliness, the scene now before us. See what endless fields of wheat waving in the gentle south-west breeze! Here plenty reigns and revels. Come hither, thou who art fond of the beautiful, and say, didst thou ever look on such a scene? The interchange of prairie, and woodland, and running stream, and the variety of color, as the fields wave in the sunshine, form a picture of beauty which no painter may imitate. Come hither, ye poor, ye hungry, and look on the exhaustless provisions of nature for the supply of the wants of man. Let Europe send forth her starving millions. These prairies, if there were hands but sufficient to cultivate them to the extent of which they are capable, might produce sufficient to supply the world.

But the sunshine grows hot, and we must leave the open prairie, and take shelter in this cluster of trees. The forests are beautiful in summer. The prairie trees seem young, as if they were but children, though the oldest inhabitant here may not remember when they were not; but the trees of the woodland seem old and venerable. These oaks, and sycamores, and elms, tell of the past. There is an old elm that throws its shadow, at sunset, upon my study window. It stands alone—all its companions have fallen by the woodman's ax. Its noble trunk stands erect, and far above the tops of the trees in the forest beyond, it throws out its graceful branches against the clear sky. Its smaller limbs hang drooping, as if in sorrow for the loneliness of its situation. That fine old tree belongs to other days, and could it speak, it might a tale unfold. It stood there when the Indian roamed these woods. It stood there when the white man first built his cabin, on the spot where, since, has risen a fine town, and it stands there still, though surrounded by farm-houses and cottages. I love that old tree, and I have requested my neighbor, on whose land it stands, to spare it from the ax, and I hope I may rescue it from that Vandalism which is ruining all these fine old monuments of the past, which might, if spared, add so much to the beauty of the country.

Near my childhood's home was a plain, that seemed to me illimitable, covered with a most splendid forest of pine, fir, and tamarack. Its lively green, appearing even in winter, and more striking from contrast with the snow, was one of the first things that awoke in my heart the love of the beautiful. There came forth, from that forest, sounds, which none, who has once heard, can ever forget. A pine forest forms the harp of the winds, and when touched by the breeze it sends forth inimitable music. That forest was a favorite resort in my early days. There I rambled with buoyant spirit when a child, and there I sat under some old pine, in my maturer and studious days, with book or pen in hand. I fear, however, that should I again visit that old forest, I might find it sadly changed; for what men call public improvement has been there, and the snorting steam-horse, rushing with his ponderous car over its iron track, has scared away all the sylvan associations of the place.

What scenes of intense sublimity are sometimes witnessed, in our western country, during a summer shower!

The thunder rumbles not among the distant hills, as in New England, echoing from side to side of the mountains, and reaching the ear only after the sound is greatly diminished by repeated reflections, but it bursts upon us at once with a startling intensity, or a deafening crash. The lightnings sometimes flash out quietly from every point of the horizon to the zenith, and then, again, they dart from cloud to cloud, or to the earth, in a zigzag chain of exceeding brilliancy. The innumerable pools of water, fallen from the clouds, and covering the face of the earth, lighted up by the electric flashes, shine like myriads of silver mirrors. For a scene of glorious sublimity, give me a summer shower on some western plain. And then how quiet the sky, and how beautiful the earth, when the shower is over!

In summer we have fewer birds than in spring. The mocking-bird, the sweetest of all singers, is seldom heard in this neighborhood after June. He comes in early spring, and sits and sings all day on the topmost branch of the willow that grows near my cottage, and I have sometimes heard him all night long. Once he began to build his nest in the honeysuckle that climbs up the lattice at my door, but some passer-by scared him away. The sweet singer has now gone, I know not where, but he has left the memory of his tones in my heart. The sparrow, the whippowil, and the robin, are with us yet. The cuckoo is sometimes heard, but seldom seen, in the neighboring thicket.

I love the birds, nor will I suffer them to be injured on my premises. I envy not the heart of that man, who can wantonly, for sport and pleasure, destroy these sweet little beings that sing about our homes; for the birds are only found near the homes of man. They frequent not the forest, but live about the bushes, clusters of trees, and orchards, in the settled parts of the country. Having occasion once to visit the head waters of the Kennebec and Penobscot, some hundred miles from human habitation, in the depths of the forest, among romantic hills and quiet lakes, I was surprised at the absence of birds, and the unnatural stillness that prevailed. In conversing with the boatmen and lumbermen, who spend much of their time in those regions, I learned that when once they leave the habitations of men, they leave, also, the birds behind.

The birds are domestic beings. They love man, and should be loved by him, for they are his benefactors. A strange mistake prevails among farmers with regard to the birds. Some species occasionally do the farmer some injury by picking off a little fruit, or by picking up a little grain, and he proclaims war of extermination against the whole race. But the benefit the birds do the farmer in destroying worms, bugs, and insects, is a hundred-fold more than the injury they occasionally commit on the grains and fruits. Sometimes he kills them in the very act of doing him a favor. A speckled woodpecker is seen working away on the body of an apple-tree: the farmer, supposing the bird to be injuring the tree, kills him. Yet the fact is, the tree is infested by worms, under its bark. These would soon destroy it, were it not that the woodpecker searches them out and consumes them. The blackbird sometimes pulls up the corn; but where he pulls up one spear of corn, he kills ten worms, that might eat up a hundred spears of corn. Were the birds all killed off, the destructive insects would become so numerous as to eat up, like the locusts of Egypt, every green thing. Then spare the birds. Spare them for their own sake. Spare them for your own sake. Spare them for humanity's sake.

TO AN ABSENT CHILD.

Come home, my lovely child, come home. Too long hast thou been absent. I miss thee, my dear one—miss thee too much from thy home. I miss thee at morning; when rising from my bed I hear not thy cheerful voice. I miss thee at the table; when looking around on my loved ones I see thy seat vacant. I listen in vain for thy sweet voice, when we read in family circle, at the hour of morning devotion, the lessons of holy inspiration. I miss thee as I pass the window where thou thoughtful wert seated with thy bird and thy book. I miss thee at Rosa-bower, where the violets are blooming over thy sister's grave. I miss thee at my study in the sequestered vale, where thou didst often come, with thy sweet smile and joyous voice to cheer my sad heart. I miss thee at twilight from the garden walks around our humble cottage. I miss thee at night when I look on my sleeping loved ones, but see thee not.

I think of thee when absent—think of thee too much. I think of the hour when first I heard thy young voice, and looked on thy infant features, and clasped thee to my glad heart.

I think of the pleasant summer evenings when thou, a tiny little child, wouldst run to meet me returning home, and trip along, light as the fawn, with arms outstretched for an embrace, and lips ready for a kiss. I think of the blessed hour, on that vernal Sabbath evening, when I led thee to the altar of prayer, and saw thee give thy hand to the Church and thy heart to God. I think of the sad hour when I saw thee approach the bier, as the coffin lid was falling, forever to shut out the light of earth from the fair face of thy only sister, and imprint the last farewell kiss on her pale brow.

And now, my child, come home. Thy mother's eyes are sleepless for thy return. Thy little brother asks, "Why don't Ellen come?" And I, alas! hour after hour I wander sadly about the garden where together we picked the ripened fruit, and the forest where we gathered wildwood flowers, and I sit under the old tree at the bower, pensive and lonely. Come back, then, my child, and smile on me once more. Come back and sing me the song I love to hear. Come back, and let me hear again the halls of home resound with thy merry voice.

THE VALLEY IN THE MOUNTAIN-LAND.

From the hill, hanging over the green valley, where cozily nestled the old homestead, I often looked on the long range of blue mountains that rose, some hundred miles or more distant, in the north-west, and wondered what fair land might repose in summer sunlight beyond that misty boundary of the horizon. In summer and in winter, in spring and in autumn, at morning, at noon, and at night, a soft and mellow atmosphere seemed resting over that distant land. Did there summer perpetual bloom? Were there the skies always cloudless, and the breezes always gentle, and the sunshine always pleasant? Was there the happy land, shadowy glimpses of whose unearthly scenery so often, in sleeping dreams and waking reveries, flitted over my soul? Might I there find the ideal of my imaginings, the beautiful and the good, for which my youthful heart had long pined? Might I there meet some angelic being, for whose congenial sympathy my soul had so long yearned? Might I there find some fair and gentle one, who could read the invisible record of experience and of anxiety in a heart, whose deep emotions none had sounded, and with whose agitations of hope and of despondency no other heart had ever vibrated in harmony?

One fine morning of my seventeenth autumn, I looked again toward that mountain-land, and resolved to make my way to its mysterious precincts. With a small package in my hand, and a very few dimes in my pocket, I started on foot and alone for the north-west. After a few hours of devious rambling over the fields, through the woods, and in the pastures, I arrived on the banks of the Androscoggin, at the Falls of Lewiston, where the river, rushing, and roaring, and foaming, and boiling, pours over the rocky precipice. I sat down on a projecting rock, besprinkled with the spray of the waters, whose thundering roar I had often heard booming over the hills far away. Wild was the scene. The river came gently and quietly along, with not a ripple on its surface, till it reached the very brink of the precipice, when suddenly, as if surprised and startled, it leaped over the rocks, and went dashing on its way. Not a house nor a field appeared in sight. Nature alone reigned with unquestioned sway over the spot. There was nothing to break the spell of romantic interest thrown around the scene. Grand old forest-trees threw their dense shade over the landscape. On the rocky hight stood the oak with its full, spreading top; and on the plain rose, straight and limbless, the pine, its green tassels mournfully sighing in the autumn wind.

Leaving the falls and the river, I journeyed along over a pine forest plain. The trees stood at irregular distances, their smooth and straight trunks appearing like columns supporting a canopy of dark and dense foliage, through which came the autumn sunlight in scant and softened rays. Through their waving tassels sadly moaned the autumn wind. Beautiful, very beautiful, seemed that old evergreen forest. Beautiful was the soft carpet of fallen leaves on the ground. Beautiful stood the pines with their towering trunks. Beautiful spread the green canopy overhead. Pleasant, though mournful, was the sound of the sighing wind in the lofty branches.

Beyond the plain rose a high hill, covered from its base to its summit with a grove of noble oaks. Up the hill wound the road in many a serpentine curve. From the summit appeared a prospect beautiful, and bounded but by the horizon. On the south lay the pine forest, stretching away in one unbroken range, and the river flowing on between its evergreen banks, till in the far distance both were lost—the river mingling its waters with the ocean, and the forest plain forming the line of coast. On the east lay an undulating region of woodlands, fields, and pastures, with farm-houses, and villages, and steeples of rural churches peering up amid the variegated foliage of autumn. On the west lay sleeping in the fair sunshine, dreaming of perpetual summer, a lake of pure, transparent water—one of those little, lovely lakes forming a general and marked feature of the mountain landscapes of New England. Over the bosom of the peaceful waters was floating a soft and wavy light. From the mirrory surface was reflected the graceful forms of the pines that skirted the shores. Not a wave beat the margin, nor a ripple moved on the surface of the tranquil waters. On the north still loomed up the mysterious mountain-land. My position of observation, nearer than I had ever before attained, presented the mountains in bolder outline. Their summits seemed greatly elevated. Their sides were marked by bold ridges and deep furrows. They seemed a barrier impassable: nor could I imagine how I should reach the fairy-land, which I knew must lie beyond. Resuming my journey, on I went, downhill, and uphill, and over plain, and along valley, and across winding stream. The mountain-land lay still before me. One range of hills being past, another higher still arose, seeming to lie right along my path. But onward pressing my way, I wound around the hills, along the valleys, and over the gentle slopes of the uplands, leaving the rugged hills standing like fortifications impregnable, but too distant to arrest or annoy the invader. And thus I saw to-day far behind me the grand and gloomy mountains, which yesterday threatened an obstacle insurmountable in my path. I often wondered how I had so easily evaded the difficulty, which I might in vain hope to surmount. Often thus, in the journey of human life, our way seems impassably barred, our progress inevitably arrested, and ourselves lost in a threadless labyrinth. We become disheartened and desponding. But go on. There is a way, "which the vulture's eye hath not seen, nor the lion's whelp trod." There "is a path which no fowl knoweth." The unerring finger of Providence will direct your steps. Go forward, then, with a firm faith and a manly heart.

After some days of weary travel, I had meandered around the north-western base of a craggy hill, and reached an elevated table-land of dark forest. Passing around a point of woodland into an open glade, I saw suddenly opening before me one of the loveliest prospects that ever rose on human vision. Before me lay a valley, extending far to the north and to the south. On the east and west it was bounded by gently-sloping hills, covered with orchards, and fields, and farm-houses. Through the midst of the valley flowed a clear, rapid river, meandering through the meadows, sometimes kissing the hills on one side, and then on the other. The valley was a smooth and level lawn, over which were scattered, in single specimens and in clusters, tall old elms and vigorous young maples. The course of the river was marked by the bright gleam of its clear waters, rippling along over a pebbly bed.

I looked over the river on the eastern shore, and there stood, on a terraced plain, one of those fairy villages seen only in New England, and when once seen never forgotten. One long street, lined with magnificent elms, extended for a mile along the terraced plain. On each side of the street, shaded by the elms, and embowered in shrubbery, stood the neat white cottages. In an open square stood a venerable church, with a tall steeple, from which were pealing forth, on the still air of the autumn evening, the clear and mellow sounds of a sweet-toned bell. In rear of the church was a beautiful cemetery, in which slept the departed loved ones of the hamlet, in graves marked by tablets of white marble. Not far from the church, on a spacious plain, amidst trees and ornamented shrubbery, stood the academy, around which had clustered for many years the youth of the valley to receive instruction in the higher branches of science.

Some miles south of my point of view, at the lower end of the valley, where the river abruptly turned to the east, appeared another village, embowered and nearly concealed by grand old elms, standing on each side of the wide street, and intertwining their noble branches far above the neighboring cottages. Farther still south stretched away, in the dim distance of the plain, a forest of pines.

Turning again to the north, and looking far up the valley, I saw a most grand landscape. A circular chain of lofty mountains inclosed the valley on the north, the east, and the west, leaving only an opening south, through which flowed the river. In the noble amphitheater lay nestled the living fountains of the beautiful river. In the circular chain of mountains inclosing the valley were peaks of vast hight. On their utmost summits was falling the sunlight of evening, while all along their sides were gathering shadows, and in the deep ravines was darkness visible.

I stood fixed on the spot, admiring the beautiful, the grand, the glorious scene, till night began to throw her dim shadows over the landscape. I then made my way to a hospitable dwelling, where I spent the night. When the morning came, I arose early to resume my tour of observation along the happy valley. As I passed up along the river-side, or wound around the base of the hills, new views were constantly opening before me, and new scenes appearing on the landscape. Placid lakes of cool, transparent water lay quiet and still in the sequestered forest. Perennial fountains burst out of the hill-side, and sent a living stream along the meadow. Sparkling rivulets poured by a series of cascades down the mountain, till they reached the river valley, through whose green borders they gently meandered between rows of golden willows and weeping elms. Sheltered vales lay imbosomed among the hills, forming, from early spring till late in autumn, a paradise of birds and of flowers. There were neat farm-houses peering out through the green trees and perched on the hill-sides. The hill-tops were covered with forest-trees, their verdant sides were cropped by bleating flocks and lowing herds, and the valleys at their base were waving with the ripened corn. To me my fairy visions seemed realized. I had reached the mysterious valley among the hills, to which I had so often looked with admiring interest. Beautiful, very beautiful, it proved to be, yet not altogether such as my youthful fancy had pictured it. Perpetual spring smiled not, nor summer bloomed always there. The autumn came with its falling leaf, and winter ruled there often with an iron scepter. Around those mountain peaks the storm sometimes terribly beat, and along the valley the winds often piped a merry whistle.

Happily, cheerfully, joyously passed in that fair land the years of my youth, till there came on me the responsibilities of manhood. I then emerged from my sequestered retreat, and rushed out into the busy world. And many, very many years—years numbering nearly a generation of human life—have passed over my head, since the morning of my departure from that fair land of youthful affection, yet my heart nestles there still.

There yet hangs in the inner chamber of my soul a fadeless picture of the whole landscape. The mountains are as blue, the valleys as soft and dreamy, the river as clear, the cascades as lively, the cottages as white, the hills as green, and the ravines as romantic as when they all stood within the circle of my visual horizon.

Strange, mysterious seems the conceptual power of mind, by which we create at pleasure spiritual images of the objects of sense, the perfect counterpart of past perceptions. By what daguerreian process are the forms, lineaments, and even color of beautiful objects drawn and fixed on the soul?

THOUGHTS ON THE CAREER OF MAHOMET.

THAT all events in the progress of human history are under the control of a superintending Providence; that men, though free to will, and free to act, have no power to determine the final result of their agency in human affairs; that the almighty One *can* use, and the omniscient One *does* use, the good, the bad, and the indifferent, as instruments, willing or unwilling, to promote his own glory and the interests of humanity; and that, in the final consummation of all things, the grand result will appear consistent with the power, wisdom, and benevolence of the Deity, however untoward may have been the spirit and perverted the ways of men, are truths taught by revelation, by reason, and by observation.

In looking over the history of the world, we may frequently, after the lapse of a few centuries, trace clearly the course of Providence in educing good from evil. Sometimes, however, the final result of the events evolved from human history may not appear for many thousand years. Yet he who believes in Providence will never suffer himself to despond of good amid the changes and revolutions of time.

In tracing the strange career of Mahomet, and in observing the surprising fact, that, the great cycle of twelve centuries having passed away, his system of religion, false and worthless as it appears to Christians, does yet retain much of life, of power, and of influence, we are led to inquire what could be, and what can yet be, the designs of Providence in permitting so extensive a range, so vast an influence, and so long a period of time to Islamism?

Mahomet was born at Mecca, in Arabia, about the middle of the sixth century. At the time of his birth his father was absent on a journey. While on his way home he fell sick, and died at Medina, without once looking on the face of his only child. Some little property was left; but being, according to Arabian law and usage, all appropriated to the brothers, the widow and orphan were left homeless and penniless. The mother of Mahomet, by her own energies, protected and maintained him for six years, when she died, leaving him to the charities of his grandfather, a very aged man, one of the hereditary guardians of the sacred temple of Mecca. After about two years, the venerable man also died, leaving the poor child, at the age of eight years, utterly alone. From family pride, more than from love to the orphan, one of his uncles consented to give him a place in his tent.

The sorrows and bereavements which he had so early suffered; the knowledge of his father's influence, which was lost to him, and property of which he had been unjustly deprived; the memory of his amiable and beautiful mother, who had died in her youth of a broken heart; and the ever-present reality of his own lonely and dependent condition, induced in him habits of serious meditation and anxious thought. He would wander away alone over the hills, and sit for hours in some hidden cave, brooding over his hapless lot. At times he would feel conscious of inherent energy and personal power yet to rise, in spite of fate, to a station of influence among his people. He resolved not to yield without a struggle to the force of unfortunate circumstances. "Misfortune," said he, "shall not triumph over me, if I can help it." He began to exhibit indications of an excitable mind, of vivid imagination, of brilliant wit, of quick perception, and of sound judgment.

As soon as he became of an available age, he was put by his uncle to business, in mercantile expeditions over the desert. From the age of thirteen to twenty-five, he was constantly engaged in traffic, and in crossing and recrossing the desert with caravans, from Mecca to Damascus. This kind of life afforded no means of acquiring knowledge from books, but great opportunities foı becoming acquainted with men. All these advantages he improved in the best possible manner. He observed and he inquired. By the evening fire, and in the noontide shade, he listened to the stories of his fellow-travelers, rehearsing the wonderful things they had seen and heard in many an adventurous expedition. In the marts which he visited, he met strangers from places various and far distant, and often learned from them new and valuable facts. He frequently met Jews and Christians, and learned from them the story of Moses and of Christ. All these things he treasured up, and pondered in his heart.

At the age of twenty-five, having become expert in the usual mode of mercantile dealing, he was appointed agent of a wealthy widow, who was continuing the business of caravan traffic, in which her husband had been engaged. By his business talents he won the respect, by his honesty the confidence, and by his amiable deportment the love of the lady, and she offered him her heart, her hand, and her fortune. The offer was gratefully accepted; and Mahomet found himself in possession of property sufficient to raise him to distinction in Mecca, and of a wife whose mind and person proved a greater prize than her fortune.

Being no longer obliged to work for a living, he had leisure for retirement and meditation The religious office held by his grandfather may have made him early conversant with sacred rites, and disposed him to divine contemplation. Though brought up, as were all his people of that age, an idolater, yet he had learned from the Jews and Christians that great truth, fundamental of all religious truth, that God is One. Idolatry he knew to be wrong in spirit, and degrading in practice. Yet idolatry was the established religion of his people and of his country—idolatry, with its horrid rites, even human sacrifices—idolatry, with its long train of barbarous usages and cruel superstitions. Infanticide, the most unnatural, the most shocking of all crimes, was only one of the fruits of idolatrous, Arabic superstition in the sixth century. Mahomet's own grandfather had escaped sacrifice in infancy only by accident. The terrible destiny of infant sacrifice fell more often on the lovely and beautiful of the race—the female child. The fair and delicate being was permitted to grow up in the family to the age of five or six years, and then, when it had become most interesting to the household and most fond of life, its own father, with his own hands, would thrust it alive into the grave, reckless of its fearful cries and its imploring entreaties, smothering the voice of weeping, and shutting out forever the sunlight from the fair face of the youthful innocent. Such was the religion, such were the dreadful customs, of the people, among whom was cast the lot of Mahomet. Such a religion he determined to subvert—such customs he resolved to abolish. Poetic in temperament, ardent in feeling, sensitive to emotion, imaginative in conception, strong in thought, and bold in enterprise, he applied himself with all his power to the work.

He had no adequate notion of the great scheme of the Divine revelation, of the nature and office of Christ, of the plan of redemption, of the way of salvation, and of the institutions of the Gospel; yet was he in advance, far in advance, immeasurably far in advance, of his people. He felt strongly solicitous to reform the national religion, to destroy idolatry, to abolish the cruel rites and ceremonies of the times, and to bring the people back to the primitive faith and pure worship of the patriarchs—of Abraham, and of Ishmael, and of Moses. His interest in the subject became intense; his retirement became protracted; his meditations became deep and serious. He felt called to become a reformer among the people. He was moved by influences he could not resist, to undertake the hazardous enterprise of changing the opinions and of subverting the long-established usages of the nation. In the rapturous ecstasies in which he fell, during his hours of lonely meditation, believing himself called by the sovereign One, Creator of the universe and Ruler of men, to subvert idolatry and restore the pure worship of Jehovah, he might easily fancy himself favored with heavenly visions.

Returning home one evening, from a day of dreamy reverie, spent in a solitary cave among the mountains, fasting, lying on his back on the ground, his face enveloped in a mantle, engaged deeply in prayer and meditation, he told his wife there appeared to him a miraculous manifestation—the angel Gabriel—announcing to him the appointment as prophet of the Most High. He expressed, however, some doubt of the reality of the manifestation. It might be a dream, though it appeared to him a reality. To his devoted wife his character had always appeared perfect, his motives sincere, and his conduct honorable. She had unlimited confidence in him. To her his unimpeachable character seemed satisfactory evidence of his divine mission. Joyfully, therefore, she received him in his new character as prophet of God, and encouraged him to doubt not the heavenly vision, but to go boldly forward in the work committed to him.

Cheered by the influence of his amiable wife, he ventured to communicate the revelation, which he, no doubt, sincerely thought made to him, to a few of his personal friends. He soon gained three other converts to the new faith---his servant, Zeid; his youthful cousin, Ali; and Abubeker, a respectable citizen of Mecca. He then determined to proclaim openly his mission. He invited his kinsfolk to a feast at his own house. There were present about forty persons. After some time spent in eating and in social conversation, Mahomet solemnly arose in their midst, and declared to them his mission He exposed the folly and the wickedness of idolatry, severely ridiculed the absurdities of popular belief, eulogized the faith of the ancient patriarchs, and told them he was commissioned by God to reclaim them to the religion of Abraham, and of Moses, and of the prophets. But they laughed him to scorn. They pronounced him a fanatic, to whose visionary harangues no sane man should for a moment listen.

Mahomet, however, stood dauntless, and confident in the truth of his doctrines and the divinity of his mission. Being rejected by his kinsfolk, he appealed to the people, and boldly proclaimed his mission, and unceasingly lifted up his voice of warning in the streets of Mecca, and in the public places. He was zealous and eloquent. He plied the force of reasoning; he appealed to the conscience; he touched the heart. The people listened, and many of them believed.

The tribe of Arabians to which Mahomet belonged was of priestly prerogative. To it was consigned the administration of religious affairs. They began to fear their craft might be in danger. Mahomet was becoming popular. Should he succeed in undermining and overthrowing the established religion, their occupation would be gone. They resolved, therefore, to crush him. They first charged him with heresy and apostasy. But he still made converts. They then entered into a vow of proscription, withdrawing all business and social intercourse from him and his family, till he should cease inveighing against the religious usages, and declaiming against the religious faith of the country. But the league, though faithfully kept and strictly enforced by the confederates, had no influence on Mahomet. Still he preached, and still the people believed. Then they resolved to end his troublesome pretensions by assassination, and appointed a large committee to carry out the plot. The conspirators surrounded his house in the night, intending to assassinate him whenever he should go out in the morning. But he had been informed of the stratagem, and had escaped, and hid himself, with his faithful adherent, Abubeker, in a cave. In the morning the assassins, finding he had eluded them, went in pursuit of them, and passed right by the mouth of the cave in which the fugitives were concealed. As Abubeker heard them tramping about the cavern, he whispered in terror to Mahomet, "There are many of them, and only two of us." "Say, rather, three of us," said the fearless Mahomet; "for God is here." As soon as his pursuers were gone, Mahomet arose, left his cave, and fled, in great haste, to Medina, where he was gladly received and chivalrously protected. The flight to Medina is called the hegira, and is the era from which time is reckoned in Mahometan countries.

Immediately on getting fairly established in Medina, he built, laboring at it with his own hands, a house of worship, in which he preached and enforced his doctrines. Converts were rapidly multiplied. He soon found himself at the head of a powerful and enthusiastic party, ready to go with him to battle, to prison, or to death.

Thus far we find in his course little to censure and much to approve. But the means which he afterward used to increase his influence, and to propagate his religious system, were "evil, only evil, and that continually." With the design evidently of imposing on the credulity of his followers, he pretended to receive frequent revelations from Heaven; and for the purpose of punishing his persecutors, and enforcing his doctrines, he marshaled his followers, and went forth to battle against the unbelievers, whom he conquered in a series of brilliant engagements, till all Arabia lay prostrate before him and submissive to him.

Far be from me the disposition to approve of imposture or of war, yet would I not withhold my admiration from one who, in a dark age, and among a barbarous people, by the energies of his own mind, without the influence of friends or the advantages of education, dared to undertake, and succeeded in establishing, reform in the religion and the usages of his people. Nor would I require of Mahomet a character founded on the model of Christianity, or of the Greek and Roman philosophy Of Christianity he knew theoretically little, and experimentally nothing. Of Grecian literature and Roman civilization he was profoundly ignorant. More justly might we compare him with the Montezumas of Mexico, or the Incas of Peru, or the Indian brave of the North American forests. Nor would I withhold from him the meed of praise for many private virtues. He maintained, according to the moral code of the country and the times, an unsullied reputation. In the midst of his elevation and his power, he lived in very simple style, affecting no dignity of state, putting on no airs, and indulging in no luxurious living. Considering the age in which he lived, and the society with whom he associated, I must pronounce him a remarkable man, of consummate talents, and of many amiable virtues.

But whatever estimate we may place on the character of Mahomet, none *will*, none *can* deny, that his system of religion, even in its worst form, was vastly superior, both in theory and in practice, to the Arabian idolatry. Nor was Mahometanism confined in space to Arabia, nor in time to the cycle of the sixth century. His successors ran a brilliant race, and erected a throne of dazzling renown, of irresistible power, and of indefinite duration. A century from the death of the Prophet had passed, and the Mahometan empire extended from the Indus to the Atlantic. Eight centuries had passed, and the renowned empire of the eastern Cæsars, with all its wealth and magnificence, was absorbed in the Saracen domain. Twelve centuries have passed, and the end is not yet. The crescent yet waves over the palaces of the city of Constantine, on the Bosphorus, over the valley of the Nile, and over Jerusalem, once the city of the great King.

It may yet be too early for us to solve the providential problem presented in the history of Mahometanism. Some other observer, placed on a point of time thousands of years now future, may be able, looking back over the past, and reading the observations there recorded, to calculate the end, both of time and of purpose, which the omniscient and almighty One has fixed for the winding up of the matter, and for the solution of the mystery. Till that day we must wait, patiently wait, knowing that with the Lord a thousand years are only as one day. In our interest and curiosity we may inquire, as did Daniel, the prophet, "O, my Lord, what shall be the end of these things?" And we may receive the same answer, "Go thy way, for the words are closed up, and sealed till the time of the end."

THE CHILD'S FUNERAL.

As I was returning from the east, I arrived toward evening at a village at the foot of the Alleghany Mountains, near the head waters of the Potomac. Desirous of crossing the mountains by daylight, I determined to remain in the village till morning. After resting for a short time, I sallied forth for a ramble, and spent an hour or more in climbing the hills, and in admiring the romantic scenery of the place. I then returned to the hotel, and was sitting at my window, when I saw passing a funeral procession. At the head of the procession walked the minister of God, with the sacred book in hand. Next to him followed four young and beautiful girls, dressed in pure white robes, with long white vails spread over their heads, and suspended over their faces. They bore on a bier a little child, over whose coffin was spread a white pall. After the bier followed the father and mother of the child; and the procession was closed by a small company of neighbors. I arose and joined the procession; for I never shun a funeral, though it revive in my own heart recollections which I would gladly let sleep. We wound around the crowded streets of the busy village, and entered a neglected graveyard, near an old church. I stood by while the coffin was lowered, and the grave filled. No service was performed at the burial, except a brief prayer; but my thoughts were busy and my heart full. The parents appeared plain, simple-hearted people, apparently poor. This child might be their only one—their sole earthly treasure. They uttered not a word, but they looked the picture of grief and sadness. How many hopes had perished with that child! What bright visions had vanished! When the little mound was heaped up over the lost one, the company, without ceremony, dispersed. But the parents stood, looking with intense agony at the grave. I stepped up to them, took each by the hand, and was about to speak a word of consolation; but my heart forbade my lips uttering a word. We all three wept together for a moment, then silently shook hands in sympathy, and separated never to meet again. They left the graveyard by a retired street. I stood looking after them, and saw them enter a small but neat cottage, in full view of the very spot where they had laid their child to sleep. How desolate to their hearts was now their home! Cheerful might blaze the fire on the social hearth, fair might bloom the flowers in the door-yard, green might wave the trees over their cottage, lovely might the fertile valley spread out before them, and beautiful the blue hills might loom up around their home; but the light of the bright eyes of their only one was quenched forever. A fairer flower than blooms in earth's garden was withered and faded. A sunny brow was shrouded in the deep darkness of the grave. Ringlets of fair hair were twined about a head that lay low in the ground. Lips that once smiled were closed forever, and a voice of sweetness and melody was silent. O, who can gauge the deep agony of bereavement that distends the heart of the childless one! Mock not with words the spirit of the mother, who has buried her only one. All the streams of human affection will seem to center about the lost one. The whole house, and all the grounds about it, become a mirror, in which she sees only the image of her child. She listens again for the voice of her child. She expects to hear the light footfall on the floor. But all is silent. She throws up her window, and looks out on the grass plot, and about the garden walks; but all is deserted. She opens the little chest that contains the apparel and the playthings now unworn and unused. Here is the little dress that never again will cover that lovely form. Here are the shoes that no more will protect those little feet. Here is the toy that those delicate fingers will handle no more

"Take them away. I can not look
 On aught that breathes of him—
O take away this little cup;
 His lips have touched its brim—
Take the straw hat from off the wall,
 'Tis wreathed with withered flowers;
The rustling leaves do whisper me
 Of all the loved, best hours.

The rattle, with its music bells,
 O do not let them sound;
The dimpled hand that grasped them once
 Is cold beneath the ground;
And turn that picture to the wall;
 His loving, mournful eye
Is piercing through my very heart—
 Again I see him die."

Slowly and sadly wears the day away. Wearied with watching and with weeping, the mother lies down on her lonely bed. She sleeps and she dreams—she dreams of her child. She stretches her arms to encircle him, and draw him to her bosom, but he is not there. She awakes to vacancy and to tears. And then she hears the wild winds whistling about her door, and the rain pattering on the roof, and thinks of her child as exposed to the wintery wind and pitiless storm. She even imagines him waking from his long sleep—waking in the grave—and reaching forth, as he was wont in his bed, his little hands to her, saying, "Mother, are you here?"

O, chide not—chide not the bereaved one! Tantalize her not with comfortless words!

"Go, let her weep; there's bliss in tears."

MAY-DAY.

Delightful is the merry month of May. In its annual visit it brings along pleasant associations of the past. To me it brings back the feelings, the thoughts, and the pleasures of childhood and of youth. On my native hills, swept as they are by the mountain wind, "winter lingers in the lap of May," and May-day is usually but the first opening of spring. The snow-drift on the mountain side yet gleams in the bright sunshine, and only in the sheltered dell may be seen the delicate footstep of spring. On the morning of May-day, all the children and youth of the rural region are up betimes, to go on a search for wild flowers in the woods; and fortunate is the fair one

> "Who may chance to spy
> Some small star-flower, with its silvery eye,"

peeping out under a dry leaf on the sunny side of a hill.

I well remember my last May-day excursion. The world might, even then, have called me no longer young; for many a gray hair had already appeared on my temple. But my heart was yet young, and I went forth with the children, myself a child among them.

> "A lisping voice and glancing eyes were near,
> And ever-restless feet of one, who now
> Gathered the blossoms of her fourth bright year;
> There played a gladness o'er her fair young brow,
> As broke the varied scene upon her sight,
> Upheaved and spread in verdure and in light;
>
> For I had taught her, with delighted eye,
> To gaze upon the mountains, to behold,
> With deep affection, the pure, ample sky,
> And clouds along its blue abysses rolled—
> To love the song of waters, and to hear
> The melody of winds with charmed ear."

Beautiful was the scene of our rambles. Gentle reader, I would that I could exhibit to your eye the picture of that lovely landscape, as it is daguerreotyped on my own heart. Suppose you take a walk with me to the summit of the "overlooking hill." Here is afforded such a panorama of hill and dale, mountain and valley, forest and field, streamlet and lake, as is not often presented to the eye of the traveler, even in Switzerland, or far-famed Italy. On the north there rises a range of grand mountains, stretching away toward the east, till their dim outlines are lost in the distance. The morning sunbeam is now lighting up their bleak summits, while night yet lingers among their dark ravines. Beyond is another range, on which hangs the blue mist that distance always throws over mountain scenery, while still beyond is another, raising its snowy peaks far up toward the blue sky. Beyond that farther range, as the adventurous hunter tells us, is an unbroken forest, stretching away in gloomy grandeur and dreary solitude far toward the Arctic Ocean. A little to the west of that long range, you see a lone, white peak, gleaming bright in the morning sun. You might at first mistake it for a cloud on the verge of the horizon. There yet tarries winter in stern severity. Around that bleak summit oft gathers the wintery storm and oft the summer thunder-cloud. There sits old Æolus on a throne of granite.

There is an interesting variety in the ever-changing appearance of mountain scenery. Sometimes the summits are covered with snow, sometimes with clouds, and sometimes they are surrounded by a thin vail of inimitable blue. Distance "lends enchantment to the view"—the asperities are smoothed—the rough appears plain—the precipitous cliffs and dizzy ravines are not observed. A nearer approach changes the scene from the beautiful to the sublime. I have stood on the overhanging rock at

Niagara, and seen the waters tumble over the precipice, and listened to the deep bass of their incessant monotone, with feelings such as no pen may describe. But still more intense was the emotion of the sublime, when I stood, as I once did, on yonder distant peak, which you may just see on the utmost verge of the horizon, and found myself, though yet the summer was scarcely past, suddenly enveloped in a furious storm of wind and snow, and obliged to grope my weary way to the plain over rocks thrown together in the wildest confusion, and along the verge of dizzy precipices walling up dark ravines a thousand feet deep.

Those glorious old mountains, how they stand out as living monuments of the power of God, and as emblems of his immutability! The works of man, what are they, and how unequal to the task of resisting "decay's effacing fingers!" The cities of the Nile, of the Euphrates, of classic Greece, and of sacred Palestine, have crumbled away, and are leveled to the dust. But these old mountains stand, defying the storms, and even time itself. They, too, have a language, and their history is written in hieroglyphics older than those of the Nile, reaching back to the time when the morning stars first sang together, and the sons of God shouted for joy.

> "O, mountain land, how my young spirit leaps,
> After long years, to tread thy hights again,
> And with the clouds to hang along thy steeps,
> And watch the river sweeping to the main!
> Long years! but not the necromance of time
> Can dim the shapes of memory sublime—
> Thy cliffs and waters—when with shivering breath
> I gazed through vistas of the rocking pine,
> And saw below the silent gulf of death,
> And over me as near the realms divine."

But you may be weary with looking on that mountain scenery. Let us, then, turn to another part of the landscape. Here opens a view toward the sunny south. At our feet is spread out a tranquil lake. Its bright waters reflect the light, like a mirror of silver. Its shores are fringed with evergreens. The pine, the fir, the cedar, and the larch are growing there together, giving to the scene a beauteous variety, such as art may in vain hope to imitate. From the foot of the lake issues a small stream, which meanders through a quiet meadow, and then empties its clear waters into another lake. Beyond you may see a lovely vale, stretching away between the hills, till it spreads out into a broad plain. On that plain the light falls mellow and soft. The blue tinge of distance is diffused over the whole scene. It would seem that there might be the "happy land where care is unknown." A thousand times have I looked on that lovely valley, and yielding up my reason to my fancy, imagined it some fairy-land, some region of the blest, some paradise of flowery beauty, where the winds blow not, the storms never come, where the sunlight of spring always shines, and sorrow is unknown.

But we must bid adieu to this scene of beauty. On the landscape we may look no more. The mountain, the vale, the lake, the stream, the garden, the greenwood, the neat village, with its white dwellings, the church, with its Gothic spires, and the cottage on the hill-side, with its shrubbery and flowers, we must leave forever.

Yet beauty exists every-where. Our western homes may not afford us a distant prospect. The surface of our country is too level for any extended views. We have no mountains, and few lakes. But so fertile, and so easy of culture is our soil, so genial our climate, and so easy is it to cultivate fruits, shrubbery, and flowers, that we may, with little expense, and no great labor, render our homes so beautiful, that we may have no need of depending on our neighbors for a beautiful prospect. I would hope, gentle reader, that your home is not in the crowded city, where you are hemmed in on every side by an unsightly mass of brick and mortar, with scarcely room on your premises to plant a tree or a shrub. I like not a city residence. It is said that God made the country, and man the town; and for my part I like the works of God much the best. Instead of brick, and mortar, and lumber, I would look on the green woods, and the verdant pastures, and the waving cornfields. Instead of thumping drays, rattling carriages, and the hum-drum of discordant voices, I would listen to the music of the waterfall, and the song of the birds. Instead of paved streets, and crowded sidewalks, I would ramble along the cow-path over the pastures, and along the winding brook in the wild woods. If I must do business in the city, still let me have a quiet little home in some retired, suburban spot, where my children may have a little play-ground in the open air, and where I may retire at evening to commune with nature.

Reader, are there *children* in your family? Have you little sons and little daughters, or little brothers and little sisters? If you would have them interesting in mind and in body, accustom them early to cultivate the love of the beautiful in nature. Take them out at morning and at evening, and let them see the glories of the season. For their sake, make your home beautiful. Embower it with shrubbery, crown it with flowers, and ornament it with shade-trees. If your home be pleasant, your children will be contented with it, and will not be inclined to go abroad. Nothing can be more injurious to the moral habits of children, than the practice of running about the neighborhood and the town for recreation and amusement. Let them have something at home to interest them, and it will be easy to keep them there.

A home made pleasant by fruits and flowers, will promote the cheerfulness of children. Cheerfulness is a virtue, and it should be cultivated by ourselves, and encouraged in our children. All nature is cheerful. The plants put on their beauteous colors, such as Solomon in all his glory could not boast. The insects are so happy they hardly know what to do with themselves. The birds sing a merry tune, all except the moping owl. Of all beings man should certainly be the last to be sad and melancholy. Most of all should the good be cheerful. If any should be sad, let it be the bad; for they have reason for it; but the good should promote cheerfulness in themselves, and especially in the little children intrusted by Providence to their care.

Home made pleasant by cultivated grounds promotes the health of children. Their nature requires exercise in the open air. Confine them to close rooms, restrain them in their play, and you do them a lasting injury. Entice them out into the garden, the orchard, the ornamented yard—accustom them to run about the garden walks, and to perform such labor as may be suited to their little hands, and you will develop a healthy body and a sound mind.

Familiarity with the beauties of nature has much effect in refining the taste and developing the mind. A child brought up amidst shrubbery and flowers can not well be coarse in manners, uncultivated in mind, and deficient in taste. The superiority of the ancient Greeks and Italians over other people, was greatly owing to the influence of nature over them. Their country was beautiful, their skies serene, their climate mild. By nature they were initiated into the love of the beautiful, and thus were led to excel in literature and in art. Their beautiful mythology, stripped of its poetic drapery, was but a deification of the powers of nature. The works of nature illustrate the wisdom and the goodness of the Deity. The argument for the existence, the wisdom, and the benevolence

of God, drawn from the proofs of contrivance in nature, may be made perfectly intelligible to the mere child, and will have more effect on him than a thousand dry moral precepts. Then, if you would give your child an idea of the supreme Being, and a conception of the most interesting of his attributes, take him with you into the garden, and show him the flowers, and the marks of contrivance and design they exhibit.

We have another inducement to render, so far as possible, the home of our children pleasant to them. We thereby furnish them an inexhaustible fund of delightful associations in after life. Home, "be it ever so homely," is still the sweetest word in the English language. When, however, there is associated with that word the idea of good taste and beauty, it has an inexpressible charm, that binds the heart, as by a spell, for all future time. I would not lose the word from our language—I would not lose the memory of it from my heart, for the wealth "of Ormus or of Ind." Though from the home of my childhood my friends are all gone, though the stranger's foot is on the threshold, and I hear no familiar voice, and see no familiar face within the halls, yet my heart often instinctively turns to the spot. My reveries by day and my dreams by night carry me back to the play-ground of my childhood's sunny days. Dear to my heart is the little brook that flowed by the door, the lone old apple-tree that grew in the field, and even the rough granite rock that lay poised on the hill-side. While thus memory points me back to youth, a faculty of mind, for which we have no name in our language, points me on to age, and I see my own children, then grown to maturity and scattered over the prairies of the west, turning back their thoughts to the little white cottage, the spring in the locust grove, the thicket of evergreens, the trellis of vines, and the bower of roses.

SUBSTANCE AND SHADOW.

I DO not wonder at the philosopher who doubted the reality of material existences. Indeed, the material world is only a world of shadows, of unsubstantial phantasms, of transitory appearances. Sensuous objects flit before us, and are gone. The form, the organization of the object changes, and its very individuality vanishes. And when once the material organization has passed the crisis in any stages of its existence, return to its former position is impossible.

So rapid are the changes of material nature, that it is doubtful whether we ever see the same object twice of the same form and substance. The landscapes familiar to us, the home of our childhood or of mature years, slowly yet surely change, as day succeeds day, and year follows year. The changes so gradual may not be observed while we are incessantly looking on the scene; but returning after a few years, or even a few days of absence, we shall find the changes really perceptible.

The child that grows up by our side passes through changes which, from our constant intercourse, we rarely appreciate, till a period of separation makes us sensible of the sure and unerring effects of time. Not alone the corporeal form, but those qualities of mind which constitute individuality of character, are affected, often radically, in the course of a few years.

Never in the history of nature or of man has there been any restoration of things, when once changed, to precisely their former condition. Successive have been the changes on the surface of earth since in the beginning God created it; but no two geological periods have been the same, if, indeed, they have been in any respect similar. In no two periods of human history have the same circumstances existed, or the same events transpired. No two men have been produced precisely alike. The world has seen but one Moses, one Solomon, and one Paul; one Alexander, one Cæsar, and one Napoleon; one Homer, one Bacon, and one Newton.

The most evanescent and transitory appearances of nature are but emblems of the rapid mutations of the most enduring works of man. The magnificent cities, the gorgeous temples, and the elegant palaces of antiquity have wholly disappeared from human vision. The empires, the kingdoms, the political institutions, the religious organizations, have all ceased to exist in any substantial form. They have passed away, cities, kingdoms, and all, like the vapory creations of sunset.

The forms of visible things are often preserved long after the original object has disappeared, by the skill of the sculptor or the painter; yet the marble is not imperishable, nor may the colors on the canvas always retain their truthfulness to nature. The statue and the picture may, therefore, finally prove as unsubstantial as the forms whose image they were designed to perpetuate.

The ideal world is really the world of substance. Spirit forms alone retain forever unchanged their original impress. The conceptual existences of mind are immortal and changeless. The conception once entertained by the mind of a beautiful object, a landscape, or a "human face divine," becomes an imperishable and inalienable picture in the gallery of intellect. The ideas suggested to the mind by external objects of perception, by reading, or by reflection, become real, indestructible existences, subject to none of the changes and accidents which befall material objects. There may be oblivion, but there is no obliteration of knowledge. And the reign of oblivion is only temporary. The surges of her waters may fill up imprints made in the sand, but can not erase thought traced and graven in the imperishable tablet of mind. Forms of beauty once conceived in the mind become changeless. Images of loveliness once daguerreotyped on the soul become effaceless.

What a glorious gallery of lovely pictures may the observant mind in one short life collect; pictures of natural beauty, of thousand-tinted flowers, of green hills, of fair vales, of smiling plains, of brooks winding amid verdure, of lakes embowered amid grand mountains, all forming a landscape more beautiful than fairy ever saw or poet ever dreamed; pictures of moral beauty, scenes of magnanimity, of virtue, and of goodness; conceptions of the beautiful, the grand, the sublime, with all of pure and indestructible thought, accumulated through life! All these conceptual images we may classify, distribute, and arrange so as to form for ourselves a world of beauty in which we may forever luxuriate.

The treasures of thought laid up in the impregnable storehouse of mind remain secure from stratagem or ravage. Into that treasury thieves may not break. From it they may not steal. Men may take from me all of external I have—my property, my liberty, my life; but they can not take from me the acquisitions of knowledge. They have neither key to unlock the storehouse, nor force to demolish it, nor power to drag thence the possessions.

Rich, surpassing rich is he, whose is the ideal world, the world of conception, the world of thought. All of beauty and of good, all of present and of past, is his. He ranges over earth; he ransacks the old and dilapidated repositories of the past; he collects all of thought from the archives of humanity; he constructs a world of his own, and furnishes it with the choicest products of nature and of art. Within the precincts of that world there is no decay, no change; there is only accumulation, as thought after thought is added to his possessions. Not, then, in the external, but in the spiritual world, the world of conception, of thought, must we look for reality, for substance. All else is shadow.

LITTLE ROSA.

Do you remember, little Rosa, the evening when first we met—the pleasant summer evening, when at twilight you stood with your youthful, widowed mother before our cottage door, having come a long journey of a thousand miles? Do you remember, Rosa, the garden, the orchard, the grove, the brook, and the bower, and how you rambled with me, your little hand clasped in mine, along the flowery walks of our western home? Do you remember how, after you had returned to your Atlantic home, I went to visit you with cousin Ellen, and you, meeting me at the gate, threw your arms around my neck, and in the ecstasy of joy could only exclaim, in infant accents, "My father!" Alas, poor child! he whom God had given you for a father by nature, had been, from your earliest infancy, sleeping in the church-yard, and you seemed to feel an instinctive desire for one on whom your young heart could rely.

Do you remember the pleasant day we spent on the Atlantic beach, looking at the ships, picking shells, and running before the surf? Do you remember the hour of parting, when pressing you long to my heart, with tearful eye I looked what I could not speak, farewell, and turned away toward my distant home.

Little Rosa, shall I ever see thee again? I can not cease to grieve for thy absence. Slowly and sadly passed the autumn by. Winter came, and again passed away. Spring, with its budding beauty, its fair flowers, and its music of birds, came, and went again. Summer came, and is gone. Autumn came again, and strewed the walks of Rosabower with fallen leaves. Yet thou, Rosa, returnest not to me. Wilt thou come again, sweet child, to my home—come to my heart? Come, and in spring we will roam together the woods, and pick the anemone as it peeps out from under the fallen leaf. We will recline upon the lawn, beneath the pine which we planted, and gather the early violets. We will follow the little brook along the valley, and listen to the birds singing on the willow-trees. In summer we will sit beneath the shade of the old beech at the bower, enjoying the fragrance of the rose and the lily, and breathing the bland zephyr. In autumn we will gather the fruits of the orchard, luxuriating amidst pears and peaches, and apples and grapes. When winter comes, with his frosts and his snows, we will heap on the wood in the old fire-place, and before the blazing fire pass the long, cold evening, defying the peltings of the storm.

Come, Rosa, and we will welcome you to our home in the west—to our clear skies and bland atmosphere. Come and live among our grand old forests, and look on our illimitable prairies, and drink our pure and cool streams. Come, and go with us on the quiet Sabbath to our beautiful village church, whose sweet-toned bell calls us at the hour of worship to our devotions. Come, and with your little cousins pursue the path of knowledge, gathering along the way flowers fairer than the spring violets or summer roses. Come, and be my child, since she, whose name you bear, can return to me no more.

Alas, Rosa! hard seems the lot that separates us. I greatly fear thou art to me lost forever. With passing years thy beauteous features are changing; and should I, after a long time, again see thee, I might not, in thy mature countenance, recognize the lovely image of childhood, daguerreotyped on my heart. Thy heart, too, Rosa, may be changed. The outgushing fountain of childlike love may become the deep and stately current of mature affection, directed in a channel far away from my secluded heart. Thy pure love may then be to me among the things that were, but never can be again. Long is the distance that now separates us. Between us mighty rivers flow, and lofty mountains rise, and great lakes extend their watery domain. And I may never see thee more. So, little Rosa, with deep regret must I give thee up. Farewell, my Rosa, beauteous child, lovely one, farewell!

THE HEAVENS.

How glorious must have appeared the nocturnal sky to the Chaldean philosophers and the dwellers along the Nile! In the pure atmosphere and clear sky of the plains the stars shone out bright from the concave firmament, seeming like a thousand lamps hung on high. The diurnal motions of the stars could not escape the notice of the observer for a single night. When the sun had disappeared, he saw myriads of lights scattered over all the heavens. Of those in the eastern horizon, in the zenith, and in the west, he could but remark the motions even in a single hour's observation. Those in the east would ascend by regular movements, those in the zenith would descend, and those in the west would set. The Chaldean shepherd, as he watched his flocks during the summer night, would observe, as the hours passed away, stars continually rising one after another, and following each other over the firmament. When he looked toward the north he would observe a variant phenomenon. The star at the pole would appear stationary, and all in its neighborhood revolving in circular orbits about it.

The observer would naturally search for the cause of these appearances. He would easily perceive that the diurnal motion of the stars might be real or only apparent. If the earth be motionless, then the stars move. If, however, the earth revolve on its axis, then the motion of the stars is only apparent, their rising and setting being caused by the revolving earth interposing its rotund surface between the star and the observer.

The observer could not long fail to remark the unchanging relations which most of the stars retain among themselves. Certain clusters, occupying definite relative positions, retain those positions night after night, week after week, month after month, and year after year. The individual stars, forming these clusters, seemed associated permanently together. These clusters they designated constellations. Names were early given the constellations—names either of persons or animals, founded on some fancied resemblance of shape or some story of mythology. At what time the constellations first received names is unknown. Homer, who lived about one thousand years before Christ, mentions the constellations Pleiades, Hyades, Bootes, Arcturus, and Orion. Hesiod, who lived near the time of Homer, mentions the same, with the addition of Sirius.

But neither Homer nor Hesiod mentions planets distinct from stars; nor is it known at what precise time the planets were distinguished and named; yet the difference between them and the stars must have been early observed. The stars maintain, year after year, precisely the same place among themselves, and the same with respect to the sun and the earth. But the planets were observed to change often their position relative among themselves, and relative to the sun and the earth.

Pythagoras had some conception of the revolution of the planets about the sun, and a tolerably correct idea of the various distances of the several planets from the sun. He fancied he saw some analogy between the distances of the bodies of the solar system from each other and the divisions of the octave in music. He supposed that the planets in their motions about the sun caused musical vibrations, and the sounds, owing to their regular intervals combining in harmony, formed the music of the spheres. A passage in the book of Job seems to recognize this idea: "The morning stars sang together." In that music what powerful bass must be made by Jupiter rushing through space, while Venus would pour fourth her delicate and melodious tones!

What an hour of deep and strange interest was that, when Gallileo, receiving a hint from a spectacle-maker, had, with much ingenuity and labor, contrived the wonderful telescope, which has affected such a revolution in modern science! When he had completed his instrument, he turned it toward the heavens, and pointed it at the planet Jupiter. To his astonishment, he discovered what had never before been suspected—four moons accompanying the planet, as our moon accompanies the earth. He looked at Saturn, and saw encircling the planet enormous rings, whose nature or purpose he could not determine. He looked at Venus, and perceived that she suffers changes of phase precisely as does our moon. He looked at the moon, and discovered on her surface prodigious mountains, dizzy precipices, and fathomless ravines. He looked at the sun, and saw on its surface dark spots, from whose changing position he inferred the rotary motion of the orb of day himself. Similar observations soon proved the diurnal motion of Jupiter and Mars.

Wonderful have been the triumphs of science in measuring the distances of the heavenly bodies. The exact distance of any planet, whose plane is within twenty millions of millions of miles from the sun, may be, by well-known mathematical rules, easily calculated. But there are bodies in the heavens at distances so immense, that no certain means of computation have ever been discovered; yet enough is known to prove that the nearest of the fixed stars must be so distant as to require more than three years for light, though traveling nearly two hundred thousand miles in a second, to reach us from their surface. Indeed, by observations lately made, it is rendered probable that from no star does light reach the earth in less than nine years. By similar observations it is inferred that the polar star, the star better known than any other in the heavens—the star that for ages has guided the sailor over the deep—is so far from the earth as to require twenty years for light to pass from its surface to the human eye. Let, therefore, at this moment, that glorious star be struck from the heavens, and its light would still stream on for twenty years.

The number of stars is inconceivable. The number visible in both the north and south hemispheres with a good telescope is computed at five and a half millions. Yet every one is supposed to be a sun, as large as our sun, and may have a planetary system moving about it. And these bodies are all in motion. The moons move around their primary planets; the primary planets of each solar system move around their sun; and the system, our sun with its attendant planets, and the five and a half millions of other suns with their planets, are moving round a great common center in the heavens. A distinguished astronomer supposes he has discovered that center, near the Pleiades, around which our system is moving at such a rate as to make one revolution in eighteen millions of years, and other systems in other times, but all in regularity, order, and harmony. Omnipotent far beyond human conception is He who, from nothing, created this sun, these planets, and this innumerable host of stars, each itself another sun with its attendant planets. As yet we are far from having explored the utmost depths of space. Our telescopes have only reached a limited distance into the regions of the heavens. There lies a depth beyond the lowest depth, a hight above the utmost hight, and a length beyond the greatest length yet reached by human eye or philosophic glass. There may lie as many stars, as many suns, as many solar systems, without as within the range of the most powerful telescopes yet invented. To space there is no bounds. And space seems full of the handiwork of the Almighty. Omniscient, as well as omnipotent, must be He who hath given all these bodies their orbits in the heavens, and who, from age to age, regulates their motions and prevents collisions. In our system, one sun, nineteen planets, counting the newly-discovered asteriods, at least twenty moons, and an unknown multitude of comets, have been, for many thousand years, moving in the heavens, each subject to attractions and disturbances from all the others, and yet no collision has ever occurred. The millions of stars, so far as we can discover, pursue their way eternally in the heavens without interference or collision. Wise is the mind, and strong the hand, to control and regulate so many immense and rapidly-moving bodies.

It is impossible now to conceive how widely the sphere of human knowledge may yet be extended in the heavens. Wonderful were the revelations made by the telescope of Gallileo, imperfect as was its construction. Sir William Herschel constructed with his own hands a telescope much superior to that of Gallileo, and immediately therewith discovered a new planet, new satellites, and innumerable new stars. The Earl of Rosse has lately constructed one far superior to that of Herschel. By it the most wonderful sidereal pictures are afforded. Spots in the heavens, appearing in common instruments only light, misty clouds, are resolved by this telescope into distinct, beautiful, magnificent stars.

There is no probability that human ingenuity is yet exhausted, or that science has reached its terminus. Other telescopes of higher power may yet be contrived, and other observers may detect new planets and new stars. Our amount of knowledge respecting those parts of our own solar system already discovered may be vastly increased, and our view into the depths of space may be greatly extended. While *we* see on the surface of the planets only lofty mountains and dark ravines, *others,* with better instruments, may see green trees, and waving harvests, and cities with towers and steeples, and living men.

Would you like to visit these planets, and suns, and stars—these monuments of the glory and the handiwork of the Almighty? Conveyance may now be found difficult, and all known means of locomotion entirely too slow. It would require the rail-car, at its utmost speed, five hundred years to reach the sun, twenty-five hundred to reach Jupiter, four thousand, seven hundred and fifty to reach Saturn, nine thousand, five hundred to reach Uranus, fifteen thousand to reach Neptune, seventy millions to reach the nearest star, and four hundred millions to reach the polar star.

Take, then, the wings of the morning, mount a sunbeam, and away on your adventurous journey. You would even then be eight minutes in reaching the sun, forty in reaching Jupiter, one hour and a quarter in reaching Saturn, two and a half hours in reaching Uranus, and four hours in reaching Neptune. Should you venture to the stars on a beam of light, your journey would be in going to the nearest three and a quarter years, to the polar star twenty years, and to Alcyone, the central star of the beautiful Pleiades, five hundred and thirty-seven years. If therefore, in your future state of spiritual existence, ye are disposed to visit and explore the works of God, ye need never feel want of employment—ye need never have occasion, as did the conqueror of earth, to sit down and weep over the lack of more worlds to visit, more wonders to admire, and more glorious exhibitions of Divine power and wisdom to observe.

THE MINIATURE.

Before me lies a daguerreian group of three little girls, of beauteous feature, and childlike drapery. The picture has faded some little in color, but the outline is yet perfect, presenting the little angel-band just as it appeared, years ago, gathered about the cheerful fireside. The pictured group alone remains, the living originals being scattered to distant homes. On looking on the picture, I am deeply impressed with the changes which a few years have effected in the form and features of the beauteous sisterhood, who used to sing so merrily about their home. Day by day, and hour by hour, have the features of childhood been yielding to replacement by those of maturity. There is now on that serious countenance hardly a trace of the merry and careless gladsomeness of childhood. The mind is changed not less than the feature. The feelings, the taste, the opinions, are all modified, and more or less changed. Not even the features of the countenance, nor the affections of the mind, remain constant. It is vain to expect the tastes and the sentiments of childhood to be reproduced in maturity. Each period of life—childhood, youth, maturity, and age—has its own resources of pleasure, and its own chosen associates; nor usually do the same persons prove spirits congenial with us through more than one period of life. The memory of early friendships may never be lost. But often the continuance of our partiality is owing only to the pleasant associations of childhood's remembrances. Permanent and unchanging congeniality can only be secured by continued familiar intercourse, and similarity of mental direction, and moral cultivation.

On meeting, after a separation of years, with a friend of childhood, we are often grieved and disappointed at the mutual change in our relations. We can not call back the ecstasy of pleasure we reciprocally enjoyed in our early intercourse. We are changed, and we are conscious of the change. The change is affected by a law of nature, a law including in its folds the physical and the moral constitution.

The only method of securing ourselves against disappointment, is to bring ourselves constantly nearer the great standard of moral perfection and holy love, on which the eye of the soul should be always fixed. Only by becoming every day better and better, and by approaching nearer and nearer the standard of human excellence, may we hope to preserve the relations of congeniality, which often spring up between the ingenuous and pure-minded.

There have been, perhaps, those among us, whose souls seemed born in the same mold as our own. God sometimes gives us, to cheer us for a while on the pathway of life, some companion, of peculiar congeniality with ourselves; some angel visitor, in human form, appears, walks gently by our side, becomes the sharer of our joys and sorrows, reciprocates our love, and thoroughly understands and comprehends us. The soul is satisfied, and we are happy.

A sad change comes over us. The congenial being is called away to another sphere, and we are left again alone. Like old Jacob, when bereaved, or Rachel mourning for her children, we refuse to be comforted. Despairing of earth, we look forward in hope of reunion, in a better world, with the loved one of the heart gone before us to the spirit-land. That hope of reunion, and of a renewal of happy intercourse, can only be realized by our incessant striving for the good and the true. And even though we labor diligently for improvement in moral goodness, the earlier saved may become far in advance of us, and, though younger in years, yet greatly our superior in goodness. Then, if the gentle and lovely one whom Providence sent,

"More than all things else, to love us,"

has been early removed from us to heaven, we must, in hope of a happy reunion, strive for great proficiency in moral goodness, that, when we meet again, there may not be found great disparity in our moral tastes.

THE POETS OF THE WEST

THOUGH few volumes of poetry have been published by writers residing west of the Alleghany Mountains, yet there is scattered, through newspapers and magazines, every year, a sufficient amount of first-rate poetry by western writers to make a volume of respectable size. Some of our female writers have produced stanzas equal, in beauty of conception and harmony of measure, to any thing I have ever read in the English language.

Few, if any of our writers, whose productions have never been collected in a volume, have written more or better than Mrs. Sarah T. Bolton. Her poems are found in various papers and magazines, and exhibit extraordinary talent and taste. Her history, though brief, is one of interest. She is a child of the west. She was born in Newport, Kentucky, on the banks of the Ohio, near Cincinnati. When she was yet a mere infant, some two or three years old, her father, with his family, removed into the interior of Jennings county, Indiana, and settled in the wild woods.

There are in Indiana beautiful and lovely spots—groves delightful as those of Arcadia, vales delicious as Tempe, and fields fair as that

> " Of Enna, where Proserpina, gathering flowers.
> Herself a fairer flower, by gloomy Dis
> Was carried off."

But no such groves, nor vales, nor fields were found in that remote and cheerless region, where little Sarah T. Barrett spent the days of childhood. There were no hills and vales, and few running brooks. Beyond the cleared opening of her father's farm, there stretched away on every side an expanse of flat beech woods. The nearest neighbor was three miles distant, and the next nearest, six miles. To provide for his family, the father toiled on from day to day, clearing the land, sowing the seed, and reaping the harvest. The mother, within the rude walls of the log-cabin, incessant plied her industrious hands, in preparing for the use of her family the materials of food and of clothing which the father had provided. The children, as soon as they could handle the lightest implements of labor, were employed in assisting the father and the mother in whatever department their services might be available.

There would not seem much poetry in such a place and such a life; yet little Sarah, before she had attained her ninth year, and while as yet she knew not one letter of the alphabet, had actually composed a poem, which she used to sing, alone in the woods, to a tune of her own making. The circumstances under which she composed her first poem are curious. There came along one of those primitive preachers, who, in the order of Divine providence, have followed the pioneer settlers of the west to the most remote frontiers, and preached the Gospel in every neighborhood, before the first log-cabin was hardly roofed. He was a man of tall and commanding form, and of powerful yet melodious voice. To the small congregation of settlers gathered in the woods from far and near, he spoke with as much zeal, and, perhaps, as much eloquence, as did Massillon before the court of France, or Whitefield to the thousands at Moorfields. His theme was the *judgment.* He depicted the magnificent and awful scenes of the last day. Among the auditors sat enchained and spell-bound the little Sarah T. Barrett. To the measured and melodious tones of the preacher's voice her own ear vibrated in harmony. The scenes of awful grandeur, of terrific sublimity, so vividly portrayed, aroused in her soul, from its unconscious state, the spirit of Poetry. On leaving the place, she retired to a sequestered retreat of the forest, and wove the rude descriptions of the preacher into melodious verse. So soon as she learned the letters of the alphabet, her first literary exercise was the writing down of her poem in large capitals. It is a pity the copy was not preserved. It would doubtless be a curiosity now even to herself.

Though Mr. Barrett had probably little, if any, conception of the value of the rare gem that sparkled among his household jewels, yet was he not indifferent to the education of his children. For the purpose, therefore, of affording access to the means of instruction, he removed, when Sarah was nine years old, to Madison. No sooner had he become settled at Madison, than he procured for his children such advantages for education as the place afforded. The school which Sarah attended was at North Madison, on the hill near the upper terminus of the inclined plane of the Madison and Indianapolis railroad. To reach the school-house she had to clamber daily up the hill, and, when the school hours expired, return to her home by the river-side. But to a child such as she, of vigorous health, buoyant spirit, and poetic fancy, a daily ramble over the Ohio hills was far from being disadvantageous. The physical exercises added strength to her constitution, and the romantic scenery nourished the genius of Poesy, which the itinerant preacher's description of the *last day* had aroused in her soul.

During her early school-days she wrote several little poems, which Colonel Arion, a gentleman of whom she ever speaks in the kindest terms, was pleased to publish and to praise in his paper. While yet a young girl, she became known, through her poetic effusions, to Mr.

Nathaniel Bolton, a printer, who was then publishing a paper at Madison. Mr. Bolton first solicited from the youthful and talented fair one her poetical contributions for his paper, and after that, as any man of taste might reasonably and naturally have done, he solicited her hand.

During the disastrous storm that swept over the business community in 1837 and 1838, the financial interests of Mr. Bolton were nearly wrecked. To extricate himself from his difficulties, he opened a tavern on his farm, a short distance west of the city of Indianapolis. Mrs. Bolton, then scarcely seventeen years old, found herself incumbered with the care of a large dairy and a public house. To aid as much as possible in relieving her husband from embarrassment, she dispensed with help, and with her own hands, often for weeks and for months, performed all the labor of the establishment. Thus for nearly ten years this child of genius, to whose spirit song was as natural as to the bird of the green wood, cheerfully resigned herself to incessant toil and care, in order that she might aid her husband in meeting the pecuniary obligations which honesty or honor might impose.

During these long and dreary years of toil and self-denial she wrote little or nothing. At last the crisis was reached, the work was accomplished, the liabilities were liquidated, and the bird, so long caged and tuneless, was again free to soar into the regions of song.

The most of her poems which have come under my observation, have been written within the last three or four years. There is among them great variety of subject and of measure. There are songs of the affections, elegies, songs of patriotism, songs of philanthropy, and numerous occasional or miscellaneous poems with a wide scope of subject.

From her songs of the affections we will present a few

stanzas, as specimens of her genius and taste. The delicacy of poetic conception, and the simplicity and beauty of style, in the following lines, can but be admired by every reader of taste:

"THE FLOWER AND THE STARLIGHT.

"From its home on high, to a gentle flower,
That bloomed in a lonely grove,
The starlight came at the twilight hour,
And whispered a tale of love.

Then the blossom's heart, so still and cold,
Grew warm to its silent core,
And gave out perfume, from its inmost fold,
It never exhaled before.

And the blossom slept through the silent night
In the smile of the angel ray;
But the morn arose, with its gairish light,
And the soft one stole away.

Then the zephyr wooed, as he wandered by,
Where the gentle flowers grew,
But she gave no heed to his plaintive sigh;
Her heart to its love was true.

And the sunbeam came, with a lover's art,
To caress the flower in vain;
She folded her sweets in her thrilling heart,
Till the starlight came again."

The following stanzas contain poetry and philosophy in melodious measure:

"Cloudlets, with their brows so fair,
In the summer weather,
Wandering through the fields of air,
Meet and blend together.

Moonlight, from its throne above,
In its fond devotion,
Trembles, with a smile of love,
O'er the mighty ocean.

Zephyr ranges summer bowers,
Fearless and unbidden,
Wooing fragrance from the flowers,
Where the dew is hidden.

Then the joy affection brings
  Try no more to smother;
Taught by brightest, fairest things,
  We should love each other."

Over the threshold of Mrs. Bolton's cottage the angel of death has never passed; at the fireside of home all of hers meet; at the family table no seat is vacant; the deep fountains of her heart have never been moved by the swelling tide of bereaved affection; yet, true poet as she is, she has written some of the most touching elegies in the English language. The following lines on the death of William Quarles, one of the most generous and noble men that ever trod the soil of Indiana, are, both in expression and in measure, surpassingly beautiful:

"Mournfully, mournfully toll for the dead:
He passed from our side in his manhood's pride,
  Ere the glow of his rainbow hopes had fled;
When his sky was bright with meridian light,
Death bore him away to a dreamless night;
  Mournfully toll for the dead.

Silently, silently let him sleep on:
From the hurry and strife of the battle of life
  A victor away to his home has gone;
Gone, gone from the tears, from the sorrows and fears,
That come to the heart on the tide of years:
  Silently let him sleep on.

Hopefully, hopefully lay him to rest,
Where the dew-bright flowers, in the long still hours,
  Will weep o'er the sod on his pulseless breast;
Where the breeze will sigh, as it wanders by;
Where the starlight comes from its home on high;
  Hopefully lay him to rest.

Solemnly, solemnly bow and adore:
An angel of light, on a pathway bright,
  Conducted his soul to the viewless shore;
His dust from the gloom of the silent tomb,
Shall arise again in immortal bloom:
  Solemnly bow and adore."

From an address to a lady on the death of a darling

daughter I extract the following stanzas—polished and perfect gems:

"She was a radiant star, mother,
That made thy pathway bright,
Till a cloud passed o'er thy summer sky,
And stole away its light.
It stole away the light from thee,
And hid it up on high,
Where the fairy flowers never fade,
And the lovely never die.

This world was far too cold, mother,
For such a heart as hers,
And she left it ere her eyes were dimmed
With sorrow's bitter tears.
And though, around thy quiet hearth,
She comes and sits by thee,
Her form is far too glorious now
For mortal eyes to see.

Upon thine aching heart, mother,
She lays her radiant brow;
But her angel touch is soft and light—
Thou mayest not feel it now.
She sings to thee the dear old songs
Thy lips had taught her here,
But her voice is all too sweet and low
To reach a mortal ear."

The reader will, I trust, excuse me for inserting the following elegy, which has appeared in a western magazine since this article was written:

"IN MEMORY OF EMMA ROSABELLE LARRABEE.

RESPECTFULLY ADDRESSED TO HER PARENTS.

"Pale and silent lies your darling,
In her little snowy shroud,
And ye often weep beside her,
But ye never speak aloud;
For there is a holy quiet,
In the sunshine and the air,
And ye know the white-robed angels
Keep their sleepless vigils there.

Never more will dewy daisies
Feel the pressure of her tread;
Never more will her slight fingers
Cull the berries, ripe and red;

Never more will her sweet laughter,
  And her artless lisping words,
Be mistaken for the warble
  Of the joyous summer birds.

Spring-time flowers have bloomed and perished;
  Summer moons have waxed and waned;
Autumn leaves have faded, fallen,
  Mournful winter winds complained,
Since ye laid the gentle darling,
  That affection could not save,
Very softly, very sadly,
  In the shadow of the grave.

Still your home is very lonesome,
  In the long bright autumn days,
When the sun sets, blushing crimson,
  Through the Indian summer haze.
And when dismal rains are falling,
  As the wint'ry nights come on,
O how fondly memory whispers
  Of the lovely cherub gone!

And ye often stop to listen
  For her footstep on the floor,
And ye see her shadow passing
  In the sunshine by the door.
And ye lead her through the meadow,
  By the coppice and the stream;
O sweet phantasies—ye awaken
  But to find it all a dream.

Where the gentle starlight watches,
  Through the balmy summer eves;
Where the violets, in their dreaming,
  Listen to their whispering leaves,
In the dim, old, solemn forest,
  Where the night-dews softly weep,
And the low-voiced winds keep sighing,
  Ye have laid her down to sleep.

Yet, while other little children
  Gather pebbles by the rills,
Laughing, dancing in the sunshine,
  And the shadow of the hills;
While they chased the fairy hum-bird,
  Or admired a meteor star,
Little Emma has been singing,
  Where the blessed angels are.

Would your longing love recall her,
  To this world of care and strife?
From the golden streets of heaven,
  To the paths of human life?
No, be thankful that our Father
  Took her to the glorious goal,
Ere a grief had dimmed her spirit,
  Ere a sin had stained her soul."

Mrs. Bolton's power of description is very great. The following picture of the battle of Monterey is hardly inferior to Byron's masterly description of the battle of Waterloo:

"O, there were trembling hearts, and sighs,
  And shrieks of deep despair;
All bloodless cheeks and tearful eyes,
  And wild confusion there,
When first the cannon tolled death's knell
  Upon the troubled air.

On, on they came, the free and brave;
  I saw their ranks advance,
Their starry banners proudly wave,
  The war-steeds gayly prance,
And all along the solid lines
  The unsheathed weapons glance.

There was a sound that seemed to rend
  The strong old earth in twain,
And then the battle smoke did bend
  Its wings above the plain,
As though it strove to hide from heaven
  The gory, ghastly slain.

Among the wounded and the dead,
  Along the crimson street,
I heard the soldier's measured tread,
  The sound of flying feet,
And words of bitter parting said
  By friends no more to meet."

The description of "A Gallop on the Grand Prairie" makes us feel, from its peculiar measure, as if we were really bounding away over the plain:

"Away, away, on our coursers fleet,
Where the grass is green, the air is sweet,
Where the earth and sky like lovers meet,
          On the Grand Prairie.

Now we are leaving the forest-trees,
Flying along like the fairy breeze,
Midst budding flowers and humming bees,
On the Grand Prairie.

On, on we speed; there is naught in sight,
But the bending sky so blue and bright,
And the glowing, sparkling sheen of light,
On the Grand Prairie.

The oppressor's tread may never stain
The glorious soil of this lovely plain,
For Liberty holds her court and reign
On the Grand Prairie."

The following stanzas afford another example of measure peculiarly appropriate to the sense. Indeed, the poetry of Mrs. Bolton generally is remarkable for well-constructed measure:

"Genius is a mighty fountain,
Gushing from a cloud-capt mountain;
Talent is a pleasant rill,
Winding round a sunny hill.

Genius is forever pouring,
Rushing, foaming, seething, roaring;
Talent sings a pleasant lay,
As it glides along its way.

Genius from its wild endeavor,
Stoppeth, resteth, never, never;
Talent loiters oft to play
With the rainbow on its spray."

I can not withhold from the reader the following inimitable lines, which express so truly, so beautifully, and in so sweet numbers, the pleasures of the ideal:

"Oft when the world is cold and dark, in seeming,
When friends I loved too well have changed or flown,
I wander far away in spirit, dreaming
Of light and beauty in a world my own.

In that transcendent realm, my soul's elysian,
I hide me from misfortune's simoon blast,
And realize hope's fondest, fairest vision,
And live and move amid the shadowy past.

I see again, in those bewitching trances,
The brightest, dearest scenes of other years;
And revel, in wild dreams and glowing fancies,
Till I forget life's cares, and toils, and tears.

There are the pictured forms of loved ones sleeping;
There are the eyes that once spoke love to mine;
And there is faithful Memory, fondly keeping
Her vigil o'er the treasures in her shrine.

The song of birds in dim old forest bowers,
The murmur of the stream where first I roved,
The music of the breeze, the breath of flowers,
Memory hath hoarded all that childhood loved.

The latest ray of loveliness, that lingers
Around my devious pathway, may depart;
But O, forbid that Time's effacing fingers
Should mar the sacred record on my heart!

When somber clouds along my life-sky darken,
When in the future not a star appears,
Still let me love the past--still let me hearken
To the sweet melodies of other years."

Mrs. Bolton is a philanthropist—a philanthropist of high and holy aspirations. In her poems are exhibited the yearnings of a spirit thrilling with sensibility to human suffering, and a soul overflowing with the love of humanity. In illustration of her devotion to the cause of active benevolence, we would be glad to quote the whole of her poem, "Awake to Effort," but we must content ourselves with two stanzas:

"Awake to effort while the day is shining;
The time to labor will not always last,
And no regrets, repentance, nor repining
Can bring to us again the buried past.
The silent sands of life are falling fast;
Time tells our busy pulses, one by one;
And shall our work, so needful and so vast,
Be all completed, or but just begun,
When twilight shadows vail life's dim, departing sun?

The smallest bark, on life's tumultuous ocean,
Will leave a track behind for evermore;
The lightest wave of influence, set in motion,
Extends and widens to the eternal shore.
We should be wary, then, who go before
A myriad yet to be, and we should take
Our bearing carefully, where breakers roar,
And fearful tempests gather; one mistake
May wreck unnumbered barks that follow in our wake."

The inequalities in human condition, the wrongs in the present organization of society, and the contrast between the noble and the peasant, are thrillingly described in the following poem. Let the reader also notice the perfection and beauty of the measure:

"TWO SCENES.

SCENE IN A PALACE.

"Over the moorland the wind shrieketh drearily—
Ice-jewels glitter on heather and thorn—
Pale is the sunlight that flashes out fitfully,
Over a dome where an infant is born.

Fold silken robes round the little one carefully;
Lay him to rest on his pillow of down;
Watch o'er the sleep of that scion of royalty,
Born to inherit a scepter and crown.

Shut out the light, that the room may be shadowy;
Fold silken curtains around the proud bed;
Ladies in waiting step softly and silently;
Let not a word in a whisper be said.

Joy in the palaces lighted so brilliantly,
Beauty and bravery are reveling there;
Wine in the jewel-wrought goblet foams daintily—
All things proclaim that the king has an heir.

Joy in the villages—church bells ring merrily—
Rockets are lighting the sky with their glare—
Bonfires are crackling, cannons are thundering,
Children are shouting, long life to the heir.

Downtrodden millions, go join in the revelry—
Go, in despite of fetters you wear—
Vassals and beggars, and paupers, right joyfully
Flutter your tatters, the throne has an heir.

SCENE IN A HOVEL.

Over the moorland the wild wind wails mournfully—
Ice-jewels glitter on heather and thorn—
Pale is the sunlight that trembles out fitfully,
Over a hut where an infant is born.

None heeds his wailing, although it sounds pitiful,
None shield his form from the wind, cold and wild;
Heir to privation, scorn, misery, and poverty,
Dark is thy pathway before thee, poor child.

Child, with the spirit to live through eternity,
  Born to the yoke of the tyrant art thou;
Even the bread that is dealt to thee scantily,
  Thrice must be earned by the sweat of thy brow.

Cold is the hovel, the hearth-stone is emberless—
  Creaks the old door as it moves to and fro;
O'er the poor bed, where the mother lies shivering,
  Busily flutters the white-fingered snow.

Pale is the cheek of the plebeian sufferer,
  Passing from poverty's vale to the grave;
Better by far had she died in her infancy,
  Ere to the millions she added a slave.

Yes, she is pale, and her voice sounds huskily,
  Begging in vain for a morsel of bread:
Hush! it is over; her heart slumbers silently;
  Grim famine stands by the pale mother dead."

In the following lines the sickness of heart, the wild despair, the raving insanity, and ineffable agony of the ruined one, are depicted in language and in measure which cause the soul of the reader to thrill with intense emotion:

"Above us the clouds are wild and black,
The winds are howling on our track;
The shivering trees are bare and bleak,
My heart is sick, and my limbs are weak,
  Wandering wearily, wearily.

They turned me away from the rich man's door,
Haggard and hungry, and cold and poor,
There was feasting, laughter, and song within;
But they turned me away, in my tatters thin,
With thee, thou pledge of my shame and sin,
  Away, where the wind sobs drearily.

My heart was cold, and the demons came,
With their livid lips, and their eyes of flame;
They told me to murder thee, child of shame,
  And laughed till my brain whirled dizzily.

They followed my path through the drifted snow,
Taunting, and mocking, and gibbering low,
'There is peace and rest where the cold waves flow,
  Far down o'er the white sand busily.'

I felt their breath on my tortured brain;
They tore my heart, and shrieked in vain;
They whispered, 'Death is the end of pain;

Fly, fly to the grave's security—
The world will turn from the hideous stain
That mars thy womanly purity.'

They bade me remember the bright old time,
My cottage home in a foreign clime,
The friends I lost by my love and crime,
Till smothering my soul's humanity,
I grasped, in the strength of my deep despair,
Thy neck, my babe—it was soft and fair,
But the warm blood curdled and blackened there,
To witness my wild insanity.

How quiet, and rigid, and cold thou art!
I lay my head on thy fainting heart,
And kiss thy lips, with a quivering start!
My hand! God! let me not think of it!
I have seen thee smile, I have felt thy breath:
Can I feel it now? O death, pale death!
Thy Lethean cup, let me drink of it!

We'll make us a bed in the snow so deep;
The frosts with a shroud will cover us;
The winds will lull us to a dreamless sleep,
And the stars, in their far-off homes, will keep
Their beautiful night-watch over us.

* * * * * *

But where is the father of that dead child,
That sleeps where the winds wail mournfully?
He left the woman his love beguiled—
Is the monster loathed, contemned, reviled?
Does the world regard him scornfully?

He is reveling now, where the lamps are bright;
Where the hours go by in festive flight,
And the gleeful song rings merrily;
They wish him joy, on his bridal night,
And warm, young hearts beat cheerily.

The bride is a creature of love and youth;
With an eye of light, and a lip of truth,
And a fair form molded slenderly:
Her heart is a fountain of kindly ruth,
That flows for the suffering tenderly.

O, little she dreams that a wretch defamed,
Deceived, dishonored, betrayed, ashamed,
By the strength of the bridegroom's oath once claimed
The love she is fondly cherishing.

For he is a model of manly grace,
With the sounding name of a noble race;
He has power, and fame, and fair broad land,
And there is no blood on his jeweled hand
  To tell of the lost one perishing.

Where the censers breathe, and the jewels shine,
They pledge him now in the rich red wine;
But never, by token, or word, or sign,
  Allude to his victim's history.
No, fill the cup to the sparkling brim,
With life, and pleasure, and fame for him:
The future is bright, let the past be dim,
  And wrapped in fearful mystery.

In the penal code of this righteous world,
  Justice, I ween, is a rarity;
At the kind, but frail, the lip is curled,
The bitter taunt, the sarcasm hurled,
  With sure, unvarying parity;
But over the monster mean and vile,
Whose heart is a canker, festering guile,
Who kills with the light of his serpent smile,
  We throw the pure mantle of charity.

And many a heart that faints and fails,
And many a beautiful cheek that pales,
And eyes that weep at fictitious tales,
  Of sorrow, and wrong, and misery,
Will turn from the pallid brow that vails
  A deeper and wilder agony."

We do not claim for the poems of Mrs. Bolton, more than for other human things, perfection. The measure is nearly faultless, and the rhyme generally good; but the rhetoric of some lines and some stanzas might be improved. We, however, have no great propensity for fault-finding, especially where there is so much excellence. We could hope that she would collect, correct, and publish in a volume her productions, now scattered through the columns of magazines and newspapers. It is true she may hereafter write more. But we know not how she can write any thing better than are some of the verses which she has committed to leaves, as frail and evanescent as those on which the Cumean Sibyl wrote her prophecies. It is our deliberate conviction, that, of her scattered and fugitive productions, there might be collected a volume, which, for variety of subject, beauty of conception, purity of sentiment, and perfection of measure, would be fully equal to any volume of poems yet published by any American writer.

THE EXCELLENCE OF MIND

"How fleet is a glance of the mind!
Compared with the speed of its flight,
The tempest itself lags behind,
And the swift-winged arrows of light."

SITTING beneath the branches of this forest tree on this lovely evening of early summer, my mind, quicker than the sunbeam now glancing by me, bounds away to my childhood's home, on the Atlantic shore. The old-fashioned mansion, with its hoary timbers, and rudely-carved wainscoting rises before me. The old elms are spreading their venerable branches over me. The pines that cluster on the hill-top are sending forth, on the evening breeze, their plaintive monotone. The lambs, returned with the flock from the pasture, are skipping on the hill-side. And there is the ocean, its surface spotted with white sails, and its wild waves dancing on the beach. Before I may have time to greet one old friend, or shed one tear over the past, the scene disappears, and I bound away over the mountains of the setting sun, and stand on the shores of the western ocean,

"Where rolls the Oregon, and hears no sound,
Save his own dashing."

Before I am aware, I am sailing over the shoreless sea of Jupiter,

"Whose huge, gigantic bulk
Dances in ether like the lightest leaf,"

or standing on the rings of exiled Saturn, or streaming through space with the eccentric comet, or rambling among the gardens of the Pleiades, whose distance geometry fails to estimate. And then again, gentle one, I am with thee, in thy city mansion, or thy prairie cottage, or thy forest cabin, communing with thee on the past, the present, and the future—on the ideal and the actual—on the beautiful, the good, and the true.

Mind regards not time. The past is its own. It goes back to the beginning, "when the morning stars sang together, and the sons of God shouted for joy." With the first-born of earth, it wanders among the groves of Paradise. With the father of the faithful, it communes with the angels of olden time. With the patriarch of Palestine, it goes down into Egypt, and is present at the busy and exciting scenes, when hundred-gated Thebes is pouring out its countless warriors—when the Memnon is reared to greet the morning sun with its tones of music, and when the granite block of gigantic dimensions is moved from the quarry to build the pyramids. With the shepherds of Judea, it hears the song of the angels at the Savior's birth. With the wise men of the east, it follows the star of Bethlehem, and with the disciple whom Jesus loved, it stands by the cross. The future is its own. With its eye I look on ages yet to come—on glorious ages of light, of knowledge, of liberty, and of religion.

Mind regards not physical force; but by its own power controls all created influences. The winds, the waters, and the lightnings are directed by it. The strength of the lion and the flight of the eagle avail not against its power. Look at the war-horse, "whose neck is clothed with thunder. He paweth in the valley, and rejoices in his strength. He mocketh at fear, and is not affrighted, neither turneth he back from the sword. He swalloweth the ground with fierceness and rage. He saith among the trumpets, Ha, ha, and he smelleth the battle afar off, the thunder of the captains and the shoutings;" and yet he submits himself to man, and suffers the little child to mount him. The elephant, whose "bones are like strong pieces of brass or bars of iron, "brings his incomparable strength to the service of man. The sea-monster, whose teeth are terrible round about, who "maketh the deep boil like a pot," and his path in the ocean shine after him, suffers man to "put a hook in his nose, and bore his jaw through with a thorn."

Mind knows no limits to its development. The body, by the law of its nature, may be developed only to a certain extent. It has its youth, and its maturity, and then its decline. But mind knows no old age—no decline. God, in his pleasure, made all things mortal, but mind. The earth herself may grow old and die—the hills and the mountains may melt away—the rivers may cease to flow, and the ocean be dried up—the very elements may melt with fervent heat; but mind is subject to no decay—no death. Through its endless existence, the works of God will furnish it the exhaustless means of knowledge. I know not but this is the design of the vastness and the profusion of the works of God. In our spiritual and immortal state, we may visit in person the distant worlds, now dimly seen by philosophic eye. We may go, with a speed which the sunbeam never attained, to that polar orb, which, perhaps, so strangely to our comprehension, has, from the first time its light fell on our childhood's eye, maintained the same place in the heavens, having never, like other stars, sunk to repose beneath the horizon. There will be time enough in eternity to visit all the bright worlds that have been circling the celestial vault above us, till they have become familiar to our mortal eye. And then there will be time enough left to visit those far beyond the reach of mortal eye or philosophic glass. And no matter where the spirit may go, it will find a home every-where. The innumerable multitudes of worlds in the universe are but mansions in our heavenly Father's house.

Mind never loses what it may have once acquired. Impressions once stamped on it become indelible. Ideas once acquired become, from the very constitution of mind, immortal as mind itself. There may seem to be, sometimes, oblivion of the past. But it is temporary, not permanent. There is no lethean stream, of which we may drink and forget. There may seem to be loss of knowledge once acquired. But the loss is only apparent, not real. There is a power in mind by which it may call back every wandering idea, and renew every fading picture, and revive in all their freshness and vigor all past feelings and emotions. I have somewhere read a beautiful story of the magician's mirror. Whoever looked on that mirror's polished surface saw again all he had ever seen—his early home—his childhood's play-ground—the hills, the valleys, and the streams of his native land—the friends of former years—friends long since dead, and buried, and forgotten. In that mirror, as the story goes, the Wandering Jew, who has, as the legend tells us, been wandering over earth for eighteen centuries, and who is doomed still to wander till the Savior comes again, desired to look. The magician held it before him. The wanderer saw on its magic surface all the incidents of his life in the long centuries past, and far behind all a lovely landscape reposing in quiet beauty beneath the sunny skies of Palestine. There appeared a vale shaded by trees and watered by running brooks. A flock was feeding on the green grass, and beneath a palm-tree's shade was sleeping a child of surpassing beauty and loveliness. In that landscape the wanderer recognized his own home of centuries ago—in that flock the sheep that had fed in that quiet vale under his care—in that child his own beloved daughter, his sweet little Marian, the idol of his heart.

There is such a mirror in the human soul. It needs no magician's wand to bring forth its power. The images it presents may sometimes be faint and shadowy. Present objects flitting before it may obscure our view of the past. Our position may not always be such as to present the image distinct. But the mirror is always there, and occasions will come when the bright and beautiful forms of the past will flit before us. Let the vail of mortality be taken from our eyes—let the busy forms of present objects take their places among the images of the past—let us look with undimmed and immortal eye on that mirror of the soul, and we shall see the bright and undying images of all our past experience.

Tell me not of the dignity which depends on wealth, or station, or pomp, or circumstance. The world can not confer true dignity. It belongs not to externals. It belongs only to mind. Tell me not of the diadem of royalty, sparkling with gems and with gold. The bright scintillations of human intelligence eclipse the most dazzling of earth's productions. Mind alone is precious. Let no mention be made of coral, or of pearl, or of rubies, or of diamonds. Tell me not of earth's treasures. Mountains of solid gold and oceans of melted silver are naught compared with mind.

THE SACRED ASSOCIATIONS OF PALESTINE.

In reading Lynch's "Expedition to the Jordan and the Dead Sea," I have been forcibly impressed with the unsatisfactory results of all attempts to identify the places of sacred associations in Palestine. Some few, and only a few places, may be identified. The Dead Sea, the Sea of Galilee, and the river Jordan of modern geography are doubtless the same as those bearing the same name in ancient times. The modern city of Jerusalem unquestionably stands on the ruins of the ancient city. The general features of the country, the mountains, the plains, the valleys, and the larger rivers are still there, as in the days of Abraham, of Solomon, and of Jesus. But the outlines only and the profile of the country retain resemblance of the ancient land of Palestine. The filling up of the landscape has wholly changed. The lights and shades of the picture have commingled and changed places, till probably no Jew of the times of Solomon, or even of John the Baptist, should he, with the full exercise of his memory and all his intelligence, return to earth, could possibly identify any place, however familiar it might once have been to him. Nor is there any thing miraculous in the changes which have come over the physical appearance of the country. Precisely such changes do physical agencies always produce on hills and valleys subjected to the circumstances which are known to exist in Syria. The country is a region of numerous hills and narrow valleys. The hills, like all hills in countries of primitive geological formation, are mostly of rock thrown up by volcanic influence. In ancient times these rocky sides and summits were covered with soil, which supported a heavy growth of vegetation. Gradually the forests disappeared by means of the ax and of raging fires, which often sweep with terrific fury over mountain regions. Whenever the roots of the trees on the summits and the sides of the mountains decay, the soil is easily washed away by the rains, till there is nothing left but solid and naked rock. You may see this tendency of denudation on the summits and sides of any mountain range in America. Thus by mere natural causes the hills of Palestine, which were once covered with groves on their summits, and with gardens and pastures on their sides, have been reduced to mere naked, barren rocks. Their appearance, therefore, has wholly changed. The landmarks which distinguished one hill from another have become wholly obliterated.

The destruction of the forests and the denudation of the mountains has, by exposing so much surface of rock to the sun, so increased the evaporation as to dry up the streams, which irrigated and rendered fertile the valleys. Sterility, therefore, in the land of Judea has taken the place of fruitfulness from causes sufficient to produce the same result in any country. Instead, therefore, of being, as once it was, a land flowing with milk and honey, it has become a land burnt, dry, and sterile, exhibiting scarcely more resemblance to its former self than does the grim and ghastly skeleton to the being of beauty and of life which was once associated with it.

And what matters it, though we may not see, in the present decayed and ruined region, even the lineaments of that fair land in which dwelt the patriarchs, and the prophets, and the Savior? What matters it that the manger, in which the Virgin mother laid the infant Jesus to rest, is no longer distinguishable among the thousand others in Bethlehem? What though no man living may designate the field in which the shepherds were watching their flocks, on that auspicious night in which the angels, with heavenly music, gave them a serenade? What though the landmarks of the garden of Gethsemane be wholly obliterated, and even the tragic hill of Calvary be undistinguishable among the mountains that are "round about Jerusalem?" What though even the place of the holy sepulcher, for whose empty possession the powers of Europe and Asia contended so long and so bravely, can not be certainly identified?

For me it is enough to know, that the Son of God took on himself the nature of man, that he died for the world, and that, rising again in triumph from the grave, and ascending on high, he ever liveth to make intercession for sinners.

I would not much care to travel in Syria. I would not like to have tarnished by contact with the present the conceptual pictures of the past, painted, on the ever-enduring tablet of my soul, by the living pencil of divine inspiration. I would not have disappear, in the blazing radiance of a Syrian sun, the shadowy twilight that floats in my eye over the mountains and the vales of Palestine. I would not have broken the spell nor dissolved the charm which youthful fancy threw around the ideal of that fair land. Let there remain, undisfigured by random touches from the coarse and common pencil of modern observation, the pristine picture, drawn by imagination, of Zion's hill, of the vale of Sharon, and of

> "Siloa's brook, that flowed
> Fast by the oracle of God."

How vain is the hope of man in attempting to restore the past! The Jew yet lingers about the land of his fathers, expecting a day of restoration will yet come. But not to him nor to it will ever return the glory of the ancient times. His father-land is irretrievably desolate and utterly hopeless. Of it nothing remains but the skeleton. All that gave it beauty and life is gone, forever gone.

In the physical and the moral economy of the universe each organization of matter and each act of mind has its part to perform, and then they each return through dissolution to their original elements. Syria was the cradle of the human race. To the civilized world that country is now of as little use as would be the infant's cradle to the full-grown man. The Jews were once the chosen people of God—chosen and set apart for a specific purpose. The purpose being answered, they are no longer needed in the economy of grace. And vain are all their hopes of future power for themselves, or renown for their primeval country.

THE SEASONS.

How full of variety, full of instruction is the changing year! Each season has its own distinctive characteristics, and furnishes us its peculiar moral. Spring has its beauties, summer its glories; but autumn, with its fruits, and winter, with its reign of snows and storms, suggest to the thoughtful moral reflections of grave import. Interesting as appears Nature in her delicate robe of spring, or in her brilliant and flowery costume of summer, yet to most observers she seems still more beautiful in her autumnal shroud. Tinged with colors foreign to their healthy and primeval nature, the leaves, though beautiful still, all betoken decay. Indeed, to the elements of decay they seem to owe the extraordinary beauty of their colors. And it would seem a general rule in nature, that the process of dissolution should develop beauties unseen and loveliness unappreciated during the period of vigor and of growth. Who has not been deeply impressed with the surprising exhibition of strange beauty in the face of the dying and the dead? While looking on the features of the departed, often far more lovely than in life, we can not believe that death has really done its work; we suspect there must be some deception in appearances; we fancy the living spirit must yet animate the beautiful form; we look with anxious expectation for the eyes again to open, for the lips to move, and for the sleeper to arise; we listen for the sweet sound of the voice to fall again, with its familiar tones, on our ear, and for the light footstep to echo again along the hall; but these appearances are only the natural and legitimate results of death. They are only indications of the first stages of decay. The golden-tinted leaf of autumn, though wondrously beautiful, can never again resume the freshness and life of spring, nor may the unearthly loveliness of the youthful dead ever again give place to the bright and rosy hue of health.

Winter is the season of rest. Winter as well as night is essential to the development of living forms. Nor man, nor animals, nor vegetables could well attain physical perfection were there no night, no interception of sunlight, no diurnal season of rest. Winter seems less essential than night, yet its influence for good in the economy of nature is marked and efficient. Though in a tropical zone vegetation may luxuriantly thrive, yet the demand for periods of rest, so conveniently furnished in temperate zones by winter, is clearly observed in the habits of every species of plant. The evergreen of the north and of the south equally sheds once a year its old leaves. The principal difference between an evergreen and a deciduous tree is found in the fact, that the evergreen, whether northern or tropical, retains its old foliage till it has manufactured and put on its new dress, while the deciduous lays aside its garments, and retires for its winter rest, and in spring arises and dresses itself in new robes.

During the resting period of winter the vegetable creation is accumulating resources, and acquiring energy for its summer progress; the buds and sap are maturing. When the allotted period of rest shall have passed, and the returning influences of spring shall have penetrated the abode of vegetable life, and awakened the spirit from its sleep, and broken the spell which winter's magic wand had thrown over it, then shall we see the whole vegetable world rushing forward with renewed speed on its career of progressive development. There is a winter in the affairs of men. Periods of doubt, of darkness, of discouragement, of disappointment, and of ill success, are often only the natural recurrence of the wintery season, which may prove essential to our success. There often occurs a *winter* season in the history of reform and benevolence. During this season of wintery weather, amidst the blasts and storms, ephemeral enterprises die. But those enterprises founded on the principles of true charity, of pure benevolence, of Christian duty, and demanded by the nature of man, though they may suffer a temporary cessation of visible progress, or even an apparent reverse, will most surely elaborate and mature during the wintery season the elements of success and triumph. The seed of reform, of virtue, of Christian enterprise is endued with immortal life. Long may it be buried in the ground, or covered with rubbish, yet it never loses its vitality. In the revolutions of time it will yet come to the air and the light, when it will thrust deep in the ground its roots, and protrude through the rubbish its stock. You may trample down the plant, but it,

"Crushed to earth, will rise again."

On it may beat the pelting storm, but its power of endurance will prove exhaustless. It may be swayed to and fro by the rude blast of the furious winds, but it will again recover itself, and even acquire firmness in the struggle. The heaving frost may penetrate about its foundations, and attempt to throw it out of its place of lodgment, but its roots strike too deep to be reached during the temperate winter of indifference or the Arctic winter of persecution.

There are periods of winter in human history—periods during which, to superficial observers, the progress of humanity seems retrograde. Such a period was what is usually called the dark ages. Dark those ages may seem to us, but only because we usually look on the wrong side of them. Dark seems sometimes the moon to us; but while to us, who look on one side, she appears dark, to other beings, who look on the other side, she seems bright and fair. Dark seems the cloud to us, when we look only on its earthward side; but to those on the mountain summit it may appear lighted up in gorgeous reflections.

The dark ages were to human progress what winter is to vegetable development. It was the period of rest, of accumulation of resources, of elaboration of instrumentalities. It was the season of preparation of mightier, of better directed, and of more successful effort than humanity had ever made. To that winter there succeeded a glorious spring, followed by a gorgeous summer, in whose light we of the present age, with appliances and privileges peculiar only to ourselves, are most luxuriously basking.

THE REINTERMENT OF HOWARD.

FROM the climes of the south, where waves the flag of the lone star, they have brought back to his home all that to earth remains of Howard, the great, the good, the beloved Howard, the nation's representative, Indiana's favorite son. Not as he went forth from among us comes he back to us. He went from among us, one of whom nature might be proud; of form tall and manly; of eye beaming with philanthropy, and sparkling with the scintillations of mind; and of voice of surpassing eloquence. He comes back—alas, how changed! Prostrate is the form; dimmed, forever dimmed, is the eye. Over it have passed the films of death, nor may we tear them thence. Silent, forever silent, is the voice once so powerful to move the people. Never again shall its deep and musical tones delight the listening multitude, nor answer the call of trusting childhood. Pulseless is the heart once so respondent to human sympathy. Indiana loved him when living, and she honors him when dead. Yet is he not conscious of the respect she shows him, nor does he listen to the lament she makes over him. Deep are his slumbers, unbroken by her voice of praise or regret. As the escort has moved along through her cities and her villages, and over her beautiful plains, her noble sons have come forth to honor him, and her fair daughters have shed over him many a bitter tear; yet he slumbers still. Her pealing bells have sent forth on the still air their sad tones; music has breathed her plaintive notes; the long procession has been formed, and the eulogy pronounced; yet still he wakes not. Over many a hill and dale familiar to him in former years, across many a verdant intervale and rapid stream, whose native beauties he was wont to admire, they have borne him to his own village, to his neighbors and friends, to his own home, to the wife of his bosom, and the children of his heart; yet still he sleeps on.

Long has Indiana mourned him. From her prairies and her woodlands, and along her meandering streams, the wail of woe has gone up for him. From her village mansions and her frontier cabins the notes of sadness have come forth for him.

> "Her spirit yearns to bring
> Her lost one back—yearns with desire intense,
> And struggles hard to wring
> The bolts apart, and pluck the captive thence."

But in vain. Death yields its victims back,

> "Not to the streaming eye, nor to the broken heart."

There is no Orphean lyre, at whose sounds the unyielding powers of dissolution cease their work. There is no Promethean fire, by which to kindle up again the light that once beamed from that brilliant eye. There is no magic wand which may break the spell that death throws over all who enter its dark domain.

* * * * * * * *

Providence seems occasionally to send on earth beings highly gifted with lofty aspirations after something nobler and holier than can be found in the present condition of humanity. They are men of deep, generous sympathies, of lenient views of human errors and frailties, and of universal philanthropy. Such a man was Howard; he had faith in man—unfaltering faith in the human race. He believed in progress, in movement, in the development of human nature. He belonged to that school of philosophic philanthropists who believe and teach that man is capable of much more enlarged civil and religious freedom than he has ever yet enjoyed; that the race is endowed with a perfectible nature, and is from age to age advancing in civilization and virtue. He had traced the history of civilization from its origin in the east, through classic Greece and iron-hearted Rome, down along the course of modern empire, till in our own land human liberty seems reaching its highest condition of perfection. In all history he saw evidence of progress—of the advancement of humanity in virtue and in happiness. In the darkest times he never despaired, nor lost his faith in man, nor his trust in Providence.

He looked forward to a more glorious day of light, of knowledge, of liberty, and of virtue. He saw a day when the hand of tyranny shall be palsied, and the arm of oppression broken; when ignorance shall disappear before the onward march of universal education; when human liberty shall exist in its most perfect state; when the human race, regenerated, emancipated, and disinthralled, shall arise in its majesty and its glory, and go forth in its career of universal improvement.

Happy is he who, with high and noble views of human philosophy, has the power of eloquence to move the people in favor of his principles. Few men in the west, few in the east, few any where, have so many elements of eloquence as had Howard. His personal appearance was dignified and commanding. He stood among us as did Saul, the son of Kish, among the people of Palestine. His tall and elegant figure, his keen black eye, his large and well-formed features, the general expression of his countenance, lighted up with benevolence and hope, yet slightly shaded by a tinge of sad and serious thought, commanded at once, whenever he arose to speak, silence and attention. His voice was powerfully effective. Its deep, full, distinct, and solemn tones fell pleasant on the ear and melodious on the heart. His style was always chaste, generally beautiful, and often sublime. He assumed in his arguments no false positions, dealt in no sophistry, nor availed himself of any popular prejudice. He made no attempt to speak for mere effect, nor ever fell into the errors of most popular orators, using a style bordering on coarseness, and sometimes on profanity, but he spoke at our common public gatherings, in the court-house and in the woods, as if he had been addressing the polished Athenians in the time of Pericles, or the dignified Roman senate in the time of Cicero, or the British house of peers, in company with Burke, and Pitt, and Fox.

I have never known any man, of any party or profession, so deeply and universally loved, as was Howard. The utmost bitterness of party strife could not neutralize the warm affection entertained personally for him. And this great personal popularity was founded not merely on his eloquence, but on his elevated and pure character as a man. He was entirely above and beyond all suspicion of unfairness and political intrigue. He breathed a pure and holy atmosphere, uncontaminated by the breath of dishonor or distrust.

Howard was a Christian—theoretically and practically a Christian. He had faith in God, faith in Christ, as well as faith in humanity. A holy influence of deep personal piety was shed all around him. Vice, whatever form it might assume, stood ever sternly rebuked in his presence. With the mildness and gentleness of spirit for which he was so distinguished, was united an uncompromising disapproval of every thing mean, profane, or immoral—a disapproval which failed not to make itself felt and respected in whatever company there might be occasion for it.

His faith in Christ failed him not in the hour of death. As the beautiful visions of earth faded from his material eyes, the glorious scenes of heaven seemed opening on the eye of the soul. He died, as the Christian would die, in the triumph of faith, and in the unfading hope of a glorious immortality. In the prime of life, in the utmost vigor of manhood, with his splendid mind not yet expanded to its full capacity, the shadows of death came over him. Far away from his home, from his wife, his children, and his friends, before he had scarcely entered on the work of the mission for which his country had sent him, he suddenly sickened and died.

For him we must weep. It is right we should. It is the dictate of nature—of the nature God has given us. The wife weeps for her princely husband; the children weep for their honored father; Indiana weeps over the untimely bier of her honored son.

* * * * * * * *

Take him, and bury him among you. Bury him where the primrose and the violet bloom in vernal beauty, where the rose of summer sheds its fragrance, and where the leaves of autumn fall to protect the spot from the cheerless blast of the wintery winds. Bury him in that rural bower on the hill-side, within sight of his quiet cottage home. Bury him by the side of the "pretty child he loved so well," the beauteous little girl who years ago died suddenly, when the father was away from home. Bury him now by her, that child and father may sleep side by side. Ye need erect no costly monument, with labored inscription, over his grave. On a plain stone inscribe the name of *Howard*, of *Indiana's Howard*, and it shall be enough.

AUTUMN.

Summer is gone, and Autumn is throwing her sober drapery over nature. The early frost has touched the maple with its crimson pencil. The leaves of the beech look brown. The locust-leaves are falling along the foot-path. The ripe and mellow apple is dropping from its parent branch, and the ripened corn hangs earthward from its stock. The summer flowers are all gone. On the hill, and in the valley, I find nothing of bloom, but the bright golden rod, and the purple aster. I miss the flowers that all summer have bloomed along my path, and shed their fragrance about my solitary study. I miss the summer birds, that built their nests among the trees of Rosabower, and sang to me morning, noon, and evening, in gentle and plaintive tones, chiming in harmony with my own emotions. The birds that passed along in spring, and tarried with us a day, are come back again. The very same little sparrow, that sung for a day on the cedar bush by my side, seems to have returned again on her southern migration. She has been north, perhaps, to build her nest in the evergreen bower endeared to my heart by the recollections of childhood. Poor bird! she is alone, and the tones of her song seem unusually plaintive. Bring you tidings, sweet bird, from my native bower? Flows the brook by as cheerful, bloom the flowers as beautiful, shines the sun as mild, and are the firs as green, as in the joyous and halcyon days of yore? Hast thou sung a requiem over the grave of some dear friend of mine—the friend of early days—the ever-true, and reliable, and unchanging friend—the same in age as in youth, the same in adversity as in prosperity, the same absent as present? Is thy subdued and plaintive note, so congenial to my heart, designed to betoken bereavement? Leave me not yet, little bird. I will harm you not. Sing to me awhile, then go your way, trusting in Providence. When again you go to the north, to spend the summer, sing for me one song from the pine, that, years ago, I planted over the grave of the gentle-spirited and affectionate one, who led me by the hand in tottering childhood, and, by her counsel, protected my youthful heart from vicious influences. Pass on now, little bird, pass on to a milder clime; and may He, without whose notice no "sparrow falls," protect thee from harm!

Sad are the remembrances which this autumn brings to many a heart. The summer has been beautiful, gorgeously beautiful; the skies have been clear, the atmosphere temperate, and the fields green; but sickness has fallen, like a blight, over all the west, and death has swept many thousands to the grave. Strange is it that the fairest climes should be the most fatal to human life, and the most bland breezes the most deadly. Who would expect sickness and death to be floating on the mild and gentle zephyr that breathes so softly over the fair landscapes of the west? Yet the wail of woe has gone up from many a home, as one after another of the household has fallen a victim to the insidious destroyer.

Autumn reminds us of the changes which time has wrought on objects of the dearest interest to our hearts. What is the lesson which the incessant changes of earth are designed to teach us? Is it the design of Providence to attract our affections away from earth to heaven? It may be so. How hard it is to cease to love, even after the object of love is removed forever away! Alas! who that has felt can describe the power of human affection? In the buoyancy of youth, while the heart is versatile, and new objects of interest are ever presenting themselves, we feel but slightly the effects of earth's changes. Bereavement, if it fall upon us, seldom affects us so deeply as in maturer life. But, when gray hairs creep over our temples, and the renewing powers of life and of the affections grow less active, we feel more keenly and more permanently the pain of sundering the ties that bind the heart to the objects of love. And it seems strange, too, that in mature life the memory of objects of endearment, that lived and died long ago, returns to us with saddening vividness. It is not true that time heals the wounds that sorrow makes in the heart; at least, it is not true of all. The memory of the loved and the lost will rush upon us in spite of all the guards we throw around us. Pictures of beings animate and inanimate will revive, even after we suppose time must have effaced every lineament, and dimmed every color. There gathers around us, at last, an oppressive accumulation of sad remembrances. The old apple-tree on the hill-side, beneath whose fruitful branches, in childhood, we played, now decayed and removed; the grand old elm before the door, now fallen by the ax of some vandal clown; the pine, transplanted by our own hands from the woods to the garden, now branchless and prostrate; the evergreen bower, where, in childhood, we kneeled before God in solitary devotion, now swept over by fire, or occupied by a cornfield; the house—our home in infancy—now torn down, and every vestige removed; the little brook, that meandered in wild beauty through the vale, now dammed and arrested, and forced to carry a noisy mill; these all return to the chambers of memory, and utter in the ear of the soul sad and mournful tones. There are other objects of early attachment, whose memory sometimes returns in age—the pet-lamb; the playful kitten, the faithful dog, and the gentle horse.

But with a deeper thrill, and more overwhelming power, comes back the memory of the protectors, companions, and friends of the past. Say you, who were left motherless in early life, does the memory of the mother fade away from your soul? Loved one, have you forgotten the little brother and the little sister, who passed, long ago as you can remember, to the spirit-land? Childless one, will you, can you ever forget, or cease to regret, the beauteous beings that once clustered about your fireside, but now lie side by side in the church-yard? The heart that is a heart, and not a stone, or a lump of metallic coin, can never forget the objects of affection. In the busy whirl of life our conceptions of the past may be invisible, even to ourselves; but there are occasions on which they will stand out bright and vivid, covering with their well-marked forms and proportions all the tablet of the soul.

It can not be the design of Providence that we should forget objects once dear to us. Had such been his design, he surely would have given us a constitution of moral nature in accordance therewith. Some good is surely intended by this constitution of undying love for even the inanimate objects of nature, and still more for the sensitive beings ever crossing our pathway along the journey of life. Even the sadness and melancholy that sometimes throw their deep and motionless shadows over the soul of the sensitive, are not without their benign influences. By the sorrows of life the mind is mellowed, and the soul refined, and rendered more impressible by religious influences.

THE MEMORY OF AN EARLY FRIEND.

Among my correspondents of olden time, was a lady, whose last letter was written twenty years ago this very day. I first became acquainted with her while I was teaching a small school in the interior of New England. I well remember the day I first passed her dwelling. A funeral procession was forming at the door, and there was borne over the threshold a little child, arrayed in its beauty and loveliness for the grave. I was but a youth—a mere boy, among strangers, friendless and alone—trying to acquire, by teaching school, the means of paying my own expenses for a few weeks at the academy. The lady, the mother of the lost child, a few days after my arrival, invited me to her house. Of course, I went; for I felt greatly the need of sympathy and kindness. Indeed, few know how much the young man, especially the student, away from home, pines for a mother's affection and a sister's love. I found her surrounded by wealth and friends, and a large family of lovely children. On entering her house, I was received with a welcome so hearty as to make me feel at once perfectly at home, and to win my most implicit confidence. I felt that I was captivated; for such a woman could wield over me an influence irresistible. And how judiciously did she use that influence! She became to me all that a mother could be. She was a woman of much intelligence, of excellent taste, of generous sympathies, of philanthropic liberality, and of deep religious feeling. After my engagement at school-keeping was out, and I returned to my studies, she became my weekly correspondent. Her letters would form a good-sized volume, and are worthy of being read, and reread again and again. From no means, in the whole course of my intellectual, moral, and religious training, did I receive more aid than from her letters.

For some two years was this correspondence regularly kept up; and I had, also, an opportunity, during vacation, of spending, once or twice a year, a day or two in the family. During one of my visits—it was twenty summers ago—I saw on the cheek of my gentle one, whom I had learned to look on as a guardian angel, unmistakable indications of the approach of the destroyer of the beauty and the bloom of New England—consumption. She seemed unconscious of danger, nor were her family at all apprehensive of any thing in her condition of health requiring attention. She had taken cold, and was troubled with a slight cough. But I had learned to watch the approach of that pale specter, that had already summoned away from my side many a loved one.

A few weeks were sufficient to develop the disease in its most fatal form; that form, under which the patient, without pain and in cheerful spirits, gradually, but surely, descends to the grave. She soon saw the inevitable result, and calmly, as the child would repose in its cradle, she resigned herself to death. To us, in health, how strange seems the composure with which the Christian goes to the grave! To die—to leave this beautiful world—to go from our home to return no more—to leave our children and all on earth we love—who, in health, can think of this with composure? But God, in mercy to the human race, sends on us disease, whose great design seems to be to reconcile us to death. The afflictions of earth become thus blessings. This good woman looked on her journey to the spirit-world, with as much composure as she would on the journey of a day to visit some friend. She only felt interested to provide for the education of her children. In my last interview with her she expressed a hope, which she said she had long indulged, that, when I had finished my studies in college, my circumstances in life might admit of my superintending the education of her children, the eldest of whom was then but about sixteen.

Thus died, when scarce her youth had passed away, one of the loveliest beings I ever saw. We buried her, in a spot selected by herself, beneath a vigorous old apple-tree, in the orchard. Two of her younger children soon followed her, and the others came to maturity.

Many years after her death—perhaps twelve or more—I stood again, on a fine autumn evening, beside her grave. It was one of those seasons peculiarly fruitful in reflections. The landscape about me was one on which I would gladly look again. I stood on a lofty green hill, covered with orchard and meadow, and flocks and herds. On the north was the grand range of White Mountains; on the south lay, spread out in the far distance, the broad and ever green plains of Brunswick; on the east appeared, just in the horizon, the blue hills of the Kennebec, among which lay, embowered, my own cottage home, in which my children were then at play. And I was standing by the grave of one who had been my friend, when friends I needed, and who had been sleeping there for twelve years. But to me it was a consolation, which I can never describe, that, during that twelve years, each and all of her children had found, in succession, a home in my family, while pursuing their studies at school. My heart still beats quick at the memory of that estimable woman. Connected with her by no ties of family or kindred, my heart was won by kindness, by goodness, by virtue. I looked on her, while living, as an exemplification and a personification of goodness, of virtue, and of religion. Her own children knew her not as did I; for they were too young to appreciate her worth, or estimate their own loss. And when she was gone from earth, I still continued to think of her as some guardian angel, commissioned by Providence to watch over me for good. And now, eight years more have passed away, and in that time her honored husband has been laid to sleep by her side, and my early friends have fallen all around me,

"Like leaves in wint'ry weather;"

yet still her memory is cherished in my heart, as if it were but yesterday I had left her at her own fireside. Her children are scattered far from each other, and from me. Her daughters are well educated, pious, happily settled in life, and some of them occupy important positions. From one of them, who is said greatly to resemble her mother, I have lately received a letter, from which I am inclined to present the reader the following extract:

"Years, long years have passed away, since last we met. Yet, of those years, not a day has passed, when I have not thought of you, the friend and teacher of my childhood, the dear friend and correspondent of my sainted mother, and father, kind and honored, who both now sleep their last sleep, quietly side by side, in that cherished inclosure, a few yards from the place where I am now writing, at that same, dear old homestead, once so precious by their presence, now so lonely, so desolate. I can not describe the tender associations connected with the memory of your name. Do come and see us. Come, and make old friends so glad. You will find change—change stamped on all around; but the deep affection of the heart is, I trust, yet fresh and green as ever."

"All changed but the deep affection of the heart!" Alas, it is even so! And I have sometimes thought even human love, in its purest form, might change; but perhaps not. Affection, founded on goodness, on gratitude, and on congeniality of spirit, may survive all the changes of time; but will it survive the changes from time to eternity? Does that good woman, whose memory has brought on my soul such sweet influences every day for twenty years, yet regard, in her heavenly home, the child of earth, whom she once loved with all a mother's love? It often happens, in our intercourse with human society, that affection, pure and fervent, arises from similarity of pursuits and of tastes. The vicissitudes of life separate us for years. We meet, after long absence, and expect a renewal of former joys; but, to our disappointment, one or both may seem changed. We have no longer the same mutual desires, and similar tastes, we once had. How will it be when friends on earth, separated long by death, meet in heaven? Will the loved and the lost, who were all the world to us, and to whom we were all the world, meet us in the spirit-world, with the same love they bore us in this life?

NIAGARA.

READER, did you ever see Niagara—the indescribably-grand, ineffably-sublime, and overwhelming wonder of earth? All other sights, all other sounds, all other scenes of nature and of art, may disappoint your expectation by failing to equal your imagined conceptions. But Niagara can never be imagined till seen and heard. To appreciate the scene you must go and stand on the Table Rock, or pass up in the gallant and daring skiff to the misty regions near the precipice, or ramble along the shores of the island, listening occasionally to the deep tones that come up from the abyss. Those sounds can never, when once heard, be forgotten. They can be imitated by nothing earthly. If the spheres, as the far-famed sage avers, do, in their cyclic revolutions, make music worthy to be heard by angels, surely Niagara might furnish bass enough for the whole orchestra. No words can describe the emotions which must rise in your soul as you stand on the brink of that abyss, and look and listen on the sights and to the sounds which there only are seen and heard.

The Niagara river, from the outlet of Lake Erie, near the city of Buffalo, to the head of the rapids, a distance of about twenty miles, flows on with a strong but equable and smooth current, between very low banks. There is in the appearance of the river nothing to indicate the existence, within a few miles, of the most wonderful scene of natural sublimity on the globe. As you approach the small village near the Falls, the rapids are concealed from view by a strip of forest. Leaving the cars at the depot, and passing directly on through a fine grove of oak, you arrive, after a walk of only a few rods, at the very brink of the chasm, below the Falls. Looking up, you see the mighty mass of waters, pouring, with inconceivable power and stunning sound, over the precipice.

Having remained for some time standing on the brink, and lookward on the scene, till my soul was well-nigh overwhelmed with repeated waves of sublime emotion, I proceeded down the covered staircase to the bed of the river. Stepping into the ferry-boat, I was carried by the skillful oarsman rapidly over to the Canadian shore. The ferry is about half a mile below the Falls, which are in full view as you are borne along in the boat. From the ferry-landing on the Canada shore there winds its devious way up the hill a fine carriage road. As you pass along this road you often catch a fine view of the Falls. Arriving at the table-land at the top of the precipice, I proceeded directly up the river to the Table Rock, on the brink of the Falls. The greater portion of this remarkable rock had fallen into the abyss but a few days before my visit. I wondered it had stood so long. Twenty years ago I had stood on the rock, and observed the immense seam in the ledge becoming wider and wider by the action of frost, and I then called the attention of a friend by my side to the imminent danger of the whole mass overhanging the abyss falling, at no distant day, into the foaming waters. The event then foreseen had now occurred. The immense ledge, several rods in area, undermined by the waters beneath, dissevered by a gaping seam from the adjacent bank, and pressed by its own immense weight, had suddenly, with a terrific crash, tumbled down. Fortunately no one was standing on it, though a carriage had been driven over it but a few moments before it fell. The interest of this spot is not diminished by the fall of the rock. There is yet left sufficient space to stand, and to obtain a fine, perhaps the finest, view that can be obtained of the Falls. On the remaining fragment of the rock I was standing within a foot of the precipitous cliff, and but a few feet from the falling column of dark blue water. I was looking up the river at the foaming rapids. A long strip of dark clouds seemed pointing one end to the water and the other to the sky. Suddenly, and without the slightest warning, a most powerful current of lightning, of the most intense brilliancy, dashed from the cloud to the water, followed by an astounding peal of thunder. The lightning current passed so near as to give me a perceptible shock, and to send me, by an instinctive leap, farther from the brink. Before I could recover myself, there poured from the cloud incessant torrents of rain. I had seen Niagara under various phases—I had seen it on a clear day of autumn—I had seen it on a misty morning of spring—I had seen it by summer moonlight; but never had I stood on its brink in the midst of thunder, lightning, and torrents of rain. Such lightning, such thunder, and such a shower can add, if any thing can, sublimity to Niagara.

GREENWOOD.

On a pleasant summer day I crossed over the Brooklyn ferry, took a seat in the omnibus, and after a pleasant ride of a few miles, along the shores of the delightful bay of New York, I arrived at the large, cumbrous gateway that opens from the busy world into the silent resting-place of the dead.

The surface of the inclosure is remarkably diversified by hills, valleys, small lakes, open glades, thickets of shrubbery, and groves of forest trees. Nearly the entire ground is laid out in lots, of various shapes and sizes, and ornamented with iron railings, and monuments, and statuary, according to the cultivated or the capricious tastes of the several owners. It would be impracticable to describe, without resorting to a technical catalogue of names, the various shapes and styles of monument erected in that ground. There are unassuming headstones, there are plain slabs, there are monuments extravagantly costly—some with beautiful and others with grotesque and fantastic designs—and there are Grecian and Gothic structures like moderate-sized dwellings. The most expensive decorations are about the grave of Charlotte Canda, who died "by a fall from a carriage on her seventeenth birthday." Though the extravagant costliness of this monument seems inappropriate and useless, yet we may say of its form, and of its various appendages, what we can in truth say of very few of the monuments in Greenwood—that the design seems conceived and executed in good taste.

I can hardly see the appropriateness of going back, in search of suitable designs for a tombstone, to the ruins of Egypt, and deforming the monuments of the dead with monstrous forms of winged globes and unsightly images of serpents. I can see little to choose between some of these images so common in Greenwood, and the dismal skeleton faces on the old gravestones of the Puritan church-yards.

There are some points in Greenwood from which the view is splendid. There is one on the southern border of the cemetery, from which the ocean prospect is most glorious. For miles to the right and to the left, and as far as the eye can reach in front, you may look off on the blue deep, reflecting from its mirrory surface the tints of the overhanging sky, and whitened frequently with the swelling sails of numerous ships.

The sun was setting, and I was about leaving Greenwood with disappointment. The effect, on the whole, was not pleasant. There was much effort at pomp, and show, and circumstance. There was too much ambition in the proprietors of lots to outdo each other in expense of decoration. There seemed evidence of attempts to carry the artificial and conventional distinctions of society beyond life, even to the grave. The most of the names that figure largely on the costly-decorated lots are not the names known as philanthropists, or benefactors of the race, or even as contributors to science and literature. But they are names of such as have acquired wealth by manufacturing "sarsaparilla," or pills," or other equally-interesting articles. One very tall monument bears, in great capitals, the name of some one, "packing-box maker, at —— Gold-street." All these attempts to glorify, by extravagant expense and bombastic eulogium after death, the names of those who, in life, were distinguished only for acquiring wealth by some fortunate accident or artful speculation, seem to me in bad taste. Nor do I like the publicity of such cemeteries as Greenwood. The place is thronged with the thoughtless and the curious. The thoroughfares are scarcely less crowded than Broadway or the Bowery. I would not, when I go to kneel and to weep over the grave of my heart's loved one, have a hundred idle passers-by gazing at me, and, by their profane presence, disturbing the sanctity of the place and the quiet of my meditations. No. Let my friends sleep, and, when life is over, let me sleep with them in the quiet church-yard of the rural village.

I was about leaving Greenwood with feelings of disappointment and dissatisfaction, when my attention was called, by the friend who accompanied me, to a distant corner of the ground, wondrous thickly dotted with little graves. On approaching the spot, I found it the public burial-place of little children. There were strewed side by side nearly a thousand graves, all of children apparently under two or three years of age, and all made within the last few months. The little ones sleeping in this unadorned spot were children of parents too poor to own a lot in these grounds, and too poor, except in a very few instances, to afford the smallest stone on which to inscribe the name of their lost one. But indications of affection, touching indications, were not wanting. Some of the little graves were strewed with flowers. The flowers were in every stage of decay, from withered and dry to wilted or fresh, showing that often came the hand of love to scatter the emblems of youth and innocence over the grave. On other graves were arranged the toys and playthings of the lost little one. Others were covered with sea-shells, gathered probably by the poor sailor father on foreign shores. And these little toys, playthings, and shells were all the poor parents and sisters could afford in memory of "the little boy that died," or the little girl that, like the dew-drop, "sparkled, was exhaled, and went to heaven." These simple tokens of affection in the poor awoke in my heart emotions which the costly monuments of the wealthy had failed to excite.

A RAMBLE BY THE SEA-SHORE.

On a pleasant summer day, with a good, cool breeze blowing directly down from the White Mountains, I started with my friend for a sea-side ramble. We soon reached the coast, where the open Atlantic incessantly dashes against the rocky cliffs. We clambered along over the precipice, and stood on the rocks that had for six thousand years withstood the force of the ever-returning waves. The sky was clear, and the atmosphere was affected only by a pleasant land breeze, yet the ocean was, as it ever is, unquiet and restless. Wave after wave, in long succession, would come rolling in, dashing against the rocks, and rushing into all the crevices, coves, and caves, bellowing and roaring with stunning and deafening reverberations. Often we had to look out for ourselves, or the rock on which we stood would be submerged by some wave more daring than its predecessor, and we should find ourselves uncomfortably bathed. The grand old rocks around us seemed venerable with age and with hard service. Their face was furrowed, and seamed, and scarred in many a hard-contested battle with the sea. They had been worn into uncouth and fantastic forms. Weather-beaten, gray, and grim, they yet stand the impassable barrier between the domain of sea and of earth. How many scenes of thrilling interest have these same old rocks witnessed! Often have their caves resounded with the cry of the shipwrecked mariner, and their sides echoed with the thunder of the cannon, as foe met foe in gallant ship on the neighboring waters. Within their full view the *Enterprise* and *Boxer* met in deadly conflict, in which the youthful and gallant commanders of each ship fell. In the cemetery of the beautiful city, in full view from this spot, the traveler may observe, side by side, two graves, covered with plain slabs, on which are inscribed the names of the gallant chieftains, who fell in that sanguinary battle, and who, for half a century, have been sleeping as quietly together as though they had never handled the weapons of warfare. But these old rocks heed not the cry of sailor in shipwreck, nor of chieftain in battle; but they echo, echo, echo on to the thundering tones of the Atlantic.

Did you ever, reader, watch the motions of the sea from the cliffs or the sandy beach? The surface motion only you see. There is another motion invisible to you, an undercurrent, known only by its effects. This *undertow*, deep and powerful, is always in a direction opposite to the visible motion of the surface waves.

Like the waves of the sea are often the emotions of our own hearts. We are not all what we seem. There are undercurrents of emotion and of feeling, whose waves break not upon the visible shore, but roll on, deep, strong, and resistless, toward the invisible, the unknown, and the ideal.

Having satiated ourselves with the wonders of the rocky point where first we commenced our observations, we passed on along the coast, over cliffs and rocks, and along precipices, and by chasms and ravines, escaping danger only by care and agility, till we reached a little sequestered cove, with a pebbly beach. It was a delightful spot, securely sheltered from the winds, and secluded from all human observation. The shore was covered with beautiful, clean, neat pebbles, polished, smooth, and fair, and of every variety of color. The sea, however, was restless even here, and its waves came rolling, rolling, rolling in, and breaking gently on the beach. We could not here resist the temptation to indulge in the luxury of a sea-bath. It was so quiet, so secluded, the waters were so cool and clear, and the beach so neat and clean, that we could but dally, and sport, and play, and dash about the waters, and suffer the surf to trip us from our feet, till we began to feel as amphibious as the Sandwich Islander. We got thoroughly salted, and carried off a large quantity of salt in our hair.

Rambling on some miles farther, we came upon a long stretch of sandy beach. For miles the beach stretched away in a curved line. The sandy surface was hard and firm. The surf was still dashing incessantly on the shore, making music in perfect time, though rather monotonous.

In our ramble along this beach we had the good fortune to light on a fine deposit of beautiful shells. There were many varieties; some very delicate and perfect. We spent some hours in gathering and culling the best of them, and then pursued our way along the shore. Is it fact or fancy that the sea-shell, for years after it is removed from its ocean-bed, echoes in its hollow chambers to the sound of the waves? It is a fact, and no fancy, that the heart of man never ceases to echo, in its inmost recesses, to the sound of early tones.

Along the clean-washed beach of hard sand for many a mile we made our way, till we were arrested by a deep and broad river, which we had no means of crossing. Reckless had we rambled on, not knowing whither our way might lead. We had spent a long summer day, and traveled we knew not how many miles. The city we had left far behind. We had scarcely seen for the day, in our wild and wayward rambling, a living creature larger than a cricket. We had heard no voice, except that of a wild barking fox, whose territory we had invaded as we passed through a thicket of firs. It was now nearly night; and as we could go no farther along the coast, we concluded to follow up the river-bank, supposing we must arrive somewhere. On our way we passed through a most splendid grove of evergreens. The deep and dark foliage presented a curtain impenetrable to the sunlight. The ground was strewed with the fallen and dry tassels of the pine. Occasional spots where oozing moisture from the hill-side slightly watered the sandy soil, were enlivened by a beautiful patch of green moss. In such a scene of sylvan beauty might I fancy the grotto of Calypso, where, if any where, Ulysses might have ceased to pine to see the "rising smoke of his native land."

Emerging from the forest, we stood in the open land, on the summit of a hill, from which was afforded a prospect, which, for extent, beauty, grandeur, and sublimity, excelled all I had ever seen, or of which I had ever dreamed. The scene was wholly unexpected. It burst suddenly on us. Spontaneously and simultaneously we raised our hands, and uttered loud exclamations of admiration. On the east and on the south stretched away in unbroken expanse the sea. On the west, bordering the ocean, extended far in the dim distance a magnificent plain of evergreen forest. On the north, looming up in the clear sunset, appeared range after range of the grandest mountains on which, as it then seemed to us, human eye ever looked. The nearest range could not be less than fifty miles distant. It was darkened by the shadows of night. Far beyond it, gleaming in the bright evening sunbeam, arose another, magnificent, lofty, sublime. Its distance could not be less than one hundred miles.

What a landscape was that on which to look in the bright sunshine of a summer evening! It was worth a voyage to the moon or to the distant disk of Jupiter. We stood entranced at the glorious prospect, till the deep shadows fell on the scene, and the gathering darkness of night reminded us that we had rambled far from the city; nor knew we where we were. Observing a cart-road not far from us, we struck into it, and followed it, till we arrived at a comfortable farm-house, where we were kindly welcomed and hospitably entertained. In the morning we found our way back to the city.

Thus ended our ramble by the seaside. It was a day of romance—a day long to be remembered by us—a day bringing within our view more scenes of beauty and of sublimity than any other day I ever spent.

THE OLD HOMESTEAD.

I KNOW not what can produce in the heart of man more sad emotions than a visit, after an absence of years, to the home of his childhood. The changes of earth seem not materially to affect us, when they occur gradually before our eyes. But if we are absent for a time, and then return, all the mutations of men, of things, and of circumstances, meet us at once with overwhelming power. We feel as might one returned from the spirit-land to look again for an hour on the scenes of earth.

About noon, of a summer day, I was approaching the rural neighborhood, the scene of my earliest recollections. The first thing I saw, which awoke me from the reverie into which I had fallen, was a tall column of white marble peering up in a rural cemetery, near the old church where I used to worship God. The cemetery had been laid out and consecrated when I was a boy, and I recollected being present when the first interment was made in it—that of an old man, of whitened locks and decrepit form, who had for many years occupied in the church the same seat. I climbed over the massive wall that inclosed the sacred ground, to read the name on the white column. It was that of my first classical teacher, a man of letters and a man of God, one who had first pointed out to me the way of science, and encouraged me to walk therein. In the same inclosure were other graves, some marked by no stone, and yet I well remembered them; for in one had been sleeping more than a third of a century the gentle being who first taught my heart to love.

Through an avenue of the dark forest, I saw the green hill-side that sheltered the old mansion, in which my youth was passed, and the vale through which flowed the little brook from the perennial spring, that furnished water for the household. Along the winding foot-path, up hill, down valley, and over plain, I wended my solitary way, till I stood on the spot, where once rose the venerable mansion, with its heavy timbers and spacious dimensions. But no house was there. Nothing remained but the scattered stones, which once formed its foundation. Not a sound was heard but the chirping of the cricket beneath what had been the old hearth-stone. I threw down my carpet-bag on the stone, and started for a ramble over the hill, and plain, and valley, to see if I could find any familiar imprint of the past. And more than that, I desired, if possible, to restore for one brief hour the impressions of childhood—to be, if possible, a child again—to feel once more the joyous buoyancy of other days. I went to the spring near the alder brook. It was bubbling up, fresh and cool, from its sandy bed, just as it did

> "When I a child, and half afraid,
> Around its verdant margin played."

I kneeled by its brink, and drank one long, refreshing draught. It seemed as if I had never tasted so cool, pure, and sweet water. I sauntered along by the brook that wound its devious way through the valley. The trout darted at my approach into his deep and dark retreat, just as he used to do when I was accustomed to bait for him the cruel hook. Leaving the brook I ascended to the plain, to seek out the bower of evergreens, under whose dark shade I had passed many a summer hour. The same trees were there still. The wind was discoursing inimitable music through the tassels of the same pine, that threw its waving branches over me years ago. The same robin, that used to sing on the dry limb of an old oak, seemed there still. The same swallow, that used to build its nest on the eaves of the barn, still flitted by me. The little mound, that the woodchuck had made in excavating his burrow, still remained. Tree, shrub, and flower—hill, vale, and plain—bird, beast, and insect—all appeared just as they did long ago. But myself—myself alone was changed. I could not be a child again. I tried to call up the spirit of childhood, but it would not come at my bidding. I would have drank of some lethean waters, and forgotten the sorrows and bereavements of life, but the cup evaded my lips. Wearied and sad, I lay down on a bed of leaves, beneath a cluster of pines, and slept, and dreamed of other days. I heard sweet voices, voices long since hushed in death. I saw the forms of the departed. A mother was bending over me, as I lay upon my bed, and was bathing my burning temples. A gentle playmate was sitting by me, as we were conning our lesson in the old school-house. A graceful and lovely being came and walked by my side to the old church. And then—for dreams pay little respect to time or distance—I stood at the gate of my own cottage home, far away to the west. There ran to meet me, and stood with her bright eyes peeping through the fence, a fair and beauteous child, just

"Gathering the blossoms of her fourth bright year."

I opened the gate—I rushed to my long-lost child—I clasped her in my arms—I printed one impassioned kiss on her angelic brow, and then I awoke. All the beauteous forms were gone. The mother that bathed my fevered brow, the gentle boy that sat by my side in the schoolroom, and the graceful being that walked with me to the house of God, were all sleeping side by side in the old church-yard. And the child—I had laid her, one summer evening, quietly to rest by my side. I had awoke in the morning, and found her sick. I had watched over her with intense agony all that day and the following night, and early the next morning I had seen her die; and I had buried her in a solitary grave, in a rural bower, that I might protect her place of rest from the careless tread of the thoughtless, and the rude desecration of the brute.

The sun was near setting when I awoke from my dreamy sleep beneath the pines. I had some miles to travel before I could reach my temporary home in the city. I therefore proceeded on the shortest possible route. This happened to be along the railroad track. Between me and the city lay the railroad bridge, nearly a mile long, across the bay. The cars from Boston would be along that evening, and the bridge would be an awkward place to be overtaken by them. I supposed, however, I had the advantage in time, and could get over the bridge before they came up. I had, however, got but about half way over, when I heard the steam horse ripping and rushing, and tearing and snorting, behind me. To return or proceed was out of the question. There was room enough for the train to pass me, but I did not like to come so near its wind. So I leaped from the bridge on to a telegraph post, which stood upright in the water, a few feet from the track, and clung there, like a cat frightened by dogs, till the train had dashed by me. The rush with which the engine passed overset all my notions of velocity. As soon as the train was well out of sight, I crawled back on to the bridge, and without any more hairbreadth escapes arrived safely at my lodgings.

THE BACKWOODS EXPEDITION.

To one cooped up for many long years in a small village, immured for a great part of each day in a small room, inclosed by massive brick walls, and jerked about, both in body and in mind, by a bell-rope, there can be afforded no more desirable boon than a tramp in the wild woods, or an adventurous excursion to some sequestered lake, or desolate mountain, far away from the abode and the track of man.

Partly for relaxation from mental labor, and partly for scientific observation, I made an excursion with a company of gentlemen to Katahden, a magnificent and solitary mountain, at the head waters of the Penobscot river. Our place of rendezvous was Bangor, a large and populous town of eastern Maine, at the head of the Penobscot tide-waters. From thence we proceeded on our wild and interesting excursion.

AN INDIAN TOWN.

Some twenty miles above the city of Bangor is an Indian village. There, on a small, but beautiful island of the Penobscot river, dwells the remnant of a powerful tribe. The Penobscots were a branch of the great Abenaquis, who once possessed all the east, and north, from the Saco to the Great Banks, and from the ocean to the St. Lawrence. Their language was said to be the finest on the American continent. The French, who became acquainted with them in early times, said, that if the beauties of their language were known in Europe, seminaries would be erected to teach it. They averred that if such beauties were found in the ancient Egyptian or

Babylonish dialect, the learned of Europe would be at work to display them in a variety of shapes, and would ascribe superior wisdom, talents, and knowledge to the people whose idioms were formed with so much method and skill. This powerful people once possessed a country of more than one hundred thousand square miles. They now are limited to the few islands of the Penobscot. They once could collect thousands of brave warriors. They now number, when all at home, some six hundred souls. The early annals of New England abound in accounts of their fearful power and savage bravery, and the traditionary legends, yet repeated by the descendants of the old settlers, are still more fruitful in incidents of wonderful and hairbreadth escapes from these wily and warlike people. Now they are poor, inefficient, inoffensive, dispirited people, who could hardly make efficient headway against a flock of good-sized grasshoppers.

Being delayed a few hours at Oldtown, while arrangements could be made for our departure up the river, I crossed over to the island, in order to see the town, and the people. The town I easily found, but the people were few of them at home, being gone hunting and fishing. The town consists of a very neat, and, indeed, handsome church, some twenty or thirty wooden frame buildings, much neater in their external appearance than those generally found in western towns, and an untold number of camps, or tents. These camps are built of plank roughly put together. The fire is in the middle of the camp, and the smoke finds its way out through a hole made for the purpose overhead, or through the cracks in the walls, or through the door, just as it may suit its convenience.

While on the island I had the honor of an introduction to the governor of the tribe, his excellency, the Hon. John Neptune. I had seen a white governor, but never an Indian of that dignity; and, of course, I felt some solicitude on the matter. I walked along toward the mansion, with as much dignity as I well knew how to assume, and prepared myself to exhibit suitable respect and awe, on being ushered into his excellency's most august presence. The governor's mansion was a camp, in no way distinguishable from the plebeian camps about it, except that there were more dogs to bark. The door consisted of a blanket hung up as a curtain over a space left in the wall. Through this I was ushered into the presence of the governor and his lady. He was occupying a dignified position on his chair of state, which consisted of the naked floor of naked earth. A blazing fire was glowing hot in the very midst of the room, and the governor and his lady were enveloped in the smoke. The lady, who appeared, to say the least, to be no great beauty, was diligently and honorably employed in such household affairs as must always be attended to even by governors' ladies, especially when they have to be their own help. I really entertained a much higher opinion of this lady, for seeing her thus diligently employed; and I made up my mind, at the time, that her honorable industry might, in the opinion of the governor, be a redeeming trait in her character, and probably make up for the unquestionable lack of beauty.

The old governor was quite intelligent and communicative. I remained with him as long as I could stand the smoke; and when I could stand it no longer, I made as hasty an exit, as a due regard for politeness and the curtained door would admit, and rushed out into the open air. Welcome, the open air! I hate confinement, either in the smoke of camps or of cities. For amusement and pleasure you may keep your cities, and your towns, and your villages to yourselves. Give me the plain, open country, the prairie, the woodland, the mountain. For a place to worship God, keep your close, crowded churches; but give me the grove—God's first and most magnificent temple. For a study, keep your nice little room; but give me the shade of this old beech, with the sunshine all around, and the gentle south-west fanning my cheek. The open air of heaven, how it cools the fevered head, calms the troubled heart, and soothes the agitated spirit!

As soon as I had well cleared his excellency's threshold, and taken a few deep, delicious draughts of pure air, to expel the smoke from my lungs, and to revivify my blood, I started for a ramble over the island. I soon came to the graveyard—a place I never shun; for it always suggests holy thoughts and reverential sentiments. This Indian burial-place is one of the neatest cemeteries I have ever seen. It is situated in a lovely rural spot, on a gentle hill, commanding a fine view of the entire village, and the two branches of the river flowing by the island. It was inclosed by a neat and substantial fence, laid off in small lots, and ornamented with trees, shrubbery, and flowers; some planted by human hand, and others suffered to grow as nature planted them. At the head of each grave was a small wooden cross; some plain, and others tastefully carved and painted. Many of the graves were provided with a small box, shaped like the roof of a house. In pleasant weather this was laid aside, that the warm sunshine might fall on the grave, and the gentle summer wind might breathe over it, and the wild flowers might bloom on it. But when the rough storms swept down from the neighboring mountains, and the deep snows fell, and wild winter reigned, then the poor bereaved Indian went and placed the covering over the grave of his lost and lovely one, as if he would protect the dead from the wintery winds and pelting storm. To me it seemed an affecting exhibition of human affection. I never could find it in my heart to censure those who may seem to carry their veneration for the dead too far. Their philosophy may be at fault, and, by the censorious, even their religion may be impeached; yet their hearts will be found in the right place.

There were, in this Indian burial-place, no monuments of marble, or of granite; but there were at nearly all the graves wooden slabs, so neatly painted as to resemble, at a short distance, white marble. From one of these I copied the following inscription:

"Sosepmali onemun
Iral Hassun
ke sikatnet, 18,
Ahtozi Me chine, Dec.
28, 1833, chipatok, oikel,
Tamtanial,
iho hakisitankon oizi
Al polsosepal elasun
Zitpan."

I left the burying-place, and soon after the island, with subdued feelings, and sad reflections. I had seen the descendants of the mighty people, that once possessed my native state, thus reduced to a few hundreds, limited in their range to a few islands in a wild river, and growing less in numbers and importance every year. But thus goes the world. Change follows change, revolution sweeps after revolution, and death follows behind to finish the work with us all.

THE JOURNEY.

Our journey lay through an unsettled wilderness. We therefore had to take with us all necessary provisions for an absence of some weeks. Ourselves and baggage had to be pushed up a rough, rocky river, in batteaux and canoes. The batteau is about twenty feet long, and three or four feet wide in the middle, while the extremities taper to a point, and turn up, much like the old peaked-toed shoe worn by our great-grandmothers. It is made of plank, as light as possible; for it must often be carried by the boatmen around the falls, which frequently occur on the river. It has a flat bottom, so as easily to slide over the rocks in shallow water. The canoe is made of the bark of the white birch. It is round as the tree from which the bark was taken, and, like the batteau, peaked at both ends. It is about fifteen feet long, and two feet wide. It is so light that a man can carry it on his head. In these frail vessels we first packed our camping apparatus, provisions, and mathematical instruments, and then we packed in ourselves, sitting much in the manner of the Indian governor, flat on the floor. To sit in any other more dignified or comfortable manner, would manifestly endanger the stability of our position. To manage the batteau requires two skillful, athletic men. One stands on the prow, and the other in the stern. Each has a long pole with a spike in the end. This is called a setting pole. Keeping time with their poles, they thrust them against the rocks, or on the bottom of the river, and, pushing with great force, urge the boat rapidly up against the current. The canoe is managed in a similar way, only it requires but one to work it. Our boatmen on the batteau were skillful, careful hands, well acquainted with the river, and every way qualified for their business; but they were addicted to the most horrid profanity of language. I did not before know that the English language could be tortured into such outrageous oaths. If our army in Mexico swore as bad as did our Penobscot boatmen, it is not at all strange that the Mexican general, Ampudia, wished to learn how to swear so too, thinking, as it would appear, that the victory of our army was owing to the big oaths sworn by the officers at the men. Finding every means of correction ineffectual, I chose to go into the canoe which was managed by an Indian; for though he swore, as well as the white men, yet he swore in Indian, and it did not sound so bad as in English.

A HUNTO-MANIAC.

There was in our company a very queer genius. He was a young man of good education, well skilled in chemistry, and an excellent mineralogist. He was plain and frank in his manners, always speaking just what he thought, and always taking the opposite side in debate, no matter what the question was, or by whom it was started. But his great peculiarity was a mania for hunting and fishing. The river abounded in a splendid species of trout, especially about the falls and deep holes of the rocks. When we happened on one of these fishing grounds, it was impossible to get our sportsman along. He would fish, and fish, and fish, merely for the sake of fishing, thus delaying the expedition at the imminent risk of approaching winter. On one occasion he wandered off from the river, up a dreary mountain, after game. Here he lost his way, and had to lie out all night, under the shelter of an old tree. He was perfectly reckless of personal danger. If he saw a squirrel, he would leap out of the boat with his gun, at the evident hazard of drowning. On one occasion, as we were passing along in water some four or five feet deep, with a very rocky bottom, a flock of ducks flew over. The hunting mania immediately seized our friend, and regardless of the depth of the water, or the rocks at the bottom, he leaped overboard with his gun, and lighting on a slippery rock, some two feet below the surface, he fell into the river, and went all sprawling under, gun, powder, and all. While he was picking himself up the ducks escaped.

A day or two after this our hunter got enough of the "villainous smell of gunpowder." He was trying to kindle a fire, and, as the wood did not readily ignite, he put some powder on it, and then blew lustily away at the coal.

Suddenly the powder flashed, and he received the whole charge in his face. This caused him to make a hasty somerset, keeling over most whimsically, with beard, whiskers, and hair most ludicrously scorched. He began to think gunpowder was not what it was cracked up to be, and after this the birds and squirrels had a respite.

A DINNER PARTY.

Could our friends have looked in on our dinner party in the woods, they might have deemed it quite an amusing affair. We were seated around a big fire. The earth served us for chairs, ready made, and bottomed, and cushioned. A good clean chip, or a nice piece of bark, served an excellent purpose for a plate. A tin dipper formed a fine coffee cup. As to forks, "fingers were made before them." We were not burdened with many varieties of food, taking a long time to eat, and then giving us the dyspepsia. Nor did we bother ourselves with useless ceremony, and many excuses, and much compliment. I suppose the ceremonies of civilized life must be necessary. It would seem so, from their being so very much used. I would not object to them were they not often so heartless and hollow. A dinner party in the woods is, however, sometimes a relief to one tired of the regular routine of civilization. There is something so free and easy about it, that it seems to give one a new set of ideas.

THE ENCAMPMENT.

After a journey of many days through the most various scenery, sometimes pushing the boat against the rapid current, and at others gliding smoothly over the broad lakes, into which the river frequently expanded; now going past wide and fertile bottom-lands, and again coasting along under the shadow of mountain cliffs; now opening into broad meadows of tall wild grass, and then shooting through some narrow passage, where the overhanging trees, entwining their branches from each side of the river, completely shut out the sunlight, we arrived at the place destined for headquarters, during our sojourn in this wild region. The spot selected for the encampment was a beautiful island. The river here expanded into a broad, deep, and most lovely lake. The island was covered with every variety of tree common to a northern forest. There was the magnificent elm, with its large, graceful branches; the birch, with its dress of pure white; the maple, with its limbless trunk and rounded top; the northern cedar, with its gnarled, elk-horn limbs; the pine, with its tassels sighing in the wind, and the fir, with its tall, straight trunk, and its delicate branches, so regular, as to form a more perfect cone than art ever constructed. The island was bounded by a sandy beach, extending all around it, forming a most delightful promenade. The clear waters of the lake reflected the blue heavens and the green trees so perfectly, that you seemed, when gazing on its tranquil surface, to be looking at another beautiful world, concave, below you. At the distance of about ten miles appeared, looming up far above the horizon, Katahden, the prince of eastern mountains. It stood wild, grand, and solitary before us. Its topmost peak was to be the summit of our ambition, and the end of our journey. We had come thus far to measure its hight, and study its mineralogy and its geology. We could approach it no nearer by the river. From this point our ascent must be made on foot.

The sunset view at this place was most splendid. The waters of the lake glittered like silver. The trees, clothed in their autumnal garments of a thousand hues, seemed to reflect back the crimson, and the gold, and the purple of gorgeous skies. On the east, and on the south, and on the west, the view was bounded by a circumference of blue hills, just rising above the horizon. On the north was Katahden, "monarch of all it surveys." It stood alone, rising from a vast forest plain, like an island from the illimitable ocean. It seemed composed of alternate ridges and ravines—the ridges protuberant, like immense ribs, and the ravines of unknown depth. In many places there appeared the path of immense avalanches, or slides. These extended from the top to the base, a distance of many miles, sweeping down, in their headlong rush, rocks, and trees, and acres of earth. The light of sunset, reflected from the ridges, and from the naked path of the slides, and the shadows of night gathering dark and deep in the bottomless ravines, presented a mingled picture of brilliant beauty, and awful grandeur, such as I may never hope to see again.

The sunset faded, and the autumn twilight threw its soft radiance over the scene. And when that, like all things beautiful of earth, had faded too, the moon arose, and shed her mellow light over lake, and forest, and mountain. I rambled away, at a distance from the bustle of the camp, and sat down on the sandy beach, to enjoy the scene. It was not the place, nor the time for me to enjoy society. It was the place and the time to commune with nature, and with the past, and with the departed loved ones, whom I can not believe, at such times, far distant from me.

ASCENT OF KATAHDEN.

As soon as morning dawned, we arose from our bed of boughs, and made preparation for our excursion to the mountain. Concealing from the bears and wolves such baggage and provisions as we did not wish to take with us, we left the island, and glided over the smooth waters of the lake to the eastern shore. Here we drew up our light skiffs, and hid them among the wild shrubbery on the bank. The mathematical instruments, and the provisions, and equipage indispensable on our journey, were distributed among the company. From an eminence near by we took the bearing to the foot of an immense slide from the mountain, apparently about ten miles distant. We then, with baggage and utensil, plunged into the woods in Indian file. We soon, in the depth of the forest, lost all view of the mountain, and had to depend wholly on our compass. Our route led over the strangest variety of scenery. For some miles we passed over gentle hills with intervening valleys. From these the original forest had wholly disappeared. Some careless lumberman had, some years before, kindled a fire in the dry season, in the pine forest; and when a fire once gets started in summer among the trees of a New England forest, it sweeps every living thing before it. All, therefore, of the noble forest trees of this region had perished and fallen. There had sprung up thickets of white birch, patches of gigantic ferns, and immense fields of blueberry bushes, loaded with the finest fruit. In one part of our journey we fell into a cedar swamp. This was nearly impassable. The limbs of the cedar grew but a few feet from the ground, and the branching tops were so entwined as to render the direction of Dr. Franklin, "Stoop as you go through the world," of indispensable importance to us. Passing this cedar forest, we came to a clear cold mountain stream. It poured down from the mountain in many a beautiful cascade, and went roaring, and ripping, and tearing away, laughing outright, as it rushed on toward the river. Its bed was strewed with huge bowlders of rock, having evidently tumbled down from the mountain. I had the curiosity to measure one of these granite blocks. Its circumference was seventy-nine, and its hight fifteen feet. Borne down the stream by the rushing waters, it had struck another rock, which had arrested its progress.

The sun was near setting, when we reached the base of the mountain, at the foot of the path left by the great slide. From this point there seemed, to one looking up, a broad, straight, and tolerably smooth road to the very top of the mountain peak. The hand of man, however, has had no part in forming this great highway. It is the pathway of the avalanche. It is a groove in the mountain side, varying from two to ten feet deep, and five hundred feet wide. At some unknown period, a mass of earth, with all its trees and shrubs, was swept down the mountain, far into the plain below, leaving its pathway marked for ages to come. Up this pathway we began our ascent. The inclination was at first but gentle, and the way strewed with pebbly sand and gravel. As we advanced, the ascent became steeper, and the road rougher. Near the top we had to climb up over rocks piled on rocks. Ruin had driven her plowshare over every inch, and turned up prodigious furrows all along the way.

Night came upon us, and we rested, forming the best shelter we could. Morning dawned, and we made a scanty breakfast, and prepared to climb on. We had reached a little area of table-land, commanding a splendid view. Below us and around us the atmosphere was clear. We stopped to look on the magnificent prospect. Toward the south the clear waters of the Penobscot, as they sped away toward the ocean, gleamed like a thread of silver. Toward the west there lay spread out a succession of lakes, beautiful, bright, and innumerable. Some of them we knew to be many leagues distant, yet, from the elevation on which we stood, one might seem able to throw a stone upon their glassy surface. To the east appeared an illimitable forest plain, unbroken, silent, and desolate. On the north, far as the eye could reach,

"Hills peeped o'er hills, and Alps on Alps arose,"

rugged, savage, and drear.

But while the lower strata of atmosphere was clear, affording unobstructed view of earth, heaven was shut out from view. Clouds high in air were rapidly sailing over forest, and mountain, and lake. One, blacker than its companions, had stooped from its airy flight, and was resting on the mountain peak before us. It seemed impenetrable; yet we had to climb on into its very embraces. Our way became more difficult. Rocks of every fantastic shape lay along the path, many of them so poised, that a false step, or the slightest accident, might start them from their resting-places, and send them thundering down, carrying ruin on such of our party as happened to be behind. Some of our companions got frightened at the scene, and made their escape, while their bones were sound, to a place of safety.

At last, with many a weary step, and many a hairbreadth escape, we reached the cloud-capped summit. Cloud-capped indeed it was, and the cap drawn tightly down. The cloud, which, from below, appeared resting so quiet on its mountain perch, was all in a whirl. The wind blew so violently, that one of the company, with comic gravity, inquired how many men it might take to hold one's hair on. Nor was wind and cloud all. The snow came thick and fast, and the cold was so intense, that out of ten men, protected by overcoats and mittens, not one could unscrew the tube of the barometer, so benumbed were our fingers.

An Indian of the Penobscots, who was one of the party, averred that Pimola, the mythological demon of the mountain, had sent this terrible storm upon us, in punishment of our impiety in visiting his dominions. Pimola is the genius of Katahden, of Herculean strength, occupying a throne of granite, and reigning sole despot over those lofty peaks and dark ravines. No mortal eye has ever seen him; but his voice, as the Indians affirm, is often heard, and especially in the storm. The Penobscots have the fear of him continually before their eyes, and it is with difficulty that you can urge them to approach the mountain.

After much difficulty, we succeeded in taking the barometrical observations, and obtaining such geological information as the circumstances allowed; and then, finding that longer delay might be dangerous, on account of the intensity of the cold, and the violence of the storm, we started on our return. Starting off in the direction in which I supposed we had come up, I had proceeded but a short distance, when I was arrested by the warning voice of our Indian attendant, and informed that I was on the wrong track. I could hardly believe I was not in the same path by which we had ascended, but returning to the spot from which I had started, he soon convinced me that he was right, and that the way I had been going would have led off among crags, and cliffs, and precipices, and ravines, no one knows where. The sagacity of the Indian had induced him, on going up the mountain, to mark the path, after we left the slide, by setting up stones—a prudent expedient, that never occurred to the rest of us. By this instinctive foresight of a half-wild Indian, our whole company was saved from untold sufferings, and even death. The path by which we had come up is the only known way of access to the mountain; and had we attempted the descent by any other route, we must have become inextricably confused and bewildered, and we might have perished in the storm.

As we were passing down along the brink of one of the ravines, which I had not noticed in our ascent, owing to the dense mist surrounding us, I looked down the dizzy abyss. How wide it was I know not, as I could not in the storm see across; but it was at least a thousand feet deep, and walled up by perpendicular precipices.

The scene was intensely sublime. The emotion was indeed overwhelming. On one side was the naked mountain peak, drear and desolate, its rocks rived by the frosts of six thousand winters; on the other was the deep, dark chasm, whose recesses, formed by jutting crags and overhanging cliffs, no adventurous foot had ever trod; above us, and around us, and below us, was the storm, the wintery winds whirling the fast falling snow into many a fantastic drift. The scene made the blood run chill and the teeth chatter.

PERILOUS ADVENTURE.

About noon we safely arrived at the place which we had left in the morning. Here we found our companions, who, being frightened at the falling rocks, starting from their precarious poise in our ascent, had gone back, leaving to us the danger and the glory of accomplishing the ascent to the summit. They had provided as well as they could for their comfort and for ours. But our situation was by no means desirable. We had but one tent, having left the other on the island. It was entirely too small to afford protection from the storm for all of us. We were drenched with snow and rain; for the cloud which capped the mountain top with snow, poured down torrents of rain on the sides. We had no change of raiment. Little or no fire could be raised, for we were yet too high up the mountain to find much wood, and what little we did find was too wet to burn, and only furnished volumes of smoke to be whirled into our faces and eyes by the wind. In addition to this, we were nearly out of provision, having scarcely sufficient for half our company. Our island camp, where we had left our clothing and provisions, was nine miles distant, through a tangled, pathless forest. It was deemed impossible to reach it that night. Such, however, were the inconveniences of our position, that I proposed to be one of any number, who would proceed to the island, running the risk of reaching it before night, thus leaving more room and provision for those who might remain in the mountain camp. Two of the boatmen volunteered. Each of us took our share of the luggage, and marking our course by the compass, we started, in a straight line, through bogs and brooks, and over rocks and ravines, and by hills, and valleys, and swamps, for the island. Burdened with a part of the mathematical instruments, and with my overcoat, which had absorbed too much water for convenience, wearied with the morning's excursion on the mountain, and enfeebled by unremitting pain in my shoulder, which, on account of repeated dislocations, had become acutely sensible to fatigue, I yet, for six miles, successfully measured speed with the athletic boatmen. We had now reached the river; but our camp was still three miles below, and night was fast coming on us. My strength began to fail, and one of the boatmen took my share of the luggage, and we pressed on. Shortly my overcoat became too burdensome, and the other boatman took that. But in divesting myself of my overcoat I unfortunately dislocated my shoulder. By the aid of my companions I soon reduced the joint, as I had by experience learned how to do it; but the pain and exhaustion produced by the accident used up what little strength I had.

I requested my companions to leave me, and go on to the camp, and build a fire, and get some supper, and, as soon as I could recover, I would come on, as fast as I could. I then sat down on a rock to rest. Soon I became excessively chilled, and found that if I sat there much longer I never should rise from my seat again. I arose to go on, but every locomotive muscle seemed chilled and trembling. I, however, nerved myself up, and attempted to proceed along the river's brink. But the way was incumbered by fallen trees, and I had not strength to lift my wearied limbs over them. I therefore passed down the bank, and walked along the beach. I soon came to a place where the water approached so near the bank as to leave no passage between. Attempting to climb up, but failing in strength to accomplish it, I waded on through the water, till the bank receding left another strip of beach. After a time I found my strength fast exhausting, and myself strongly inclined to sleep. Feeble, however, as had become the powers of body, the mind yet retained its usual presence. I stood on the river shore, casting about me for some rock, under whose shelter I might lie down. But I knew that if I should lie down, wet and cold, to sleep in the storm, I might never wake again. And there were, far away, now clustering around the blazing fire of my cottage hearth, those for whom I would yet live. I therefore rallied all my physical forces for another effort, but found that, though I had yet strength enough to stand, I was utterly unable to proceed.

I was standing on the river shore, partly in the water. Around me was the howling storm, before me was the rushing river, and above me, and fast gathering over me was the dense darkness of a moonless night. There was not a human home for nearly a hundred miles. A part of my company was some six miles up the mountain, and the rest some three miles down the river. So desolate was the place, that I never could dream of a living soul in the neighborhood. Nevertheless, I thought I could but call for help. I called, and I was answered. A voice came back distinctly heard above the blast. I stood surprised. Is it an echo? May it be an illusion of my own bewildered brain, like the bell of death which we sometimes hear ringing in the ear, or like the call of my loved and lost child, that sometimes thrills my soul, and vibrates my nerves, as I wander at twilight among the bowers where she used to play? No, no, it is a real, living, human voice. And there surely is, approaching the bank on the other side of the river, a man. And just beyond are the camp fires of the party to which he belongs—a party of lumbermen, on their way to the distant lakes above. Well, there is a Providence, I know there is, and to him will I look for protection, though waves of sorrow roll over my head, and rush through my heart.

A SABBATH IN THE WILDERNESS.

The stranger, whom Providence sent to my rescue, crossed the river in his canoe, and safely conveyed me to my own camp, where my companions had prepared a roaring fire, and a bountiful supper. On my arrival I was so chilled I could not speak; but a change of clothes, a blazing fire, and a substantial supper soon restored me. I then wrapped myself in my blanket, and raising my eyes and my heart in devout gratitude to heaven for my protection through the fatigues and dangers of the day, I lay down on my bed of cedar boughs, and soon fell asleep. I was, however, too much fatigued to sleep undisturbed. The image of Katahden, with its precipices and ravines, and the snow storm, of the pathless wilderness, and the conception of desperate struggles to extricate myself from impending danger, haunted me in my slumbers.

In the morning I awoke just as the sun peeped in through the trees. All was bright and beautiful. Not a cloud obscured the sky. The winds were lulled to rest. The voice of the tempest was hushed. All was deep, placid repose. It was like the repose that gathers over the fair features of childhood when the stormy struggle of disease and dissolution is passed, and

"Before decay's effacing fingers
Have swept the lines where beauty lingers."

It was the holy day of rest—the Sabbath. It was, too, the Sabbath of the year. The equinoctial storm was passed, and mellow autumn, with her variant train, had come over the plains, while winter was sitting crowned with its wreath of snow on the mountain.

It was the sweet Sabbath day, and I was left to enjoy it alone; for my companions went to meet the lingering members of the party with provisions. I love sometimes to be alone. I love a solitary ramble in the forest, or by the sequestered lake, or the unfrequented stream. There are times when I love to hear no sounds but those of nature, and to see no sights but the green grass, and the waving trees, and the bright waters, and the blue sky. Such seasons are to me the Sabbath of the soul—a Sabbath, not the busiest day of the week, devoted, from early morn till late at night, to active exercises, and on which, having to do or to hear so much *talking*, there is no time to *think*, but a Sabbath of rest, a quiet retreat, of holy meditation. Such a Sabbath was that which I spent on that lone isle of beauty, far away in the Penobscot waters. It was one of the happiest and the most profitable I ever spent.

The next morning we made ready for our return home. Fair faces, cheerful hearts, sweet smiles, and merry voices, would greet me on my return to my distant home; but yet I could not without regret leave my little island. It seemed like the home of childhood. While preparations were making for our departure, I wandered over it, marking each remembered spot, where I had passed the twilight hour, or the Sabbath rest. And when all was ready, and I had stepped into my canoe, I went back to a lovely bower, and said, instinctively, "Good-by!"

Thus it is that the heart clings to every object associated with its joys and its sorrows. Many a year has passed since I saw that lonely isle. And I have seen many a beautiful and many a lovely spot. Yet I still love, and sometimes pine for my lonely little island.

"Still my fancy can discover
  Sunny spots where friends may dwell;
Darker shadows round me hover,
  Isle of beauty, fare thee well!

Through the mist that floats above me,
  Faintly sounds the evening bell,
Like a voice from those that love me,
  Breathing fondly, fare thee well!

What would I not give to wander
  Where my old companions dwell?
Absence makes the heart grow warmer;
  Isle of beauty, fare thee well!"

AN INVITATION.

It is a bright and beautiful day. There is spread all over the heavens a canopy of clear, blue sky. How gracefully waves the tall grass in the valley, and the ripening grain on the hill, and the delicate limbs of the trees above us! How balmy the gentle zephyr that fans my cheek and lightly stirs the hairs of my head! No sounds are here but those of nature. The village is too far removed for any of its bustle to reach me, except the hammer of a single carpenter, pounding away on a house erecting in the neighborhood.

Come, gentle one, and see my bower before its quiet is disturbed and its seclusion desecrated by the ever-busy and intermeddling agency of what the world calls improvement. I really fear, my dear reader, that the days of my rural pleasures, in this clime, are numbered. When I came here, I got as far away from the village as I well could—so far that I felt secure against all the inroads of improvement. But I see, in the valley just below me, a corps of engineers, and they are staking, for the final location, the great railroad that is to connect the east and the west, forming the great thoroughfare from the Atlantic to the Pacific. They have located the Greencastle depot alarmingly near the termination of the secluded street that runs by the bower. And our village corporation are standing on the hill, between me and the town, planning the grading of the street, the building of culverts, and the flagging of the walks. And, as if one railroad was not enough, another corps of engineers is hard by, running another road from New Albany on the

Ohio to Lafayette on the Wabash, and thence by Laporte to Lake Michigan.

What shall I do? The first snort of the steam-horse will scare away all the sylvan and fairy beings that now people this sequestered valley. I can not live amidst smoke, and dust, and steam. I see no way but I must be off. I have been thinking all day where I shall go. I recollect a place I once saw, and I think it will do. Riding along, one day, near the coast of the Atlantic, on ascending a bleak and barren hill, there suddenly appeared in the distance a scene of beauty such as has never since appeared to me. There lay, smiling beneath the clear, blue sky, a village of exquisite finish and loveliness. The streets were wide, shaded by grand old forest trees, and clean as if the people had nothing to do but to sweep them. The cottages peered out amidst the green trees, white as if the painter had scarcely put up his brush. Each house was surrounded by ample grounds, furnishing room for the nicely-mown lawn, and the tastefully-cultivated flower-garden. Immediately back of the village rose a magnificent hill, from whose top might be seen, at a distance of several miles, the ocean, covered with white sail. In front of the beautiful little paradise was a plain, spreading out over many thousands of acres, covered with evergreens. On one side appeared a clear, smooth, and tranquil lake, embosomed amid hills. Some convenient distance from this village, so far that improvement can never reach it, especially as the village was *finished* many years ago, and will probably never enlarge its borders, I remember to have seen, on one of my solitary rambles through the evergreen forest, a spot, whose seclusion I think will never be disturbed by the noise and din of mercenary life. That beautiful and romantic spot has stood there unmolested, while the *improvements* of two hundred years have been going on;

and I may safely calculate on its remaining thus for two hundred years to come, unless I, as I think I shall, build me a hermitage on it. It is in the center of an immense, uncultivated, and uninhabited plain. In the distance is a range of mountains on the one side, and the ocean on the other. The plain is covered with evergreens, each of which would be worth an acre of land in the west, but which there are unappreciated and unnoticed. The land defies cultivation, and, hence, would never be cleared unless the trees were cut off for wood, and, in that case, the young ones would grow as fast as the old ones were cut down. In the depth of the forest is a small lake. Its sides are perpendicular rock. Its depth I could never fathom. Near that lake, in the depth of that forest, with the mountains behind me, and the ocean before me, and a lovely village of refined, educated, hospitable people near enough to be visited when I want to see the world, I have concluded, on some future day, to build me a hermitage, so as to be sure to have a place that can not be disturbed by railroads, canals, depots, rattling streets, and other nuisances. When I get all things fixed to my mind, I will mark the way to my cottage by blazed trees, so that if any of my old friends think enough of me they can follow the trail.

I do not intend, however, to go away from here at present. It will be a year or two before the improvements get so far along as to annoy me. In the mean time, fair reader, I should like to see your pleasant face smiling amid my trees. If you come at the proper season I can help you, or you can help yourself, to the fruits of the orchard. At all times I can hold to your lips a cup of clear, cold, pure water, gushing perennial out of the hillside. The little brook that flows along the valley from that spring is always limpid and clear, and its banks are shaded by shrubbery and sprinkled with flowers. It is a place a naiad might choose for her home; and yet—can you believe it?—a neighbor of mine came along the other day, and wanted to put a pipe into my spring, and take all the water out of my brook, despoiling my valley, to furnish him means of driving a rattling, squealing, smoking, steam saw-mill. I told him he might drive his mill by the same force a Yankee acquaintance of mine did—*the force of circumstances.* He had scarcely gone, when another came along, and wanted to pipe the spring to carry on the operations of a *pork-house.* Horror of horrors! Tell it not in Judea! In return I asked of him one favor: just let me know when he was ready to begin to erect a pork-house in sight of me, and I would leave the country the day before.

So you see, dear reader, I have reason, abundant reason, to be alarmed, and to be looking out a more safe retreat. And if you intend to visit me here, you had better come soon.

* * * * * * * *

I am here again, reader. Night has come and gone. The morning bell aroused me from quiet slumber. The mellow toll from the college steeple called me at the usual hour to prayers. Another day has nearly passed. I have spent it, as usual, amidst equations, triangles, conic sections, and differentials, with a sprinkling of logic and ethics. For the brief hour that remains I have come to my sequestered resort, to commune with nature and with thee. The day is beautiful, but not as was yesterday. The clear blue of the sky has given place to a light, thin haze, betokening the presence of great heat. The air is still. Not a leaf stirs, nor a blade of grass waves. In the west is gathering a dark cloud, and the distant thunder is heard rumbling over the woods that stretch away toward the Wabash prairies. To me the sight of gathering cloud and the roar of distant thunder are not unpleasant. They are sights and sounds familiar to me in days of yore. They remind of the hills, and the plains, and the mountains, and the ocean, and the friends of my native land. Many years ago I was caught, on a summer day, by a thunder-cloud on the summit of a lofty, rocky mountain, where there was not even a bush for shelter. I had spent many years of my youth in sight of the mountain rearing its blue top high among the clouds, but had never visited it. I had been absent several years, and returning, I wondered how I could have lived so long at the very base of so magnificent a mountain, and never have taken the pains to look at the world from its summit. It thus often happens that scenes of beauty or of grandeur easily accessible are not appreciated by us. One might live for years within sound of Niagara, and never think of going to see it; but let him move away to the west, or to the east, and he would make a long journey back to see what he might have seen by an hour's ride at any time for the past ten years. Even home and friends become more dear by temporary absence.

One fine morning, in company with a young friend, I started for a day's excursion to the mountain. We rode some ten miles over bush and brier, and through brake and forest, our horses tumbling over rocks, and pitching over fallen trees, till we came to a cedar swamp. Fair reader, *you* never saw a *cedar swamp.* How shall I describe it? Imagine all the horns of all the deer that have ever roamed in all the forests in all the world to be piled about ten feet high, and as thick as they can be inserted in every way into an immense swamp, and then compel a poor wight to make his way through them. That would be something like the passage of a cedar swamp. The dense thicket throws out its dry and knotty limbs in every possible direction, and so close to the ground that a dog must stoop to get along. We left oul horses tied to a bush, and plunged into the swamp, and, by crawling, and climbing, and edging, and backing, with many a rent and many a scratch, we got through. We then had to ascend a steep hill-side, through a forest of firs. Gradually the firs grew smaller and fewer, till we stood on the naked rock, rising, like an inclined and overthrown wall, far above us. Up the rugged rocks we clambered by foot, and by knee, and by elbow, and by hand, till we stood on the summit. We were just taking breath, when there swept over us a thick mist, drenching us to the skin. We stood shivering in the blast, as the wind swept howling by us, and enveloped in a shroud of mist, but for a moment, when the wind ceased, the cloud descended, and the sun shone on the place where we stood, calm, bright, and beautiful. Below us the smaller hills, the valleys, the lakes, the villages, and all the plain were covered by the dark thunder-cloud, from which the lightnings were streaming and the thunders roaring. We stood for some time gazing on the scene so new to us. We had climbed to this rugged summit to see the world below, and we watched for some opening or break in the clouds, that we might at least find our way down again. In one small spot, and for a moment only, the cloud gave way, and we saw in a deep valley below us, as if but a stone's throw, and yet in reality miles from us, a lovely village, surrounded by meadows and pastures drenched with the shower. The opening closed, and the next gust of wind brought back the same cloud which had passed us, or another of the same kind, and we were again copiously besprinkled, till my companion averred that, by actual count, he could find only fourteen dry threads in all his garments.

We stood some time waiting for an abatement of rain; but the more we waited, the more it rained. As night was approaching, we thought it time to be going. But which way? Nothing could be seen but cloud, and it was impossible to tell which way we had ascended. However, go which ever way we might, we could get down; and it was not many miles in any direction to a clearing; and should we happen to miss our horses, and they have to stand tied to a bush all night, it would be no worse than for us to remain on the mountain without the shelter of a leaf. So we plunged on at a venture, and when we reached the limit of vegetation, we happened to discover the limb of a bush broken in our ascent. By this we found our trail.

* * * * * * * *

While I have been down east, the thunder-shower has followed suit, and has gone by without a sprinkle of rain. I have seen it away to the north, rushing up the Wabash, scattering its lightnings and its rain along the prairies. It has now entirely disappeared. Not a cloud is to be seen in the fair sky. The sunlight, unobstructed, reaches the earth far as my horizon extends, and one beautiful expanse of blue is spread over the whole heavens. How slight a circumstance may have governed the course of that cloud! A breath of wind may have determined its direction! And how many incidents of human life may have depended on the course of that shower! Those lightnings may have kindled unquenchable fires in some human dwelling, or may have scathed some human form, and laid it prostrate in death. That shower may have spread its fertilizing influence over the field of some despairing husbandman—despairing under the influence of heat and drouth—but now hoping and rejoicing in prospect of the abundant harvest. Circumstances not less slight than a breath of air may give rise to events which influence our whole mortal career. Beside the events that have happened to us, there are others which almost happened, and which would have marked for us a destiny of which we now dream not. From the highway of life there diverge many well-trodden pathways, and the merest chance may govern the choice we make, or may even force us into one in preference to another. And though these pathways may seem scarcely to vary from the parallel, yet they lead over very different ground. One leads through smiling meadows and lovely vales, amidst flowery beauties, and the other over dark mountains, amidst gloom and desolation. On one shines the sunlight of hope, and on the other falls the deep shadow of despair. But, however much these paths may for a time diverge, yet all at last lead to one place—the grave.

Would you, reader, if you could, have the superintendence of all the events which influence your fate in life? Would you trust your own knowledge or prudence to guide you through the dark labyrinth of human life? Alas! in this we find no thread to guide us. We wander on, and stumble along, knowing little of what is before us. But there is an unseen hand that guides us. Though we are unconscious of its presence, yet it is ever stretched out to our aid. We need not, therefore, hesitate. Though we walk through the valley of the shadow of death, we need fear no evil; for Providence is ever near us.

* * * * * * * *

Another day and another night have passed, gentle reader, and I am here again for an hour. Time, how it passes! and how silently, yet effectually, it works its changes! How imperceptibly has passed from my heart the buoyancy of early days! and how insidiously the gray hairs have crept over my temple! Time's hand is seen, not in wrath but in kindness, in the changes which are passing over this little bower, so dear to me. A rough pasture, incumbered by fallen trees, and overgrown by unsightly weeds, is transformed into a smooth lawn, with its velvety sod. Weeds have given place to lilies, and roses, and violets. Pines, firs, and spruce, transplanted from my native home on the Atlantic shore, a thousand miles and more away, are growing luxuriantly around me, throwing their shade over me, and forming a dense thicket, such as I used to admire and love in childhood. Year after year they will increase and spread their evergreen foliage, till they make this little spot a gem amidst the surrounding scenery. But what will become of my bower, and of my trees, which begin to seem like my children, when I am here no more to watch and protect them? For here my vigilant eye may not always watch to keep off the intruder, who would thoughtlessly wrench away their branches, or the unruly animal that might destroy them. The beautiful pine that now waves and sighs mournfully in the wind over the grave of my child, may soon—alas! none know how soon—play, in summer breeze and wintery storm, the dirge of him who planted it. Who, then, will come here at early morn, and at evening twilight, to watch over the trees, and the flowers, and the grave? Little do we know, when we plant a tree, who will gather its fruit, or sit under its shade.

THE END.

www.ingramcontent.com/pod-product-compliance
Lightning Source LLC
LaVergne TN
LVHW010220110826
845151LV00004B/1155

* 9 7 8 1 4 2 5 5 2 6 9 1 7 *